THE CONSULTANT'S PROPOSAL, FEE, AND CONTRACT PROBLEM-SOLVER

THE CONSULTANT'S PROPOSAL, FEE, AND CONTRACT PROBLEM-SOLVER

RON TEPPER

John Wiley & Sons, Inc.
New York • Chichester • Brisbane • Toronto • Singapore

In recognition of the importance of preserving what has been written, it is a policy of John Wiley & Sons, Inc., to have books of enduring value published in the United States printed on acid-free paper, and we exert our best efforts to that end.

This publication is designed to provide accurate and authoritative information in regard to the subject matter covered. It is sold with the understanding that the publisher is not engaged in rendering legal, accounting, or other professional services. If legal advice or other expert assistance is required, the services of a competent professional person should be sought. *From a Declaration of Principles jointly adopted by a Committee of the American Bar Association and a Committee of Publishers.*

Library of Congress Cataloging-in-Publication Data:

Tepper, Ron, 1937–
      The consultant's proposal, fee, and contract problem-solver / by Ron Tepper.
         p.   cm.
      ISBN 0-471-58211-5 (cloth)—ISBN 0-471-58213-1 (paper)
      1. Business consultants—Vocational guidance. 2. Business consultants—Case studies.   I. Title.
      HD69.C6T473   1993
      001'.068—dc20   92-34607

Printed in the United States of America

10 9 8 7 6 5 4 3 2 1

Contents

THE CONSULTANT'S PROPOSAL, FEE, AND CONTRACT PROBLEM-SOLVER

Introduction

F ew industries have changed more during the past decade than consulting. Along with those changes have come some dramatic new approaches in setting fees, billing, contracts, and generating business.

Today's consultants have not only found creative new ways to generate fees and bill clients, but they have also found dynamic ways to market their services. Consultants do everything from publishing books and newsletters to giving speeches. This aggressive new marketing thrust has made consulting a dramatic growth industry—one of the most robust in the country.

Where is the growth and why? Much of the impetus for consulting's expansion can be credited to the downsizing and outsourcing that is sweeping across U.S. industries. Companies are cutting back, requiring many employees to handle multiple duties. When a key project is launched and executives look for assistance, they call on consultants to supply that aid.

A second phenomena that is spurring the booming consulting industry, is the search by many companies to cut back and specialize in their "core" business and no more. In the 1980s, numerous companies expanded vertically and horizontally. Corporations purchased their suppliers and other related businesses. The furniture manufacturer may have bought the lumber company; the chain of supermarkets the dairy farm.

With the 1990s came downsizing and increased competition, companies sought to dump these synergistic endeavors and concentrate on their "core" business; the business that got them to where they were. The furniture store knows retailing, the supermarket consumers. Neither necessarily knew anything about lumber nor dairy farming.

Realizing that it takes additional energy and resources to run these side ventures, companies in the 1990s are selling these side ventures and going back to the core. The huge franchise company, for instance, that created a state-of-the-art data processing department, is selling off the data processing area and concentrating on what it knows best—the selling of franchises.

When these core enterprises need services such as data processing, they are turning to outside consultants to supply them. Thus, as the divestiture of related businesses continues, the dramatic growth of consulting will, too.

For an in-depth look at the industry, new billing, fee-setting, and proposal techniques, I talked to nearly a dozen of the most successful consultants in the country. Each comes from a different industry and has carved an extremely profitable enterprise in today's environment. These consultants are intimately involved in the new trends that are sweeping the field; trends that are leading to unparalleled growth opportunities.

Nido Qubein, one of the top professional development consultants in the industry, says there are four major changes impacting fees:

1. Today's consultant is dealing and selling to a higher echelon executive.

2. An executive is probably a product of the baby-boom generation.

3. An executive looks at things differently.

4. An executive demands that consultants position themselves as specialists.

Tony Alessandra, a consultant who started as a sales trainer and today commands more than $7,000 for a keynote speech, says the major change in the industry is that consultants have to think "global."

Arnold Van Den Berg, an astute money management consultant who handles more than $50 million, says the greatest change in the financial field is the growth of specialties within specialties. It no longer suffices to be a good money manager. Today, with the complex global market, financial consultants and money managers have to specialize more than ever.

Don Kracke, a top licensing and merchandising consultant, says cash is tighter and many companies are going for percentage arrangements; deals they would never have proposed in years gone by. It's risky, but it can be extremely rewarding.

Jay Abraham, a direct mail consultant, would take that risk any time, any day. He is a specialist who believes for the consultant willing to gamble, there is a bigger reward than ever at the end of the job.

Dennis McCuistion, a banking and financial specialist, maintains one of the major changes in the industry is the new techniques that consultants have found to market and price their services—everything from writing books to creating their own television programs.

Randy Pennington, best-selling author (*On My Honor, I Will*), says before a company commits to consulting services they want to know "what can you contribute to our bottom line."

Laurie Moore, a marketing specialist, stresses that there is a growing trend among consultants to build their practice and fees through speaking and writing; activities that have enabled consultants to demand higher fees.

Bill Johnson has watched his accounting/consulting practice grow to more than $3 million a year, and most of the revenue has come from consulting, not accounting. In his area, the hottest, new fee-generating activity is reorganization consulting.

Hugh Holbert, a top legal consultant, sees seminars as a growing venue in which consultants can expand their practice and increase their rates.

Joe Izzo, considered a foremost consultant in the data processing/information technology field, says some of the major changes are the new ways in which consultants arrive at fees, and the innovative methods that have been developed to pay them.

Each consultant has become an enormous success in his or her specialty, and although each deals with different audiences and myriad industries, the challenges are similar. Billing, fee-setting, contracts, marketing services, and generating clientele have changed more in the past few years than they have in the past two decades.

From the perspective of these consulting veterans, it will continue to change in the future. These professionals provide an inside look at this rapidly growing business, the unique fee-generating ideas that have been introduced, and new contracts and approaches that are rapidly dominating the way consultants operate today—and tomorrow.

CHAPTER 1

The Consultant's Role Today

The 1990s and beyond may well be dubbed the golden age of consulting. Ask William Manville. Before he entered the consulting field, Manville thought he had it made. He was with one of the largest advertising agencies in Chicago, and after 10 years he had become a senior copywriter with a growing expertise in direct response.

Still, Manville's security—as is the case with many middle class/income executives in the United States—was tenuous, at best. After more than 16 years in the industry, Manville knew the business and he could see the trends. Agencies, as was the case with virtually every company, were continually downsizing. The cutting took place whenever Manville's company lost a major account. Predictably, the week after a client left, there would be a bloodletting.

Manville survived the cuts, but he was not oblivious. He thought, however, he was protected since he was the only direct response copywriter remaining, and one of the firm's major revenue sources was through a leading mail order catalog house.

Then it happened. The agency's mail order client changed ownership. A new president and senior management staff took over. Within weeks, Manville's agency lost the prime account and the aging copywriter could see a grim future. He was right. Three days after the client cancelled, Manville was let go. His former employer tried to soften the blow with a generous severance and outplacement counseling, but the fact remained, Manville had become a victim of two of the most devastating liabilities any out-of-work executive can have:

1. He was older—in his early fifties.
2. He had been fired.

Manville searched the help wanted section of the newspaper and scoured every advertising trade paper in hopes of finding something. Nothing developed.

Two months after he had been laid off, he was sitting alone, disconsolate in his apartment when, suddenly, the telephone rang. He was surprised to find it was one of the agency's former clients—looking for a freelance copywriter. Manville had worked on the account for three years and, although the company was satisfied with his work, the firm decided to hire someone internally. The company, however, had never forgotten Manville, and when it went through a period of downsizing—and fired the internal, full-time writer—it sought freelance help. Manville immediately came to mind. The ex-corporate employee had never thought about a business of his own, but in January 1992, the former lifetime, dedicated company executive found it surprisingly easy to make the move.

Although Manville had extensive expertise when it came to copywriting, running his own business was another matter. One of the more pleasant discoveries was how inexpensive it was to "start up." All it took was a $700 fax machine, a business telephone in his spare bedroom, letterhead, and business cards. His total expenditure was less than $2,000, and within weeks, he was billing his first client $1,500 a month.

Manville's gross was nowhere near his agency salary, but it was a start. In six months, the former Chicago advertising executive was looking at billings in excess of $10,000 a month, and his overhead—with a part-time secretary—had "soared" to $1,000 a month.

IMPACT OF TECHNOLOGY

"Manville," explains veteran consultant, Joseph Izzo, "is typical of the ease with which one can enter this business today. With fax machines and computers you do not need massive office overhead. Consultants have benefited from a horde of sophisticated, labor-saving, communication devices. There's no longer a need to hire a secretary who types 80 errorless words per minute. The word processor does that for you."

As for location and the appearance of a consultant's office, prospective clients rarely inquire about either. Most of the time, the consultant visits the client. "Years ago," continued Izzo, "clients may have been interested in traveling to your office and looking over the surroundings. They based a good deal of their decision on whether to hire you on appearance. Now, clients do not have the time to travel to inspect. They establish relationships from recommendations, and the condition or location of your office is seldom a deciding factor."

Dennis McCuistion, an accomplished, highly-successful financial consultant in the southeast United States, agrees with Izzo's assessment. "There are pros and cons to working out of your home," explains McCuistion. "For the first 10 years I was in the business, I had an office. The advantage was I had an office and clients could visit. Even more important, when I left the office I usually left my work there. When I moved the office to the house,

I found I could never get away from it. When the day ended and my employees (he has three) left for home, I never could.

"Certainly, there are advantages. I can depreciate the house and my overhead is unquestionably lower. But, if you're going to get into this business, I strongly recommend you take the plunge and rent an office. It need not be anything fancy; an executive suite (a host of offices that are serviced by one secretary) will suffice, but I think it helps to keep you organized. Working out of the house, you have a extra challenge. It is too easy to get off-track."

Nido Qubein looks at things differently. "I maintain a class A building and office even though most of my clients never come to the office. It has, I believe, an impact on my company and employees. If things look good and successful, it will rub off on the staff. They are going to feel better about themselves and our company. Frankly, it increases their confidence and enables them to perform better."

Randy Pennington, who heads the Pennington Performance Group and specializes in productivity consulting and improvement, understands Qubein's point but likes to work out of his house. Pennington says most of the time "I end up visiting the client, so it does not matter where my office happens to be. If you need to meet away from the client's office, it is always easy to rent or obtain a conference room at a hotel or the airport."

Pennington, however, has reasons other than convenience for working out of his home. He was once a partner in a large consulting firm, one that generated more than $2 million a year in billings. "We had all the conveniences," Pennington recalls, "a nice office, conference table, staff, and appearance. But, you have to decide what kind of lifestyle you want. What kind of business do you want to build. Do you want a big conglomerate or a small, easy-to-manage firm?"

Pennington chose the latter. He left the partnership and scaled down from 15 employees to 2. Pennington, who today has an income in the six-figure range, has been able to leave the rigors of a medium-sized firm for the relative ease of his own small company. At the same time, his salary has increased 30%.

Bill Johnson, a long-time consultant in the accounting field, left a large firm to open his own office several years ago. He put a "cap" on the number of employees he wanted, and he has been able to stay within it. In watching the business, however, he maintains "there are more opportunities for entrepreneurs/consultants because the barriers are lower. It is not, of course, necessary to have an office, and one of the biggest boosts available for launching a low-cost consulting practice is technology. Today, it is no longer expensive."

OUTSOURCING AND DOWNSIZING OPPORTUNITIES

Equally as important, maintains Johnson, is the tremendous difference in business. "Call it downsizing, rightsizing, or outsourcing. Regardless of the tag, it has created uncertainty (and fear) among companies, and a greater dependence upon the independent consultant. These days you have employees going in and out of companies at a tremendous pace. Many corporations cannot keep up with the change. The firings and layoffs have created a greater need for the independent consultant than ever before."

McCuistion says this is especially true in financial consulting. He deals extensively with banks—institutions that have not only been impacted by the economy and downsizing, but with a lowering of pay scales. The cutbacks have created an industry that is desperately in need of expertise, but will not pay for it.

"Banks," explains McCuistion, "are deluged by an extremely oppressive regulatory environment. The government has a growing number of compliance regulations. Many banks are panicked by these regulations, and they spend time and resources hiring people (and sending them to seminars) where they learn nothing more than compliance. Ironically, it is not in the compliance area that banks need help, but they do need assistance in areas as simple as financial statements. Believe it or not, there are many bankers in the business today who cannot read and interpret a financial statement. They know compliance, but few understand the significance of the financial statement.

"Some may perceive the compliance side as the place to concentrate—it isn't. In fact, compliance can be a nightmare because of the government dealings. The opportunity is in the other areas; areas that banks have downsized; areas where they need help if they are going to survive in today's economy."

Despite the obvious need that downsizing has created in many areas, some practitioners have seen the economy undermine their profitability. Don Kracke, frequently called the "Red Adair of licensing and design consulting," is one. Kracke spends a good deal of time creating licensing and design programs for Fortune 500 companies.

"Companies always need a controller and president, but they do not need (at least in the opinion of company executives) design and licensing people," he says. "The fees in this area have grown, but the difficulty in convincing a company that it needs expertise has mounted as well."

FEE STRUCTURE CHANGE

Kracke points to another significant change in the fee structure— getting cash. "A growing number of firms are looking for alternative methods of payment. They do not want to put out hard currency if they can avoid it. Consultants are being offered more profit-sharing ventures than ever."

Of all the consultants surveyed, Carol Geisbauer, a consultant with an unusual specialty of writing proposals that nonprofits can use to generate funds, was the only one who had a somewhat grim outlook. She has seen a complete turnaround in generating fees and contracts from government agencies.

"It is no surprise, of course," she explains, "that government funds have dried up. The government used to be $20 million short in funding some RFPs (Request for Proposal), now they are $20 billion. Generating contracts and obtaining fees is more difficult than ever. Interestingly, before we saw as many grants, but less money in each grant. Now, we not only see less money, but less grants as well."

Geisbauer says consultants who specialize in the nonprofit area have to be more creative. The consultant in this field must "look more to the local community and local foundations for contracts. Corporations are no longer a source of funding for projects—not when they are laying off 1,000 to 2,000 people. The opportunity is at the local level if consultants in this field are going to survive." Much of that opportunity is in the form of "cause-related marketing," according to Geisbauer. Years ago, when a company was approached for monies to fund a project, it would look at the bottom line and if it was a decent year, the check book would come out. The same was true of employees. If earnings went up they pulled out their wallets.

Today, however, that has all changed. Corporations are running tight operations, and employees are no longer worrying about charities; they are concerned as to whether they are going to have a job tomorrow. Consequently, consultants who try to obtain funding and contracts for local projects, have to be creative. That is where "cause-related marketing" enters the field.

"It simply means," explains Geisbauer, "that a profit-making corporation wants something in return when it funds a project or donates to a charity. The Campfire sends brochures for Britannica to the parents of Campfire youth. In the brochure is a return, postage-paid card. If the recipient returns the card (to Britannica) and a sale results, Campfire gets anywhere from $175 to $300, based upon the $1,500 to $3,000 sale. The sale was made possible—in part—by the Campfire mailing."

There are other, similar, projects. Campfire alumni are encouraged to shop at Allen Paper Company, a firm noted for its party goods. They are asked to send their receipts to Campfire, and Campfire turns the stubs into Allen and receives a 10% rebate. Another example of cause-related marketing.

Geisbauer, who competed for numerous government contracts in California, recommends consultants seeking projects and funding in the nonprofit area, take the micro approach. For example, the state of California went through drastic budget cuts—yet, it still has contracts and funding available. A few years prior to the cuts, the voters passed a proposition that called for a 25 cent tax on every pack of cigarettes sold. The monies went into a fund to promote nonsmoking activities in the state. For several years, Geisbauer obtained contracts (through Request for Proposals (RFPs), which are government contracts) in which she worked with elementary children in educating them on the inherent problems in smoking. The state funded the contract.

There are other contracts available, on both a state and national level. Politically active groups representing, for example, the disabled, have been able to convince legislators to maintain funding for many RFPs. The pools of money are there. "It's a matter of knowing where to go," she says, "and watching legislation. That frequently gives you a clue."

Generating government contracts has become extremely difficult, and the consultants who specialize in the field expect this to be even more difficult in the future. Consultants in the private sector have been more fortunate. In fact, most say their business is booming. Perhaps the lesson is: When there are government cutbacks, stay out of the public sector.

Bill Johnson's profession—accounting—is the epitome of change. The procedures and fee setting have gone 180 degrees in just a few years. In the early 1980s, accountants convinced clients it was in the client's best interest for the CPA to work outside of the customer's office, bring the financial data back to their (accounting) office, put the figures on computer, run off tax returns, payroll, and other daily tasks, and return them to the client. Accountants actually increased their perceived value by taking everything away from the client and seemingly performing some sort of hocus pocus with numbers. Thus, in the early 1980s, a large part of the accountant's role was what Johnson describes as game playing.

However, as it became more likely that a client had a computer and the right software it became increasingly obvious that there was no need for paying fees to a CPA who simply provided a service bureau.

Eventually, accounting consultants began to see the inefficiency of the business. They also realized that, in time, clients would also see the foolishness of paying fees to a high priced, off-premise bookkeeper. Astute consultants began to convince their customers that the best approach was to keep the bookkeeping in-house, and use the CPA as a true consultant.

CPAs began to help customers select and install the right hardware and software. At the same time, they also expanded into other areas, such as reorganization counseling and planning; areas in which clients desperately needed help.

This new approach was an enormous breakthrough for CPAs. "We told clients," Johnson says, "they did not need us as a service bureau. We convinced them accounting could be done in-house, with proper training and guidance. The client could save thousands of dollars." And they did. There was no need to pay an outside consultant $30 to $35 an hour to gather data, when an in-house bookkeeper could do the same for $10 to $15 an hour.

For those CPAs still practicing the old procedures, Johnson cautions that "sooner or later the client will realize the CPA is simply crunching numbers—a glorified but expensive bookkeeper. Anyone can add the figures," explains Johnson, "but it is the analysis that a CPA consultant provides that is critical. That's where the accounting consultant can shine and bring true value to the service they provide."

CLIENTS WANT VALUE-ADDED SERVICE

Value-added work is what clients want from consultants today. Fees are only justified when the consultant actually contributes to the bottom line. That does not just mean increasing sales. For CPAs, it may be a better way to move cash around or handle payables. For a money manager, it may be a better investment.

Joe Izzo performed similar tasks in the data processing field. He worked at a client's location where he would analyze and recommend internal computer changes. Often, he would reorganize the department, recommend new equipment and procedures. In providing the analysis and direction, Izzo, too, was able to bring true value to the client through his services.

Laurie Moore, a marketing consultant who specializes in real estate, has seen the industry turn dramatically during the past few years. "Value is what clients demand," she says. "Every client is looking for a more effective way to reach their customers. They also want you to know the business and industry and know it well. In other words, they want you to be a specialist. Obviously, if you have a large consulting firm with people who have expertise in many areas, the specialization is not going to impact your business. But, if you are similar to most of the independent consultants in this country, you need to specialize in order to add that value."

Moore is in a business traditionally dominated by male executives, and she had to rely upon those senior managers to retain her services. "In this industry," she explains, "there is a huge percentage of women who sell homes, however, when it gets to company management, it is predominantly male. Only once, however, did I run into a situation where I felt my gender had me at a disadvantage. The key—today—is to position yourself as an expert. People respect expertise, regardless of whether it is a man or woman who has it."

Qubein agrees about the increased opportunity, ". . . but there is a caveat. The opportunities only exist for the savvy consultant. The person with business acumen. The person who has positioned himself as an expert, and the person who can communicate effectively with decision makers. In other words, I'm saying that the opportunities are primarily for the sophisticated consultant."

CHANGES FROM 1970s TO 1990s

In the 1980s, employees and their attitudes were obstacles for consultants. At best, employees within companies who found themselves alongside a consultant, viewed the practitioner with suspicion. Consultants were a threat, coming into the work environment to change things and, perhaps, eliminate positions.

Toward the end of the 1980s, however, the view of employees began to change. Downsizing had shrunk most departments to bare-bones. They no longer had to fear the consultant and what they would do. In fact, the outside consultant was looked upon as someone who was brought in to help, to alleviate the workload.

"In the 1970s," explains Qubein, "most corporations were looking for the consultant who could supply motivation to the employees. Unless you were someone with considerable expertise in a specialized area, you had a hard time making a living unless you gave motivation talks.

"In the 1980s, corporations wanted education. Don't just tell us to climb the highest mountain, but tell us how to do it.

"In the 1990s, we are seeing corporations searching for good ideas, solutions, and a consultant who can stay around and execute the plan. In the old days, consultants were advisors. Today, a successful profitable consultant must be positioned to offer turnkey solutions. That does not mean that every one of them has to do it, however, those that can offer the gamut of services are going to do much better than those that cannot."

The reason for the consultant taking a hands-on approach is a consequence of downsizing and/or rightsizing. Initially, downsizing on the part of U.S. business was an effort to cut "fat" or "waste" and operate more efficiently. Profits were being squeezed and shareholders were upset.

Downsizing—for most consultants—became a blessing and, at the same time, it was an area that many companies handled poorly. Izzo explains, "The correct way to downsize was not merely to cut employees. Companies, and the consultants who advised them, should have been looking at more than numbers. If a company had a marketing department with four people in it, and it cut two, it should have eliminated part of the workload at the same time.

"Effective downsizing does not mean eliminating employees without readjusting the workload. If there is a high level of work and the department is cut just for the sake of saving money, the area becomes inefficient. Those who remain find their prime function is reactive; putting out fires and not contributing any value-added service to the firm."

Unfortunately, many firms viewed downsizing as merely cutting personnel. They did not look at the impact on productivity. Instead, they concentrated on making the bottom line look better—in the short run. Both Izzo and Johnson agree that getting lean and efficient means more than cutting personnel. "The process (in the department or company) has to be changed."

In most cases, the process did not change. This approach created additional opportunity for consultants. Companies that were flattened by downsizing have not had the internal resources to conduct normal activities. They ended up hiring outside consultants to supplement employed staff. The banking industry is an excellent example.

While the hiring of outsiders was good news for consultants, it was also an indication that many U.S. firms were not planning for the long haul or, as Johnson says, "reacting to reality. Too many companies believe that downsizing is temporary . . . they are waiting for the next wave of prosperity to return. In other words, for the economy to turn and the hiring to begin, once again. They feel bad about laying off friends and long-time employees, and that is understandable. But, the good old days of hiring in abundance are gone forever. U.S. business—in the 1990s and into the next Century—will never be the same."

CORE BUSINESS SEARCH

The obvious economic changes are not the only reason for the opportunity in the consulting field. During the past two to three years, there has been another relatively new phenomena emerge; a development that is making consulting more lucrative. This new occurrence is rapidly becoming the buzz phrase of the 1990s—"find your core business and stick with it."

What is a *core* business and how does it impact the contemporary consultant? To understand, it helps to go back to the early 1980s when U.S. companies were hiring, building departments, and expanding. A typical expansion might be one in which an established retail chain of department stores purchased a manufacturer that made clothing for its outlets. It could be a bank that bought a residential development company in order to have a built-in demand for its funds. Or, it could even be a franchisor setting up its own data processing department in order to link its franchisees.

In making these acquisitions, the retailer, bank, and franchisor stretched resources and entered areas where they frequently did not have expertise—the retailer in manufacturing, the bank in development, and the franchisor in computers. All strayed from their core businesses: retailing, banking, and selling franchises. Thousands of companies did the same thing. They expanded internally and added staff for noncore activities. Some called it expansion, but it frequently led to companies absorbing additional overhead with little or no return.

"In the 1990s," says Izzo, "smart companies began moving back to the core. They divested themselves of these related enterprises and started to concentrate on what made them successful in the first place.

"It's happening all over. There is downsizing, but the astute companies are paring non-core areas. The good companies are getting back to the core."

In moving to the core, companies are creating opportunities for consultants. The franchisor, for instance, outsources its data processing department. It finds a firm that specializes in data processing to take over that function; a function that it (the franchisor) eliminates. Once the department is cut, the franchisor can legitimately cut its data processing staff because the work is no longer there. It saves in a sensible manner.

The core movement is aiding the consulting industry. The franchisor has taken an element of its business and given it to an outside vendor (or consultant). It no longer has the internal overhead, however, it still may have a need to provide advice or screening for its franchisees when it comes to new data processing programs. It may hire a consultant to screen and evaluate software, hardware, or other innovations in the field. Management is happy to pay the consulting fee because the activity does not take away from the company's core business. One hundred percent of the firm's resources can be concentrated on the franchise function.

The same is true of the retailer. Instead of dividing its resources and worrying about manufacturing problems; problems that are radically different from those that a retailer encounters, the retail establishment sells the manufacturing area and no longer needs the manpower to work as a bridge between the two units. It concentrates on the core—retailing—and hires an outside consultant to advise it on manufacturing concerns.

Even the bank becomes more efficient (and slimmer insofar as labor) when it rids itself of the development company. It also divests itself of a business that it does not know much about. Lending funds for a development is one thing; running a development company is something entirely different.

The search for the core has even hit the consulting field. Johnson explains: "At first CPAs set up their own service bureaus, then they convinced clients to take the bookkeeping function in-house, now the movement is to let them (the company) maintain the basic bookkeeping function, however, when it is time for a tax return, audit, financial statement or something similar, we bring in an outside, self-employed CPA to compile the figures and return the required forms to the company. This outside CPA is not an employee nor does he receive benefits. The client pays for him on a billed rate; a rate we establish."

There is no need to hire this "service bureau" type CPA on a full-time basis. Johnson, and other CPAs, have come to realize that the consulting firm needs CPAs who are consultants, not bookkeepers and tax return specialists. "We've gotten down to our core business, too. Consulting. Everyone we have on board (26 CPAs) are consultants. We did not hire them to do tax returns. This does not mean our staff is not capable of doing tax work, they are. But our prime business is providing advice in areas ranging from restructuring a company's debt (one of the biggest needs in business today), and drawing inferences from the financial data. That's where the value-added service is as well as the prime profit area for a CPA firm."

A return to its core business landed Laurie Moore one of her biggest consulting contracts. "It was a year-long marketing project for a well-known real estate developer." The developer did what he was noted for—constructed a large subdivision. Unfortunately, the project was built at a time when the market was down. Moore set up and implemented a marketing plan for the project. She took the place of an in-house marketing director, something many developers and builders find they cannot afford because they are not constructing one project after another to keep the in-house person busy. It makes sense to retain the services of an outside consultant.

As Qubein puts it, today's consultant has to be able to provide a turnkey solution and not just an analysis with solutions. They have to be prepared to do the actual work.

Pennington understands the turnkey movement. Part of the demand relates to the attitude many employees have. "I don't think anyone would argue if I said the workforce of the 1990s has definitely changed. The loyalty of the worker and the paternalistic attitude of the company is long gone. Corporations have concentrated on downsizing and improving the bottom line through it. They frequently forget that the employees who are left can make or break the company."

Pennington illustrated his point at a recent seminar, where he brought it home to a group of 200 human resource directors. He asked how many were practicing "total quality management," or continuous improvement so that their products and services would meet the demanding standards of customers. Less than half raised their hands. Pennington asked how many were experiencing less results than hoped for—every one of them raised their hands.

THE MAJOR CONSULTING OPPORTUNITY

"The area of employee commitment and building trust among people, is a major area of opportunity for consultants. We have gone through a period when 'looking out for number one' has bred tremendous mistrust among employees. There is no loyalty; little commitment to quality. The challenge for consultants in my field is to design, develop, and implement programs for organizations that will build those elements."

Pennington's specialty, building trust in the workforce, is a difficult assignment in the 1990s. The major obstacle is one that every consultant faces when they enter a downsized environment. Employees have seen so many changes, that when another comes along—even if it has been developed by an outside consultant that management hired—they tend to view it as a "temporary inconvenience."

Or, as Pennington says, they regard "the company's new consultant and his or her plan as something that will pass—just give it enough time and it will go away. And you cannot blame them. They have seen so many changes, that is, those that are still employed, they view every new program as just another management whim."

Mirroring the corporation's search for quality and dependability in consulting, is the consumer who utilizes a consultant. Take, for instance, money management, or the consultant who invests funds for a client and earns fees based upon the size of the account, and not the trades made. Van Den Berg, who manages more than $50 million and is noted for his expertise (which he displayed years ago when he invested in gold at $35 an ounce), has watched significant changes in his industry.

"This is an exploding field," he says, "primarily because of world conditions. It has become a global market. Investments have expanded into foreign markets. Even Russia and China are going to have stock markets, and it will not be long before the developing nations join in the capitalist circle. There is a wide variety of choices for the consumer/investor, especially with more and more people having discretionary income."

Another expanding consumer-related field is financial consulting for small to medium-sized businesses. "The executives in most of these enterprises," says McCuistion, "have difficulty when it comes to running the company. Many are entrepreneurs, and they do not understand working capital, the procedures in borrowing money, and other financial concerns. They find they cannot talk to attorneys, because the lawyers do not know the financial answers; they cannot talk to most CPAs, because the accountants are always focused on the past, not the future; and a good number fear discussing things with their banker. They need knowledgeable financial consultants who can guide them through statements, bank procedures, and other financially-related aspects of the business. In the 1990s, I see the demand for consultants in this significant area."

FOUR DEMANDS SPUR CONSULTING

Izzo credits the growing demand for consultants in most industries to four demands:

1. *Compression of time.* There is a need to get the product or service out faster.

2. *Managing space.* Can someone else (another company) manage the department and/or function. Can it be outsourced?

3. *Can I reduce my space?* By outsourcing extraneous departments and functions, companies will not only cut excess numbers of employees, but they will free space as well.

4. *Compression of knowledge.* When a company gets to its core business and concentrates on it, knowledge of the remaining employees all involves the same thing—how to effectively sell a franchise, not program computers or develop software for franchisees. The organization is focused and so are its employees. It will do a better job and be more competitive.

What does this mean? Opportunity—and challenge. Opportunities emerge as companies move to core businesses. If accounting is outsourced by a corporation, the outside CPA will benefit. If a lumber mill goes core and focuses solely on producing quality board, it will still need marketing expertise to help sell its product. If the automobile manufacturer abandons its high-cost training for its dealers, it will still need to retain consultant trainers.

Of all these industries, Izzo views manufacturing as one of the prime areas of opportunity for consultants. "Take many of the major automobile companies," he explains, "they are already outsourcing manufacturing functions such as painting. Consultants should be watching the leaders in their industry. Take a clue from them. What are they doing? For instance, a few years ago, two-thirds of all the information technology directors within major companies said they would not be outsourcing. A year later (1991) there was a complete reversal and two-thirds said they would be.

"Whatever the industry, whatever the function, if it can be outsourced, it will be. It's simply a matter of economics. While major companies are struggling to make the bottom line look better, the actions they take cannot help but benefit the independent consultant."

■ Case Study

It was one of the top franchise companies in the country. A relatively new firm, it had soared to number four in the industry in less than three years. From the early days in the industry, the company began to staff up. It hired trainers, consultants, and experts in every area to service its franchisees.

As the economy slowed, so did franchise sales. Management began to analyze its problems and to downsize. The goal was to shed all the unnecessary departments and companies it had purchased and to get back to its core activity, selling franchises.

From a company of more than 300, it eventually shrank to under 200. Opportunities for those within the company were not abundant, however, the downsizing created a horde of work for outside consultants. First, it closed its training facilities. Then, it gave up its data processing services and shortly thereafter its desktop publishing.

While the franchise company managed to cut internal labor costs, it provided a host of opportunities for outside consulting services. It farmed out its data processing department, contracted training and desktop publishing and hired an outside design consultant.

The actual benefits to the company are difficult to add up, however, the outsourcing created a bonanza of revenue for the four local consulting firms that took on the data processing, training, desktop and design functions. The firms that got those contracts were those that were astute enough to watch the industry, the trends and surmise what outsourcing would do. They were the first consultants in the door when the departments were eliminated, and each ended up with a piece of business.

■

Once again, as Qubein points out, every decade there has been a shift. With economic tough times, the trademark of the 1990s, the search for core, downsizing and outsourcing, are trends that will last to the end of the decade. Some would say it is indecision and that major corporations are not sure which way to go. Regardless of the reason, the opportunity is there—if the consultant looks for it. Take, for instance, the case study on page 23 of a core search by one of the country's leading franchise companies.

Everywhere, in industries throughout the country, the same move to core continues. One of this country's largest retailers— Sears—is in the midst of a battle with shareholders. The retailing giant has had some earnings problems during the past few years, and a percentage of shareholders are beginning to demand that the retailer, once the premiere marketer in the industry, return to its core business. Interestingly, returning to its core (retailing) would mean that Sears might divest itself of some of its most profitable operations.

Should Sears decide to divest itself of its nonretail entities, there could be a host of opportunities for independent consultants; opportunities even greater than those presented by the franchising firm.

The keys: monitor industries and companies. Watch for the downsizing, the first sign of a company's move to core business; and, be capable of supplying turnkey services.

■ Case History

Consulting in the 1990s is far from what it was a decade ago. If there is one thing a consultant must do in this decade, it is to keep on top of his or her industry. Ask Don Kracke, one of the most astute consultants in the licensing field. Kracke, who earns most of his income by either finding or developing unique household products that can be licensed by large-sized consumer goods companies, watched his firm's income soar and his staff grow during the late 1980s.

By 1990, Kracke's consulting group was earning nearly $2 million a year in royalties from client companies. Then the economic slowdown hit. Companies that once welcomed his ideas became difficult to see, let alone sell. Most were worried about surviving, and not taking on new products.

Eventually, Kracke had to pare staff and for the first time since he opened his doors, he found himself cutting deep in order to preserve his firm. At the same time, he also found himself cutting departments that were not necessary; departments that had grown along with the company's sales.

By early 1992, Kracke's consulting firm was not much larger than it was when he started, more than a decade before. He not only found himself personally running the smaller staff, but he also took on additional duties of finding products that were good candidates for licensing and knocking on doors of companies that were potential licensees.

Although he had more than 20 years in the field, by mid-1992 Kracke admitted that he had re-learned several things that he had almost forgotten. "When a business grows and the money comes in no one worries about paying the bills. As long as growth is there, the concern is not. That goes for the consulting field as well as for any company in any industry. During the 1980s, most industries in this country grew dramatically, as did the consulting industry.

"This continuing up-and-down recession has been a surprise to most. It is longer and more severe than many surmised it would be. It has permanently impacted the size of companies and has definitely thinned firms to the bare bones. In some areas of consulting, it has created opportunities.

"But, for many of us the business is tougher. I'm not in the accounting or financial field, our business is getting to companies and convincing them to spend dollars on merchandising and licensing projects. Unfortunately, instead of promoting four or five new products, they may only back one or two. The one or two they promote have to produce an inordinate amount of sales. If the product does not have that potential, the companies do not want it."

How much that inordinate amount is might surprise some. A short time ago, Kracke ran across a product; a product that would be ideal for one of the major housewares companies to license. Kracke obtained the rights, prepared his proposal, set his appointment, and flew back to Chicago in April 1992, to sell what he thought would be a successful new product.

To his surprise, the company turned it down. Interestingly, it rejected the item because executives at the company believed that the product's sales (projected to be $20 million the first year) would not warrant the expenditure of half the company's yearly marketing budget.

"In the old days—that is the 1980s," laughs Kracke, "there would not have been a question. The company would have jumped at the product. It might not have been a major item, but the $20 million would have been reason enough for taking it.

"What consultants have to realize is that in today's environment the rules have changed. If you are dealing with a consumer product company, remember they do not have the funds or resources they once had. Remember, too, they do not have the manpower because of the downsizing. Marketing departments have been halved and halved again. That means a company will not take on a new project or product unless it firmly believes it will be a major boon to the firm."

■

A lack of marketing dollars is not the only thing that hinders consultants. For Holbert, it was a client's desire to get the "best deal." A banker called Holbert regarding a partnership on a piece of property in which he had invested. He shared the property with several other investors and wanted to buy them out. He was calling Holbert to take care of the legal end of the transaction.

"I found out the title to the property was in disarray. Apparently, when they first purchased it, they had hired a consultant to handle the paperwork and title and the person did not do the job. The banker had an inkling that something was wrong and he called me to straighten it out. Ultimately, I did, but it cost the investors twice as much as it would have if they had retained a proficient consultant to begin with. The problem: they did not want to pay the money."

Running into clients who object to fees will always be an obstacle for consultants. Still, those who complain most are usually those who can best afford them. Then why do they complain? Perhaps, the best answer is a report that was recently released on today's consumer by Braxton Associates, an international consulting firm that specializes in attitudes.

In the report, a consumer named Harry Arnold was discussed. It seems Mr. Arnold (not his real name) is a prosperous, well-known management consultant, who vacations in the most luxurious hotels in the world, drives a top of the line Mercedes, lives in the most expensive area of Beverly Hills—and never buys anything but generic toilet paper.

Mr. Arnold may seem eccentric, however, Harry's conduct is best explained by the report that dubs him a victim of "consumer schizophrenia," a malady that retailers, service people, and manufacturers are finding commonplace in the 1990s.

Psychiatrists will tell you that schizophrenia is the "presence of mutually contradictory or antagonistic parts or qualities" and although Harry's behavior exhibits those traits he is not ready for a mental institution. Harry's characteristics are not unusual in today's environment. In fact, Harry is not an oddball. Rather he is a product of a society that began to change rapidly in the 1980s.

To comprehend these new attitudes and what they mean to consultants, it helps to look back a few years. In the "old" days, the typical company searching for a consultant usually had one driving need that dictated the purchasing decision.

Consultants could target the need and meet it. The companies fell into traditional behavior patterns, as did its executives. But, today's buyers are what Braxton describes as a "new age" purchaser, like Harry Arnold. Most do not have any one overriding motivator or need. They are, in fact, unpredictable. They have been influenced by an up-and-down economy, a time crunch, and a changing workforce. There is little that is constant in companies. Change is the everyday rule. There are millions of Harry Arnold's—all complicated with complex needs, and they make a consultant's job difficult.

Qubein has spent time analyzing this new type client that consultants face today. "The managers in the companies that retain us are primarily baby-boomers. They have a different lifestyle than we are used to seeing. They relate to consultants differently, and they see their companies as global, rather than as national.

"For the consultant, these people are more difficult to relate and talk to. Instead of selling consulting services at the middle or lower end of the corporate ladder, as it was the case a few years ago, the baby-boomers want to be involved. Thus, the consultant finds himself selling top management.

"It's a challenge . . . not only does the consultant have to analyze what the company needs, but what today's new executive wants. For the consultants who can, there is a bright, incredible future."

CHAPTER 2

New Techniques in Generating Business

H is story is well-known in the industry. For more than three years, he worked as a speaker—initially without compensation. Finally, he started generating paydays. It was a long, hard struggle, but within a few years Tom Hopkins had not only become one of the highest paid sales consultants and trainers in the country, but one of the most successful authors in the business world as well.

Although the road Hopkins traveled was difficult, in the 1990s, a growing number of consultants are finding that emulating the famed consultant/speaker/writer may actually be a shortcut to success. Instead of renting an office, sending out announcements, buying ads, writing direct mail pieces and pitch letters, a growing number of consultants are finding that speaking and writing are the road to a successful practice.

IMPACT OF SPEAKING, WRITING ON FEES

Laurie Moore has combined her consulting skills with her speaking and writing ability and has developed a thriving practice. Moore, who entered the field about nine years ago, discovered that speaking led to consulting, consulting led to more speaking, and writing increased the demand for her on both the speaking and writing circuit. Although the two skills—speaking and writing—may seem worlds apart, they do the same thing for the consultant—they build credibility and visibility in the eyes of the potential client.

When speakers are on-stage, the audience nearly always perceives them as an authority. The fact the speaker has been selected to address the audience builds his or her credibility. The same is true of the written word. If a consultant authors a book or article, it is assumed he or she is an authority on the subject.

"In many cases," says Moore, "they are. However, even if they are not, the fact they have been given the stage is all it takes. It is the same as hearing a guest on a radio or TV talk show. The mere fact they are on-the-air puts them a step above their peers and competition."

Moore originally set up her consulting firm so she could build a reputation and become a speaker. Her success in the marketing field has enabled her to build a burgeoning consulting practice and has increased the demand for her speaking talents.

"Writing and speaking feed consulting," says Qubein. "A few years ago, I would have said speaking feeds it, but the impact of writing during the past few years has been significant. Authors are in-demand."

Today, Moore does both speaking and writing along with her consulting. She is co-editor of a trade industry monthly publication, *REAL Trends.* Although she did not foresee it, editing the trade has fed both the consulting and speaking practice. One of her best marketing tools is the tradepaper she co-created. It is an industry favorite and has more than 1,000 subscribers. Virtually every one of them is a potential client.

Writing has been a boom for Pennington, too. A member of the National Speaker's Association, a group that teaches its members how to market themselves, Pennington, who recently wrote *On My Honor, I Will,* is the classic example of what publishing can do for a consultant.

Shortly after he wrote his book, a client invited him to visit. "He asked me to come down to do some consulting work. I arrived on Monday, was picked up at the airport by his marketing director, taken to a television show where I appeared on a local talk show and discussed my book, and then was taken around town to meet business leaders. They also arranged a golf game with a couple of potential clients—and I do not even play golf well."

Before he was finished, Pennington had plugged his book, earned some hefty consulting fees, and had two potential additional clients, not to mention the books he sold as a result of the television exposure. The book made Pennington a celebrity—even among his clients.

Pennington writes articles, too. Last year, he did more than a dozen for influential trade magazines in his industry. He also wrote a column for a business publication and a professional trade magazine, *Sam's Quarterly,* which has a circulation of more than 250,000.

Pennington is duplicating a technique that Joseph Izzo mastered some years ago. Izzo, who sold his data processing firm a short time ago to A.J. Kearney, the consulting giant, has long been aware of the value of publishing and the credibility that is carried with it. Izzo not only wrote columns for trade magazines, but his articles were frequently found in the opinion/editorial sections of many industry publications. He also wrote a best-selling book, *The Embattled Fortress,* which gave him instant credibility when he visited clients.

"There are few things more impactful on a prospective client," says Izzo, "than a hardbound book with your name on it. It says you are for real; you have knowledge; you have credibility."

Chase Revel, founder of *Entrepreneur Magazine,* wrote a book on mail order marketing less than four years ago. Today, as an independent consultant, it still is part of his presentation when he visits prospective clients.

Few consultants have done more with a book than Don Kracke, author of *How to Turn Your Ideas into a Million Dollars,* an amusing, witty and fact-filled work on how people can market new ideas.

Kracke's book dates back more than 15 years, but it still has impact. "Prospective clients seldom look inside the cover to see when the book was first published," he says. "The fact you were published is all it takes."

While newspaper and magazine articles may not be as dramatic a calling card, they still wield significant influence. Successful consultants merchandise them. They reprint and send the articles out months—even years—after they were initially published. The credibility remains.

Writers have to be careful, especially when penning articles or newsletters. There is a temptation to plug clients or a practice. Moore is careful not to let *REAL Trends* become a "hype sheet" for present and prospective industry clients. It would be easy to "plug" a prospective (or present) customer—something she avoids.

"In the short run," she says, "that might enable me to generate additional clients, but in the long run it would destroy the publication and the credibility I have built. If you are going to write and build a consulting practice, be sure you never mix the two."

The opportunity is also there to hype a client when it comes to speaking. Frequently, Moore—and other consultants—find themselves in front of an audience that could benefit a client. All they have to do is tie the client into the talk.

For instance, you may be invited to address agents on new marketing techniques. If you had a client who was selling a marketing or sales tools for agents, it would be relatively easy to slip the name and company into the talk, along with an example. Avoid the temptation because of the damage it could do to the credibility you have built.

"That does not mean you can never mention a client to a group of their potential customers," says Moore. "It can be done, but it must legitimately fit into the talk. It can never be hype."

Moore offers another word of caution. "Speaking and writing are excellent ways to build a practice. They give you instant credibility, but you can wipe the benefits out in a minute if you are not totally familiar and knowledgeable about the subject and the industry."

Possessing industry knowledge is critical to a consultant's success, and he or she must have an understanding and insight into the industry whether or not he or she speaks. Van Den Berg spent years studying the stock market before he got into it. Johnson had more than a decade of experience as a CPA before he opened his own practice. Holbert spent years in the real estate industry before he became a real estate attorney. Alessandra was a college professor who spent countless hours as a part-time consultant before he took the full-time plunge. McCuistion spent 20 years in the banking industry before he opened his financial consulting practice.

Without knowledge, Moore would never have been able to launch a reliable industry trade paper. "The newsletter brings business to me. I'll get a call from a prospective client who will say something like 'I know you are the editor and we enjoyed the article about such and such. We'd like to have you talk to our managers'."

How Media Helps

Why the impact? Despite the pessimistic attitude most have when it comes to the media, we still tend to believe what we read, see, and hear in newspapers, television and on the radio. Izzo says "Put yourself in the place of a prospective client who is interviewing two consultants and trying to decide who gets the business. Both have brochures, however, one has included a copy of an article he wrote. It appeared in a reputable magazine or trade paper. Assuming each has similar skills and background, which one would you choose? The consultant with the article has the credibility edge."

GENERATING EXPOSURE

Opportunities for placing articles in trade and consumer media for consultants are abundant. The first step is to find the publication that reaches your prospective customers. Izzo provides a good example (Exhibit 2.1) of how it should be done. A few years ago, he was targeting senior managers of Fortune 500 companies. Many had data processing departments that had become outdated and inefficient. Izzo could reach executives within the data processing departments by writing a meaningful article and placing it in a leading data processing publication. But, he wanted to go beyond the executives in that particular area.

"I knew it would not be the data processing (DP) chiefs who would be hiring me. I had to reach senior management so I targeted the industry publications I knew they—and not just the DP managers—read. Consultants have to be cognizant of who will hire you?" The department or division that needs the consulting help may not be in a position to hire an outsider. They may not want to, either, especially in today's economy where those within companies are concerned about downsizing and retaining their jobs. Seeking outside help may be a signal to top management that the employees within the department cannot handle things.

For a consultant to make inroads in many companies, senior management has to be reached. Generally, presidents and senior managers do not read technical trade journals. Senior managers read trades that discuss their industry, trends, competitive activities, and the industry's outlook. The president of a Fortune 500 publishing company reads publishing trades; the head of a major aerospace firm studies trades that focus on the aerospace industry. Rarely does he or she take time to study the data processing publication, even if it is talking about computers in the publishing or aerospace industry.

Thus, when Izzo wrote an article (Exhibit 2.2), he went to journals that reached senior management, not DP people. Izzo also advises consultants to "write for the lowest common denominator. Even if your subject is technical, write it in a nontechnical manner. Articles should be written so that anyone can understand. Remember, many CEOs of technically-oriented firms do not necessarily have scientific or mechanical knowledge."

One reason Izzo had so much success in placing articles was his ability to understand what type material a publication needed. He studied trades endlessly before he submitted anything. He charted the type of stories they used and built an excellent feel for the readership (Exhibit 2.3).

One of his most successful placements was in *Nation's Business,* a publication that is read by thousands of CEOs throughout the country. The headline (and theme) of the story was "Take Charge of Your Computers—Most Data Processing Problems Are Management Problems. Get in Control with These Seven Steps." He avoided technical jargon completely and by itemizing the seven steps—and explaining them in practical, how-to terms, he kept the attention of the senior managers who read the article. It proved to be one of Izzo's most effective marketing pieces and generated as many, if not more, leads as anything he ever did.

Gwyn Myers, who was a managing principal in Izzo's company, wrote an article called "How to Get Computers to Speak Your Language" for *Executive Magazine,* another publication that catered to senior management.

Izzo also recognized that articles that were self-serving and contained hype instead of information, seldom were published and rarely led to any business. Every article had to provide information, education, and pique the prospective client's interest (Exhibit 2.4).

Revel, an accomplished writer, penned a column on small business for the Los Angeles Times Syndicate. The weekly piece

EXHIBIT 2.1
Reaching Your Customers

IN DEPTH

By Joseph E. Izzo

Stuck with a problem data processing department? Let's get rid of the data processing manager!

No matter that he's working his tail off, never having learned how to say no to user requests. No matter that he's the kind of individual who seldom whimpers, even when his requisition for just one more programmer/analyst is turned down. No matter that he runs a business nearly as complex and demanding as the company it serves and that he may be tremendously overworked and underpaid.

Someone's got to take the rap for that three-year development backlog, that unforeseen 70% jump in hardware acquisition cost, the growing number of service complaints. We need a scapegoat, so let it be him.

Let me not imply that said manager is always without sin. He will, in fact, quite often lack the business skills to complement his technical know-how. To protect his domain, he may resort to high-tech jargon. He may even exude a holier-than-thou attitude. Maybe he should be let go.

In most cases though, the malfunctioning of in-house data processing organizations can be traced to more than one cause — often to a convolution of factors both trivial and significant. Terminating the silhouetted target is usually too simple a solution for a problem this complex.

Let's say that a serious problem does exist. This shouldn't surprise us because computers, despite their enormous propagation, still represent a comparatively adolescent technology and one for which economic use poses many as yet unanswered questions. How should the computer be applied? How should it be controlled? How should cost and benefit be measured to ensure a

With turnaround management, a team of two to four highly qualified managers steps into key managerial posts within and atop the client company's data processing organization. The team's foremost objective is to turn around or reposition the DP organization so that it can move forward in aggressive support of the business.

EXHIBIT 2.1 *(continued)*

This kind of attitude shift is not achieved overnight. When turnaround management is called for, it demands a considerable management commitment. In fact, it can easily take as long as a year or more to overcome initial resistance.

fair return? Few corporations have recognized that ascertaining valid answers to such questions may be absolutely prerequisite to development of a responsive data processing resource. Problems, therefore, are not that uncommon.

Available solutions — whether that means fixing a capability gone catastrophically awry or simply creating an environment in which an ailing service will flourish — are comparatively few and exhibit varying degrees of success.

We've found, for example, that the role of the sit-by-your-side consultant seldom carries sufficient authority to overcome the inertia of a major problem. A more drastic approach — that of selling off the existing capability to a facility management outfit — carries with it some more obvious worries.

"I had considered facilities management as a solution," one manager told us, "until I recognized that many of the very factors that fueled our information processing dilemma would very likely reconfront us when it came time to buy back the capability."

The remaining solution is what The JIA Management Group, Inc. calls "turnaround management." Under this concept, which we believe is unique, a team of two to four highly qualified managers literally steps into and assumes key managerial posts within and atop the client company's data processing organization.

These managers offer an average of 25 years of experience in business, computer technology and data pro-

cessing management. And they come to the client company armed with systems and procedures, largely proprietary, that have been validated by repeated application.

The team's foremost objective is to turn around quickly or reposition the DP organization so that it can move forward in aggressive support of the business. Of course, that positioning must be accomplished in such a way that the department not only performs well during the turnaround team's residency, but also becomes sufficiently well organized, staffed, educated and motivated that a high level of service continues long after its departure.

A secondary objective is to reinforce strongly the credentials and acceptance of the data processing staff by adding to the staff's technical qualifications a familiarity with the principles of business planning and priorities as they might be viewed by the firm's executive offices — in short, giving data processing a business focus. Typically, the team leader, acting as department head and establishing an empathetic interface with the firm's user organizations, is the chief instrument of this achievement.

How well turnaround management can work was demonstrated a few years back at the Lincoln Telephone & Telegraph Co. in Lincoln, Neb. Lincoln Telephone is a utility whose data processing shop — despite the best of intentions — lacked the ability to implement the modern-day, online systems so necessary to customer service improvements. Yet after

EXHIBIT 2.1 *(continued)*

about 12 months of a turnaround management contract, the department proved its ability to design and develop major software systems, and the firm's customer service record improved dramatically.

So taken with its success, Lincoln Telephone recommended the concept to a major Midwest producer of high-fidelity equipment. The company hired JIA to turn around a data processing department that, despite some 50 people and millions of dollars worth of computer hardware, simply was not functioning.

When the turnaround was complete approximately 14 months later, JIA consultants had replaced themselves with a qualified internal management team, had instituted a major training program for the entire staff and had installed the company's first set of data processing standards and procedures covering everything from proposal format to quality assurance requirements.

One of the client firm's key executives found a changed company attitude. "When JIA arrived," he reported, "everyone in our company hated the DP department. It was not reliable, it fouled up and the like.

"By contrast, the department has now gained the confidence of our organization," he added. "Now there's dependability and good communications."

Not an overnight solution

This kind of attitude shift is not achieved overnight. When turnaround management is called for, it demands a considerable management commitment. In fact, it can easily take as long as a year or more to overcome initial resistance, to educate the staff and to install new ideas, policies and procedures, while simultaneously maintaining and upgrading day-to-day operations. The greatest results are usually reaped toward the end of the contract, long after the JIA consultants are gone.

Turnaround management can also be effective on a more limited scale.

In many instances, these same methods are applied to a single unit or function within the larger DP department: to systems development, to operations, to quality assurance or to business systems planning, for example.

One of the country's largest suppliers of private-label cheese had such a need. In this instance, the client's growth required major hardware additions coupled with state-of-the-art software and a new, more sophisticated operating environment. The operations staff, then about 30 people, couldn't meet the challenge and probably faced termination if an alternative solution could not be found.

Beginning with an effectiveness review, a JIA team of two individuals tackled the development of a data center operations improvement plan that ultimately established project request procedures, planning methodology and system turnover procedures among its several facets. The team also set up the documented methods to automate tape library management, automate software production and test, establish a viable recovery and restart procedure and implement other needed operational improvements. JIA also played a key role in procurement of a major software package.

Management involvement

True and lasting success of turnaround management almost invariably demands one very significant ingredient — the direct involvement of executive management: first to establish objectives for its data processing resource and then to monitor and control the operation to ensure continued attainment of the desired cost-benefit ratio and other goals.

Classically, top executives have more or less ignored data processing as they would never ignore engineering, marketing or finance — in many cases, simply because of uneasiness in dealing with the unfamiliar tech-

EXHIBIT 2.1 *(continued)*

nology, compounded at times by the problems of technicians' jargon or aloofness. Yet in working with more than 100 client companies, we've learned that these executives can overcome this distance and learn to make correct decisions about data processing through the vehicle of the executive policy committee.

Properly framed, the data processing executive policy committee is not a discussion group, but a decision-making body made up of the firm's senior executives. Acting much as a corporation's board of directors does in serving and guiding the corporation, this group sets the data processing objectives and policies, appoints the top DP executives and approves their organizational structure, analyzes service responsiveness and reviews — for potential returns — major development projects and other proposed expenditures.

Believing that performance of the executive policy committee would depend largely on the quality of information on which it must act, JIA developed a number of innovative standards for reports and proposals to go before the committee. For proposed expenditures, the committee receives a document known as a decision package, which has proven to work primarily because it presents its case in business language rather than computer terminology. It also demands that the corporate user for whom the development is proposed participate fully in formulating the proposal.

Bergen Brunswig, a JIA client and a distributor of pharmaceutical and health-care products, had been heavily involved in data processing for many years, even operating a computerized inventory control system-president, Robert H. Martini, and other senior executives felt that until they had established the DP policy committee, they lacked the ability to manage or control the service properly.

"It seems easy to manage other parts of the business," Martini said, "but DP was always a mystical area."

As evidence of committee effectiveness, Bergen Brunswig has since reported about a 50% cut in backlog of DP projects from approximately 20 staff-years at $40,000 per year to about two staff-years . And the firm credits the committee with a drop in DP turnover from 35% to 8% in a single quarter.

Start-up situations

For the company that believes the best cure is prevention, JIA offers a start-up management service that employs many of the same principles of turnaround management. As with the turnaround service, the concepts can be applied to an entire DP department or just a new unit within the department.

In the typical situation (much like the separate case history of the Angeles Corp.), the client used outside services but reached the point where the bureau no longer seemed the most cost-effective or timely answer to data processing needs. In such a start-up, JIA can shoulder the entire burden, beginning with preparation of a detailed strategy plan for the changeover.

Subsequent functions include the actual hardware and software selection process, effecting the transfer from the service bureau, installing necessary standards and procedures, setting up an executive policy committee, designing the computer center, managing it until all the wrinkles are out and finally selecting and training the staff to replace JIA.

JIA's role in starting up a brand new unit within an existing data processing department is normally much more limited in scope. At Bergen Brunswig, JIA helped establish two new units — business systems planning and quality assurance — in addition to formation of the firm's executive policy committee.

EXHIBIT 2.1 *(continued)*

For the most part, JIA's clients are firms undergoing a key transition of some sort — entering an exciting growth period, experiencing a product demand that's difficult to satisfy, reconsidering basic objectives or market strategies or even retrenching for one reason or another. In most cases, the transition demands samurai performance by data processing.

When it comes to developing specific solutions to the firm's problems, JIA consultants have been successful almost entirely because they are in a position to apply a vast amount of directly related experience and can do so in an objective way.

Experience level

For example, attaining improved personnel performance requires a well-stocked armory of reliable cause-and-effect experiences. From their work with many other clients, they know the results of adding people, adjusting salaries, reorganizing the department or units within it or even terminating people. And their actions are convincingly objective because their finite "reign" allows them a dispassionate, detached view.

Moreover, their limited time in power demands that replacements be certifiable before that date. To ensure that happens, they begin to inform and educate the entire staff from the first day. Their initial objective is to alleviate the natural trepidation that occurs on arrival. A carefully orchestrated presentation, open to all DP personnel from managers to keypunch operators, explains precisely why they are there, what they propose to do and how long it should take.

Within the subsequent few weeks, the consultants conduct question-and-answer sessions with smaller groups. At one time or another, they talk privately with each individual about his goals and how they might best be achieved.

The consultants are always concerned about developing each staff

member to his highest potential in line with the individual's goals. Naturally, those individual wishes sometimes conflict with the client's aims, making changes imperative. At worst, and this has applied to some department heads, it may be suggested that the employee seek another job.

Most often, however, shifting the person to a different function within the organization is the better solution and often benefits the employee directly. For example, switching a middle manager from programming

Most often, shifting the person to a different function within the organization is the better solution and often benefits the employee directly.

to quality assurance exposes that individual to a new overview of the system development cycle and the tools and techniques by which the cycle is best managed. That person then ends up with a depth of business experience to complement his technical qualifications.

To illustrate more specifically the firm's approaches to real problems, several brief case histories follow. Studies of the Lincoln Telephone & Telegraph Co. and Itel Corp. demonstrate the approach to turnaround management. A look at the Angeles Corp. shows how start-up management was accomplished.

Lincoln Telephone

About 80 years of age, the Lincoln Telephone & Telegraph Co. of Lincoln, Neb., is a sparkling example of Middle America's catch-up infatua-

EXHIBIT 2.1 *(continued)*

tion with contemporary data processing technology.

Here is a medium-size utility that offers local and long-distance services to 22 counties in southeastern Nebraska. Here's a regional firm that serves some 190,000 customers and 360,000 instruments. Here's a company whose data processing organization progressed in just a few years from operation of a semiarchaic batch-oriented accounting system to modern-day, on-line processing of customer and stockholder records, toll settlements (a major source of income) and sophisticated business management tasks from what-if modeling to inventory control.

Yet in 1977, the DP outlook could not have appeared less promising. Lincoln Telephone's management — including Vice-President and Controller Laurence Connealy — had earlier recognized that the company's accelerating growth was demanding new and better ways to handle customer orders. "At that time," Connealy told us, "it took 3½ days to install service from the time a customer placed an order."

That was unacceptable to a firm that prided itself on service improvements and hold-the-line costs. So it attempted — starting in 1975 — to develop and implement a new computer-based order processing and billing system it called Cars (for Customer Automated Records System). It anticipated that Cars would be followed by other major DP developments.

But things didn't go according to plan. Off the beaten path and reflecting a somewhat provincial understanding of DP technology, the DP staff at Lincoln spent some 60 man-months in system development, forecast the need for an additional 60 and was finally judged short on system design know-how.

Desperate to solve the growing problem, Lincoln Telephone executive management considered its alternatives: the turnkey development of Cars by an outside firm, commitment to a five-year facilities management contract or simply extensive recruiting and training. The facilities management contract — under which both equipment and data processing staff would be legally absorbed by the contractor — was a drastic solution, but it looked like a front-runner in responsiveness.

"Although the facilities management approach seemed to be a good bet, it also featured some significant drawbacks," Connealy admitted. As he now recalls it, the dominant negatives were potential cost growth, lack of guarantees on return of the capability at contract termination and the utility's definite distaste for the idea of sandwiching a separate corporate entity between the utility and its customers.

Lincoln Telephone had heard of JIA and the turnaround management concept. It agreed to a one-year management services contract, with provisions for both cancellation and extension.

The contract's comprehensive work plan addressed the identified problems, called for the immediate insertion of qualified data processing management, defined a program to upgrade its employees and supervisors and specified month-by-month deliverables by which the utility could monitor and control the effort.

Connealy's recall is a bit more vivid. "JIA brought in five managers to run our shop. They moved our people aside temporarily, wrote standards, set up a project control system, prepared a personnel assessment and training plan and began a national search for a new DP manager."

Interestingly enough, while the JIA team had termination authority, no firings were found necessary. Even the displaced manager moved into a newly created quality assurance slot.

EXHIBIT 2.1 *(continued)*

Interestingly enough, while the JIA team had termination authority, no firings were found necessary. Even the displaced manager moved into a newly created quality assurance slot.

Steering committee

JIA also introduced Lincoln Telephone to the concept of the executive steering committee. According to Connealy, this group of top-level executives still meets quarterly to review DP status and proposals.

From the JIA viewpoint, the effort represented a repositioning of the data processing department and the turnaround of an intolerable situation. When the consultants went in, DP facilities could almost have been described as chaotic. Salaries lagged behind the industry, and morale was low.

When JIA left, about five years of learning had been jammed into one year; each employee had a prescribed route to education and advancement. And executive management had begun to understand and pay attention to the data processing operation.

Lincoln Telephone also whipped the order processing problem. With Cars, more than 50% of Lincoln Telephone's service orders are actually filled the day the order is received or, in the case of orders placed late in the day, within 24 hours.

Itel Corp.

Founded in 1967, San Francisco's Itel Corp. flourished in the next decade, earning Wall Street's favor for the booming revenue from the firm's equipment-leasing business — most notably in the leasing of low-cost alternatives to IBM computers.

But 1979 saw the company stagger enormously as IBM dropped some of its prices, making much of Itel's line uncompetitive. The company lost more than $400 million that year. In January 1981, it entered Chapter 11 bankruptcy.

Today, less than three years later, Itel has gained a new notoriety — this time for the apparent speed at which it has begun to recover. It has pared the number of business units from nearly 30 to only two — container leasing and rail-car operations. It cut its work force from 7,000 to 900.

Itel has installed what is considered to be a unique bankruptcy information support system — a data processing system that has, according to Itel management, contributed so much to the recovery process that it has already been marketed to at least three other Chapter 11 businesses.

However, getting that data processing system in gear was a struggle. JIA was eventually called in.

William Twomey, selected to preside over the firm during the later phases of reorganization, saw the basic problem as one of politics. "When we cut back our management staff in the fall of 1982, I — being the vice-president of finance and administration at that time — inherited several departments, including the Corporate Information Systems [CIS] Department. Unfortunately, the manager of the department held strong opinions of his own about the development and sale of the Chapter 11 software and threatened to quit."

Recognizing that the CIS manager's threat could have widespread impact on the struggling company, Twomey backed his own hand by planning, with JIA, for emergency management services.

EXHIBIT 2.1 *(continued)*

Sure enough, in a power play, three key CIS employees — including the manager — quit, giving only two weeks notice.

The task facing JIA was unusual in that the Chapter 11 reporting requirements were monumental. Itel was dealing with more than 50,000 creditors and shareholders. The reorganization involved 24,000 separate claims and more than 3,000 executory contracts.

Periodic documentation ordered by the bankruptcy court included statement of assets, statement of liabilities, statement of executory contracts and statement of affairs, also known as Information Schedule 1.

The computer was used to maintain a claims register, to handle mailings to the creditors and shareholders, to call for and tabulate votes on the reorganization plan and even to distribute newly issued stocks and bonds.

Primary tasks

JIA's primary tasks were to see the computer operation resume without a hitch, to improve service to the remaining operating companies, to develop an information systems strategic plan and to develop a business plan for the marketing of computer services to bankruptcy customers.

> *Recognizing that the CIS manager's threat could have widespread impact on the struggling company, Twomey backed his own hand by planning, with JIA, for emergency management services. Sure enough, three key CIS employees quit, giving only two weeks notice.*

> *On Angeles' behalf, the JIA team — which varied from two to five people during the contract period — evaluated equipment (eventually recommending an IBM System/38), centralized available DP resources and established a systems development methodology.*

Another significant contribution by JIA has been a major reorganization of CIS.

As recently as June 1983, the two operating companies and corporate headquarters were

EXHIBIT 2.1 *(continued)*

each serviced by a more or less independent section within CIS. Each group did its own development work, with a high probability of duplicated effort.

Under a department reorganization, all users are served by a unified group that offers several important new functions. A quality assurance and administration group, a business systems planning office and a customer support 'group were added. The small increase in total head count also accounts for a technical group concerned with network control.

In response to JIA recommendations, Itel formed a four-man executive steering committee that will soon begin to oversee CIS operations and proposed improvements.

Angeles Corp.

The Angeles Corp. is a nationwide financial services organization. Based in Los Angeles and employing about 275 people, it acts as general partner to a number of limited partnerships, investing primarily in real estate developments and motion picture productions. It also manages pension and profit-sharing funds for other corporations and for educational institutions.

As perhaps the best measure of the firm's recent success, the past three years have seen its combined investments in stocks, bonds and other financial instruments soar to $2 billion from an already healthy $500 million.

Needed unified facility

But, according to Angeles President William H. Elliott, the firm had until recently been somewhat hampered by the lack of a professional, unified data processing facility.

"We were spending a good bit of money on service bureaus," Elliott said, "not too effectively, I might add. To keep up with our growth rate, we needed to significantly enhance our systems capabilities.

"I'm a great believer in systems," Elliott maintained. "And I'm convinced that data processing should be looked upon as a management tool, not simply an accounting tool."

Considered alternatives

The need for significant improvement led Angeles to the JIA group, but not before it considered a number of alternatives ranging from big-name consultants to equipment manufacturers.

"We were offered plenty of 'free' advice," Elliott recalled, also noting that most such advice usually proves costly in the long run.

"We needed a sophisticated data center, with plenty of growth potential, and knew that we faced a painful, extremely challenging job because we were starting two or three years later than we should have."

JIA started to work early in 1980, beginning with development of a strategic data processing plan. On Angeles' behalf, the JIA team — which varied from two to five people during the con-

EXHIBIT 2.1 *(continued)*

tract period — evaluated equipment (eventually recommending a System/38 IBM minicomputer), centralized all the available DP resources and established a system development methodology.

Cost of the new facility ran to about $2 million.

The software task was one of implementing existing applications on the firm's new hardware and designing new applications. JIA also provided an extensive amount of training for the in-house staff.

As it does in the majority of instances, JIA also recommended and helped to implement an executive steering committee by which Angeles management can monitor and control the new centralized function.

How the management contract works

The management contract is one way of quickly repositioning a data processing department and developing it into a professional, high-performance organization in a short period of time. This is accomplished by placing a JIA data processing management team in the department on a temporary basis to "turn around" the performance of the organization. During its tenure, the team's major responsibilities are:

■ To effect a quick turnaround in the performance of a data processing organization.

■ To develop within the client company a strong, reliable, enduring professional data processing organization, which includes finding the training replacements for the temporary management team.

■ To install methods and practices for ensuring an ongoing, quality organization with appropriate management reporting and control.

In bringing about the turnaround of a data processing organization, the management contract has some basic advantages over the more conventional methods of hiring a new management team or promoting managers from within.

The motivation is different. Under a management contract, the goal is to develop a lean but strong organization. Since the outside management team is there for only a relatively short period of time, the interest and focus is to put in place only what is needed; there is no tendency to build an "empire."

The contract management team has no personal ties to existing members of the organization and, therefore, can be objective in evaluating an individual's performance.

The JIA staff is experienced in working as a team to accomplish major DP objectives. In contrast, if a new manager is hired, it may take a minimum of six months before he can form and test a team that can move aggressively forward.

Many of the professional methods and practices required to effectively operate a data processing organization exist within JIA and have been tested and implemented in many organizations.

Therefore, the cost and time required to develop these methods and practices is minimized.

With a management contract, the team's success is measured by its ability to make the required changes on schedule and to select managers who will maintain a high level of performance for the organization in the future. There should be no need for outside management assistance

EXHIBIT 2.1 *(continued)*

when the management contract is completed.

A management contract is not designed to provide "hatchet men," but to serve as a means of enhancing the skills of in-house talent. Individuals will be replaced only in those cases in which capabilities are below acceptable standards.

Situation dictates size

Based on the size of the data processing installation, the number of JIA managers at the beginning of a management contract will range from 2½ to five, depending on the complexity of the situation. The contract's duration could be eight to 14 months. The time period is specified at the beginning of the engagement.

A brief scenario follows. For purposes of illustration, we will assume the requirement is for four members of the JIA management staff and the duration of the contract is 12 months.

During the first three to four months, four JIA team members would be assigned to the client site. At the conclusion of that period, one member will be replaced by a trained internal DP staff member, bringing the number down to three. At about the sixth month, an additional member of the JIA staff would be replaced by another staff member. At approximately the ninth month, the third member of the JIA staff would be replaced. The remaining JIA staff

person would leave at the end of the 12th month.

This approach allows for the gradual shift from a JIA-managed organization back to a client-managed organization. The JIA management team brings about this shift and effects change while managing the daily activities of the organization.

Several other general features of the JIA management contract include:

■ The JIA staffing levels are reviewed formally each quarter to determine if reduction of JIA staff can be accelerated. An increase in JIA staff should never be considered since this defeats the purpose of the contract; the goal is to develop the people internally.

■ The contract can be canceled at any time, with 30 days' notice.

■ JIA will assume all responsibility for managing data processing within the client's policies and guidelines and report directly to the executive in charge. Outside advice and counsel will be provided to the contract management team by JIA executive management.

About the author

Joseph E. Izzo is president of The JIA Management Group, Inc., a Santa Monica, Calif.-based management consulting firm specializing in data processing.

EXHIBIT 2.2
Write for Media the Decision Makers Read

SEPTEMBER, 1987 VOL. III NO.9

INFORMATION CENTER

MANAGING THE GROWTH OF END-USER COMPUTING

*D*on't say
that you
can't devote
the time or
the money
to develop
a system
architecture;
you can't
afford not to.

—Joe Izzo

EXHIBIT 2.2 *(continued)*

Planning and creating an information system

HAROLD LASKI, ONE OF England's leading twentieth-century economists, once said, "We must plan our civilization or we must perish." In like fashion, companies that lack an overall plan for their computer system architecture seriously jeopardize their chances for growth and success in the future.

An architecture helps a company determine how, and in what form, computer technology will be implemented to achieve the firm's goals. When I go into a company, one of my first questions is, "Do you have a system architecture?" The answer is invariably, "Yes, we do"; however, in viewing that architecture, I find it relates primarily to a hardware or a communications network. Such an architecture addresses only how the technology is connected, but not necessarily the needs of the users or the business itself. I ask further, "How will the technology be used?" I am told that the users will be better able to share information and to communicate with one another. If I ask why they need to do this, or how this will benefit the company, the answers become considerably more vague.

What's the problem here? Quite simply, there is no strategy for the computer systems architecture. When I say strategy, I mean the art of planning and directing activities to achieve a goal. It is difficult to use the technology properly when there is no business purpose in mind. I have no problem with the idea of a hardware or communications network architecture nor with users communicating with each other. In fact, both are essential. But these are the means, not the end. My point is that without a strategy that produces a desired business goal the technology is going to waste.

Historically, the firm's goals and the business technology department's goals have not been the same. A primary reason is that the business people have never taken the time to develop a true system architecture strategy that responds to the overall needs of the business. This essential first step must be taken before we can begin using technology as an enabling device.

We are at a major crossroads in deciding how computer technology is going to be used in the future. The problems are detailed in frequent cover stories in every business magazine. You must make a decision about your company's computer resources. Don't say you can't afford to make the time or the monetary commitment; you can't afford not to. The problem is already

HISTORICALLY, A FIRM'S GOALS AND THE MIS DEPARMENT'S GOALS HAVE NOT BEEN THE SAME. BUT THERE IS A WAY TO ALIGN THEM. IT'S CALLED THE SKUNK WORKS.

Joseph E. Izzo

This article is excerpted from the book The Embattled Fortress: Strategies for Restoring Information Systems Productivity *to be published in October 1987, by Jossey-Bass Publishers, Inc. (San Francisco, California).* © 1987 by Jossey-Bass Publishers, Inc.

EXHIBIT 2.2 *(continued)*

costing you hundreds of thousands, perhaps millions of dollars a year in lost opportunity and overhead.

It's not that we have been without a planning strategy or methodology in the past; it's simply that the methodologies of yesterday and today are woefully inadequate. Their purpose, for the most part, was simply to help perform tasks more quickly, which at one time was probably considered a "productivity gain." But they cannot help us implement a future architecture that addresses the changing needs of the users or that helps us produce products or services better, faster, or cheaper.

OLD PLANNING TECHNIQUES

Many of the old methodologies were, in the parlance of business technology, "information-driven," such as IBM's Business Systems Planning (BSP). Others incorporated such things as "functional activity models" with "information flow models" that created "business models." The process began when the programmers-analysts diagrammed the business operation, noting where every scrap of information came from and went to. This took months, and was often frustrating and exhausting. In many cases, this data collection became so complex that it would require a miracle to design a system that accounted for every need.

Perhaps the greatest drawback to diagramming business functions and activities is that it only accounts for where a business is right now. It doesn't consider where the company is going, and so is doomed to be out of date before it is even implemented.

In most cases, the concentration is on "information." This supports the prevailing myth that information is the computer's end product. Though the various ways in which computers are able to manipulate and deliver "information" fascinate business technology personnel, there are no inherent productivity gains that benefit the business.

To underscore my point, consider this description of a seminar for executives:

This program will give executives a solid basis for directing the implementation of technology for the information age in which we live. Meetings will focus on devising strategies for controlling the costs of handling information.

There are probably some useful and worthwhile techniques presented in a seminar like this, but it's still yesterday's thinking. It promotes what I call ephemeral planning, because it makes everyone feel good for a few fleeting moments, but can rarely be implemented in the day-to-day business world. If we are going to see the benefits of computer technology as an enabling device that truly benefits the company, we must begin what I call sensible planning: not what we'd ideally like to have in a perfect world, but what is realistic and achievable.

One more point: conventional planning strategies are concerned with managing the data we have collected and plan to collect. These strategies assume we will continue to amass more and more data on more and more functions, and never address what I consider of greater importance. If computer technology can be

properly deployed, isn't it conceivable that we could reduce the amount of data we collect and retain, and perhaps eliminate some redundant functions as well?

There are certain points in a company's business cycle when extraordinary effort is required to make a major shift or change in the way things are done. At these points, standard methods for creating change are not adequate. New approaches must be sought. How to begin? By bringing the firm's movers and shakers together to plan the strategy.

THE SKUNK WORKS

Many years ago, Lockheed came up with the idea of gathering a team of people together in some off-site location for brainstorming new products. They called the idea "the skunk works." The term "skunk" comes from the notion that these people are isolated and that no one wants to be around them. It was an immediate success at Lockheed, and now many other companies have adopted the concept. Great ideas almost always emerge. One of the most famous skunk works projects was creating the MV-8000 super minicomputer at Data General, which was chronicled in Tracy Kidder's Pulitzer Prize-winning book, *The Soul of a New Machine.*

I believe the skunk works is the best environment for tackling something as important as a new computer system architecture. First of all, it allows the team to break away physically and mentally from the everyday corporate culture. It also gives them freedom to identify new ways in which computer technology can be used to support the business and help it thrive. The skunk works allows people to get rid of their inhibitions and innovate without restrictions. The goal is an environment where they can think and talk without the conventional business constraints.

Senior management should demonstrate their support, and must remain visible and involved throughout the skunk works. This is important because it shows their confidence and trust in them. The team needs that because they are changing the way computer technology is going to be used, and thus changing some fundamental ways you do business. Involvement says you are willing to accept the risks in giving them this assignment. Without that outward sign of confidence, it will be more difficult for the team to innovate or to take the risks the project needs. They must feel confident, inspired, and secure.

As their leader, senior management must initiate the skunk works project and give the team its mission and focus. Skunk works participants must be clear and precise about their task; no one should think this is just another bull-shooting session or a low-level, busy-work project. It must be clear that change will emerge. The team must have access to the firm's goals for the next five to ten years. The team must understand senior management's thinking and strategy in planning those goals. If they can grasp how that thinking came about, they have a much better chance of turning those goals into reality.

Depending on the size and complexity of the company, it may take three to six months for the skunk works to create its plan for the new system architecture.

EXHIBIT 2.2 *(continued)*

The team must understand that the project requires their full attention for the duration, no matter how long that is.

THE COMPOSITION OF THE TEAM

The members of the skunk works should be people respected by their departments and the rest of the company. These people should be in a responsible line capacity, people who are committed "doers." The ideal mix is two-thirds line people from the user organizations and one-third technology people.

The line people should be from different departments and should be people who represent their organizations and can speak for them. You want departmental line people who understand the business. You want operational people—those who meet the customers and are involved with the firm's product.

You do not want staff people who are steeped in procedures. Nor do you want backroom people who are interested in data for data's sake. You want the people who make the difference in the company.

From the technology side, you want people who are perceptive and can think in conceptual terms. These should be people who are clear thinkers and problem solvers, not those mired in yesterday's technology. They should have a broad understanding of the technology and its uses and applications, but not necessarily detailed knowledge.

The skunk works leader should be someone who embraces the concept of technology as an enabling device, who is able to create an open and frank discussion environment, and who is not encumbered by company politics. The leader should be a senior manager who understands the business in its broadest perspective, and who is highly respected by both peers and management.

THE SKUNK WORKS DEN

To be truly effective, the skunk works team should meet in an off-site environment. "Off-site" means far enough away from the daily operating environment to avoid constant interruptions about everyday matters. The actual place the team meets may be a conference room in the far corner of one of your buildings, a rented trailer, the company apartment, or in a hotel meeting room.

The team members should have only the task at hand before them: planning and designing a new system architecture. The corporate culture drives us to certain preordained conclusions, and the team must break free of them if it is going to innovate. There are constant interruptions in our daily routines for phone calls and supposedly important messages, even at the most tightly-closed-door meeting. All these influences and interruptions must be eliminated for the skunk works to be successful.

The team members work every day at the off-site location, just as if they were going to the office. Three weeks is a long time for people to be away from their normal jobs, let alone three months. Participants often grow anxious about what is going on in their absence. Some may feel they will lose their positions to competitors if they're away too long. They must feel assured that their positions are not in jeopardy. In some cases, it may be necessary to let the team go to their offices one day a week. Be aware, however, that this creates a mind shift and may slow down the creative process.

There is no question that the company pays a price by sacrificing these people for the duration of the skunk works. But there is a payback as well. First, the new system architecture will be significantly more appropriate in supporting and advancing the business. Second, skunk works members, ostensibly the rising stars in the firm, receive a broad education in the combined aspects of business and technology. This unquestionably valuable experience puts them in a strong position to offer additional benefits to the company for a long time.

Once the team is formed, the work begins in earnest. Almost. To be realistic, not all skunk works team members will be available immediately. Most will need a little time to transfer their responsibilities to others while they are gone. This need not deter the start-up phase, however. There are many preparatory steps that need to be taken so the team can work effectively and efficiently once things are in full swing.

For example, let's say the project length has been set for six months. The first two months can be designated as preparation time, and the remaining four months as the actual skunk works project. Under such a plan, the two most important tasks during this period are establishing goals and building the business model.

ESTABLISH GOALS

Of all the skunk works activities, setting goals is the most important. If the goals are inadequate in the beginning, they will produce inadequate results at the end. They should be broad, general goals, but not easy ones; each should require a lot of thinking and hard work for the team. The goal setters shouldn't be immediately concerned about whether or not the team can actually achieve the goals they set; rather, they should be good, desirable goals that are potentially achievable. One company, a diversified manufacturing concern we helped to develop a system architecture, set these goals for their skunk works team:

- Reduce the total cost of the divisions' direct and indirect nontouch labor by 30%.
- Reduce the full-scale product development schedule spans by 33% and initial production spans prior to full production by 50%.
- Reduce internally generated changes to product definition by 75%.
- Improve the time span for incorporating changes by 50%.
- Improve shop floor direct-touch labor and equipment costs by 25%.
- Reduce the factory work-in-progress inventory by 50%.
- Facilitate improved information exchange standards and practices between the company and vendors, other contractors, and the customers.

Any skunk works team member examining these goals would have no doubt about what the team's objectives were. Equally important, goals like these de-

EXHIBIT 2.2 *(continued)*

mand that people look at the computer in an entirely different way: as an enabling technology for achieving the goals set forth. And with such specific goals the business technology department will grow, not in a purposeless manner, but as an organization with a strong, directed mission.

I learned this lesson the hard way. Back in the mid-1960s, I was asked to head a project to develop an automated production control and material management information system. And that's exactly what I did. Furthermore, when we completed the design we offered it to the president with great pride. We explained how the system was going to reduce inventory by 10%. We showed how the time to build a product would be shortened by five days. Best of all, we said, the new system would produce tons of "information" that would help to manage and control various processes.

After spending more than an hour listening to our presentation, this patient and polite man quietly complimented us on the exquisite design we had created. Then, less quietly, he told us we were not to continue with the project. "If this company is going to be in business five years from now," he said, "we must reduce inventory by 30% and the time it takes to build the product must be reduced by 45 days. That's what we need, and as for the information, if some is available, well, it might be nice."

We went away, properly admonished, to reconsider what we had done. Two months later, we went back into the president's office and made quite a different presentation. Our new system was far less complex than the previous one, produced quite a lot less "information," and met every goal he asked for.

Bold, clearly stated business goals are essential prerequisites if the skunk works team is to develop a new computer system architecture. And these goals are not simply to automate a manual function or, worse yet, to create another information system. These goals are to be developed by the skunk works team, working with senior management. During the first two months, the team might meet once a week to agree upon the goals. Once the goals are set, it is the skunk works team's responsibility to develop a strategy for achieving and implementing them.

IT'S A FULL-TIME JOB

While the skunk works team's goals are being outlined, one or two of the team members are permanently assigned the task of building a high-level model of today's business practices. This is referred to as the "as-is" architecture model. Several of the business technology department staff may be assigned to this group on a temporary basis to assist in the definition. The "as-is" model is necessary as a tool to help the entire team when they meet later, on a full-time basis, to discuss the overall aspects of, and the interactions between, various business functions.

The first month of full-time involvement is hard on the team. It is also a chaotic time. People are getting used to one another and trying to become comfortable away from their normal work. They have to adjust to spending day after day together, often in one room.

They want structure and duties, which are not forthcoming unless they themselves create them.

There is also a lot of negativism at first. As the discussions begin and people start making suggestions, you hear a lot of we-can't-do-that or they-won't-let-us or that-can't-be-done comments. These are simply excuses people sometimes make up to justify flaws in the system.

This is when the leader begins to make his or her presence felt. The leader has to give the team permission to break rules, knock down defenses, and be innovative and creative. Unfortunately, the leader also becomes the team's scapegoat. It's a tough position to be in and very difficult to do successfully. At times, it's almost like conducting a group therapy session. This is why it is important to have a skilled leader who understands the business and the technology, and who knows how to lead people in this type of process. Often, it helps to bring someone in from outside the corporation. You want to do the skunk works just once, and do it right the first time.

After a while people have vented their anger and the inhibitions are gone. Gradually, they learn that there is no one there to tell them they can't do something, and if they want to do it, they can. The way this usually happens is someone lights a spark and the whole team takes off. The realization sinks in that they are in charge, they are the change agents. People loosen up, and the real communication begins. Now anything is possible. They are on their way to becoming what I call architecturists.

EXPLORING THE TECHNOLOGY

It is important that every member of the skunk works understand computer technology. In the early stage, let them explore computer technology in a free-wheeling fashion. Let them talk about the computers the firm currently uses. Let them talk about trends, new products, and new technologies until they are comfortable with them and understand them.

Often, the business people will be asking most of the questions, and the technology people will be doing most of the answering. Let this happen. They may want to discuss artificial intelligence, relational data bases, parallel processing, or local area networks. Let them go into as much detail as they want about designing, creating, and engineering computer systems, until they are thoroughly satisfied.

At this point, the leader or an appointed architecturist will ask, "If you could, how would you do things differently?" It's at this point that you begin learning how to create the new system architecture. Often the question has to be asked again and again, punctuated with, "Yes, but what if...." But the answers are invaluable.

One thing you learn during this stage is that most of your firm's departments and organizations are islands of automation. Even though they are connected to the central computer, they don't interact very much. You will learn the business technology department is an island, too; there is very little coordination in either data, functions, or ideas, and even less sharing with other departments.

EXHIBIT 2.2 *(continued)*

Designing a system architecture

What is meant by the term system architecture? It's the same process as designing a building. It is a set of design principles that define a relationship of, and interaction between, various parts of a system or network of systems, including the organization of functions. System architecture starts with a look at the business as a whole to determine the best way computer technology can be used to support the business and its mission to produce its products better, faster, and cheaper. It's not just looking at the individual functions, but the relationships between all the functions in the business.

The best computer system is a simple computer system. The way to achieve this is to disperse the computer power throughout the organization, moving applications away from the centralized computer and as close to the user as possible. The application strategy I present here is conceptual in nature. The method of implementing it into a system architecture can vary significantly, depending on the nature of the organization and its size.

Most companies don't have an overall system architecture. If they do, it usually is a patchwork of current technologies serving the existing, time-worn approach to applications. The inherent problem with this approach is that it assumes those 10- to 15-year-old applications are satisfactory. Thus, whatever exists becomes, by default, the foundation for further architectural developments.

Any future systems architecture must address three different missions: company needs for system integration of functions and data, organizational or departmental needs for applications that are responsive to their unique requirements, and an application environment that provides individual users with the tools they need to accomplish their work. I call these three levels of systems architecture enterprise level systems, departmental level systems, and ad hoc level systems.

Enterprise Level Systems. These systems maintain the primary management and operational data that cut across the company as a whole. Enterprise level systems should be limited to only processes that integrate key business functions. These systems are both a transporter of data between entities and a maintainer of data that are shared between multiple entities. I view an enterprise level system as the primary means of achieving control between various organizational entities within a business unit. This assures that a common operating philosophy is achieved.

Notice that enterprise level systems normally are not involved in creating data or in determining the manner in which data are used. These activities are best performed at the other two levels of the system hierarchy. By taking this approach, you will greatly reduce the complexity that could result from the mixing of departmental requirements with overall company requirements.

Departmental Level Systems. These are systems that are placed within a departmental or even an organizational unit within a department. Their purpose is to achieve the unique objectives of that entity. For example, consider how different the needs are for processing, managing, and controlling a purchase organization versus a marketing department or a manufacturing organization. Although these various departments may share some data, most of their data processing can be self-contained and should be treated that way. These organizations should

have the authority and responsibility to select and implement their own solutions to satisfy individual objectives.

Departmental level computer application processes deal with a variety of situations and special cases, which makes the application software design relatively complex. This complexity should be addressed by those people who are familiar with the functions their departments perform. Further, the definition and implementation of data that is created in the department should be their responsibility as well. The software design and maintenance demands of department application functions are thus isolated from the enterprise level applications.

The system hierarchy concept suggests that large central programming staffs may no longer be required. Some of these people can be moved out to the departments to directly support them. This will give departmental managers not only the responsibility, but also the capability to use their computers as they deem necessary.

Decisions about the number and capacity of the company's computers are more manageable when the system hierarchy is applied. Growth in central capacity is more easily controlled when it is no longer driven by departmental processing demands. Computer resource needs at the departmental level, on the other hand, are influenced mainly by the number of terminals and workstations those computers must support. With a dispersed computing approach, functional managers find that they can decide for themselves whether to increase computer capacity or to buy more terminals because they alone make the terminal response time versus computer cost trade-offs. Their computer cost decisions are not compromised by priority or peak processing demands of other users. Departmental managers are out in a position to better control their work.

Ad Hoc Level Systems. These are not systems in the usual sense of the word, but rather a variety of tools and techniques that let individual users set up their own systems. We have found the most innovation at this level of the architecture, so these systems have the fewest controls and permit the greatest freedom.

Here we find a high proliferation of personal computers, personal productivity software, English-like languages, and 4GLs that tie into relational DBMSs. Often we find software and other capabilities provided by the company's information center, that allow PCs to act as on-line terminals.

Even though I say control is slight at this level, it is important that users adhere to conventions established for the architecture. If the corporate standard is set for IBM PCs and compatibles, or the approved data base software is, say, *dBase III*, then all users must adhere to those products. This facilitates a degree of compatibility for future systems planning, which would be essential if, for example, a local area network were installed. It also means data can easily be distributed and shared. And last but not least, it facilitates learning efforts, because an experienced user can help the novices.

The enterprise, departmental, and ad hoc systems together make up the integrated application environment of the future. The main goal always is to move the technology out. A well-planned, well-executed, dispersed architecture is essential for using computer technology as an enabling device and moving the business aggressively into the future.   —*J.I.*

EXHIBIT 2.2 *(continued)*

It's important to keep these discussions moving ahead, for in time the team itself will recognize these islands and will want to overcome the isolation. The leader should continue asking questions about what is there and what isn't, probing until they find out what is missing and what is needed. The skunk works is creating the fertile ground in which to begin growing the new system architecture.

This exploration stage generally takes two months. Once completed, it is time for them to begin conceptualizing and designing the new system architecture.

FROM "AS-IS" TO "TO-BE" ARCHITECTURE

The business people start by discussing business practices. They explain the nature of their work and what they want to accomplish. This is a fairly general discussion. For example, they may say they want to capture these or those data, and combine them with something else. They may say they want to automate a particular function or add a graphics workstation.

The technologist ventures opinions on what can or cannot be done. Gradually, the issues begin sorting themselves out. What emerges is an optimistic vision of the future in which a new, simpler, more flexible computer system seems possible. The technologist sees the promise of computers working more efficiently and harmoniously, systems that can be easily changed when necessary. The business people see the possibility of computers that adapt to the way they do their work, that permit growth and changes in the organization, and that serve the firm's missions and goals.

The subject of these early discussions is what I call the "as-is" and the "to-be" architectures: what we have now and what we want to have tomorrow. The reason for discussing the "as-is" architecture is to create a broader understanding of how the business operates today, and to locate the weak points. The "to-be" architecture is developed into a broad schema of what the future could be if technology is appropriately deployed. Now we have an architecture that marries business goals and computer technology.

This is a significant event at the skunk works. People feel they have accomplished something and have come up with a new, promising, viable alternative to the complex, frustrating rat's nest computer system they now have. It is an achievement, and when it's accomplished, the members have indeed become architecturists.

THE NEW ARCHITECTURE

The next stage is to open discussions about the new architecture. The team must keep its focus sharply on how the new architecture will help the company achieve the goals the skunk works addressed. There is a great deal of enthusiasm and interest at this point. The team feels that is has earned its stripes, so to speak, and now they are ready to design the new system.

The work is broken into two phases. The first phase is developing the architectural concepts and then thinking through their various impacts on the organization. Many issues cannot be resolved, but the important thing is to keep the discussion moving toward a new system architecture.

When the team feels they have a preliminary architecture defined, they should prepare a report for senior management. This should explain how the new system architecture will form a solution to the goals with which the team was charged.

In the second phase, the team members must turn their ideas into reality. First, they must study senior management's critique and comments, and locate the plan's strengths and weaknesses. Then they must revise and refine the plan, over and over if necessary, until they come up with a legitimate, final architecture.

The final stage of the skunk works involves writing a report to senior management that includes the following items:

The system architecture. This explains the strategy for dispersing computer technology, how the functional or organizational applications will perform, and their relationship to other applications and processes.

Organizational impact. This section deals with the functional realignments within the company that are necessary to fulfill the new architecture's mission. It also includes an impact analysis of these changes.

Computer hardware, software, and communications network architecture. The team must explain how to develop the high-level technical architecture that will support the new system. This portion of the report describes where the computer hardware (whether centralized or dispersed) will be located, the interconnections between the hardware and the communications networks, and identifies the implementation policy and standardization requirements.

Computer technology delivery support requirements. This section deals with the organizational aspects of delivering the new system architecture. It covers what should be centralized, what functions should be dispersed, and how these various functions will interact in the future.

Costs and benefits. This section explains, in broad estimates, the costs associated with achieving the new architecture, the benefits the business stands to gain, and how those benefits relate to the original goals the skunk works was charged with.

Migration plan. Here an overall scenario is developed that recommends how to move from the "as-is" to the "to-be" architecture.

The process is neither complex nor new. It combines knowledge and understanding of today's business, corporate goals, and directions with enabling technologies, and gives us the freedom to choose different approaches to achieving tomorrow's business goals. It's the vehicle for identifying the issues and opportunities related to managing today's business and for allowing us to establish future objectives.

System architecture, once developed, becomes the road map to the future. It provides the framework for sound judgment in the development of capital, human, and technical resources, and for the achievement of a more profitable and competitive enterprise. IC

Joseph E. Izzo is Vice President of A.T. Kearney's Information Technology Group, a management and consulting practice specializing in information systems. He is a well known author and speaker.

EXHIBIT 2.3
Know Your Readers—and Your Publisher!

INFORMATION STRATEGY

THE EXECUTIVE'S JOURNAL

Volume 4   Number 3   Spring 1988

The Wages of Software Piracy

The Embattled IS Fortress: Dispersing Computer Power

Let a Thousand Voices Publish

A Strategic Tree in the Forest of IS Opportunity

No Instant Gratification from Office Automation

The Factory of the Future: Just in Time for What?

Executive Computing

Cost Management

Decision Support

Bookware

A WARREN, GORHAM & LAMONT COMPANY

EXHIBIT 2.3 *(continued)*

INFORMATION
STRATEGY
THE EXECUTIVE'S JOURNAL

Volume 4   Number 3   Spring 1988

L.R. DeJarnett, The JIA Management Group Inc
Consulting Editor

Andrew Rosenbloom
Senior Editor

Author Information: *Information Strategy: The Executive's Journal* invites the submission of manuscripts of particular interest to the senior executive striving for effective and strategic management of information systems. Potential authors and columnists can obtain general information by calling or writing Andrew Rosenbloom, Senior Editor, Information Strategy: The Executive's Journal, Auerbach Publishers Inc, a Warren, Gorham & Lamont company, One Penn Plaza, New York NY 10119, (212) 971-5000; manuscripts for publication and related correspondence should be sent to Andrew Rosenbloom in care of Auerbach Publishers.

EXHIBIT 2.3 *(continued)*

The Embattled IS Fortress: Dispersing Computer Power

Joseph E. Izzo

Control of computing resources by centralized systems technocracies hinders end users' performance of the business functions that support their employers' business goals. Even decentralized computing and distributed processing, argues the author, are centralized approaches that fail to give users the flexibility they need. The answer: dispersed computing, whereby computers, applications, systems expertise, and technical and organizational innovation are delivered to every user's fingertips.

Besides mainframes, there are super-computer mainframes, small-system mainframes, desktop superminis, briefcase microcomputers, and much more. With these options, there should be no reason why we cannot get the right computing power and the right application software into the users' hands. But the existing centralized computing scheme prohibits it. I am convinced that dispersing computer technology is the way to restore the lost promise of computer productivity to US companies.

Consider what happened when the business technology (or IS) department for a large county in a Midwestern state insisted on maintaining its centralized control over county computing. This department used an IBM 3081 for conventional offline batch processing—payroll, welfare, and voter registration. But, the county hospital needed 24-hour-a-day, online, real-time computer services. Patient records had to be updated immediately; doctors needed status reports at all times of the day and night; administrative records had to be updated daily.

The county's business technology manager, who wanted the computer power centralized, said his people could handle the hospital on their IBM 3081. Because this seemed practical and cost-effective, it was approved.

Business technology added the hospital's records to the system but found that running both a batch processing system and a real-time system on the same computer was a bad idea. The hospital's information request and response time was more than two minutes—enough time to lose a patient's life. System performance for the county offices was reduced too. Users did not get the service they deserved.

The problem was caused by the attempt to support vastly different processing requirements—two entirely different business missions—on one computer. My company recommended giving the hospital its own computer. The business technology manager didn't like it; he'd lose some control and some face. But his way of looking at computer use represents a wrong-headedness that we simply cannot afford. The cost is too great—in money, lost productivity, and lost opportunity.

Dispersed computing

Whether it's putting a mainframe like the IBM 3081 in a hospital or a desktop microcomputer in front of a CFO for cash management, I call putting computer power where it is needed dispersed computing. A large corporation can have terminals connected to a mainframe, minicomputer systems, workstation clusters, and numerous standalone machines, including desktop microcomputers or individual workstations. The centralized mainframe plays an important role, performing tasks that influence a variety of functions and business units in the corporation. But many departments, functions, and groups are

EXHIBIT 2.3 *(continued)*

Joseph E. Izzo is Vice President of A.T. Kearney's Information Technology Group, a consulting practice specializing in information system productivity. This article is adapted with permission from his recently published book, The Embattled Fortress *(San Francisco: Jossey-Bass, 1987).*

free to do their own computing, using their own computers.

There is no centralized responsibility as we know it today for all these computers; much of the computer power is under the direct supervision of the users themselves or the users' management. It may seem at first that there is no order to the plan, but a carefully crafted architecture guides the dispersal.

You may think this is no more than another variation on old architectural ideas (e.g., decentralized or distributed computing). This is not the case.

Decentralized computing. By its name, decentralized computing would appear to be the antithesis of centralized computing. Decentralized means breaking apart and scattering management responsibility for the computing function, implying: Here is your computer, now go it alone. But a scattered organization's information system becomes structured in the same way as those for a traditional centralized organization, causing services to be dispensed in the same way. The result is many smaller, centralized locations, and no change in the delivery process to the user.

To my mind, centralized versus decentralized translates into form prevailing over content. A computing machine's physical location is not the issue; the issue is how to make computer systems more sensitive to the needs of individual business functions, thereby helping that function support a company's business goals.

Consider what happened to a multibillion dollar corporation that decided to decentralize. It had a traditional, centralized business technology department whose staff thought its resources were inadequate; users felt the department was unre-

sponsive; and senior management was sure the IS department wasn't helping the company achieve its goals.

After many hours of meetings, senior management finally agreed that decentralization was the answer. But after two years, there were no significant changes. Even though computers had been moved to decentralized locations, the old problems remained.

What did they expect? They still had the same staff. They still had the same computer systems. They still had the same thinking. How could anything change?

Consider a $500 million chain of food stores. Because several divisions were unhappy with the centralized business technology department, corporate management decided to decentralize. At the last minute, my company was called in to determine if the scheme would work. We went to one division and asked, How will decentralized information systems affect your business? The answer was, At least we'll have control. Another division immediately began buying its own computers, but when we visited, we found they were recreating another centralized computing facility. To this day, not a single one of the systems is up and running.

Control is not the answer, nor is moving the computer center from one place to another. That's the old, centralized thinking. Neither one of these companies asked the more basic questions: What is our mission? How can computers help us achieve that mission?

Distributed computing. This is another commonly used term in computing, and one with which I strongly disagree. A popular college textbook on business data processing says that a distributed system is more flexible because it

EXHIBIT 2.3 *(continued)*

places computer power where it is needed. The author cites a company's distributed system that has a couple of hundred network-connected processors, thousands of terminals and printers, several hundred remote job entry stations, and hundreds of network processing systems at plant sites all over the world.

This suggests that the computer power is in the hands of the users, but that is not the case. This system and many other so-called distributed systems like it are nothing more than geographically enormous centralized computing systems. Distributed processing is nothing more than remote processing, or remote data entry. Users simply pass data back and forth to the mainframe; control remains behind the glass walls of a centralized business technology department. Computer power is not distributed; the processors are all connected in a network. The users, with no control over the computer, strike the keys of terminals and remote job entry stations. Applications are chosen and managed according to the capabilities of the network's processing systems.

In a dispersed system, there would be no need to connect so many devices into a single, complex scheme. Computer power is dispersed from the centralized computer in concentric rings, each with its own machines, its own applications, and its own support.

Dispersed computing is resource management, which includes dispersing computers, applications, technological expertise, and innovation.

Users are free

In dispersed computing, a mainframe still plays an important role, performing tasks that influence functions and departments throughout a company. But specialized user groups or functions are free to do their own computing using their own computers.

For example, a corporation established a computer-aided design (CAD) application on their mainframe. CAD, a graphics system, requires a great deal of power from a central processing unit (CPU). Within a year of installation, it became necessary to upgrade to a larger processor, an IBM 3081. The following year, they again needed more power and an upgrade, this time to an IBM 3084. It didn't stop there; the

3084 became overloaded, and response time dropped.

With a dispersed system, engineers can perform design work on their own smaller mainframe, mini, or micro without taxing the central computer. The central computer would continue to support novices and smaller groups of users. For more sophisticated users, the CAD drawing data base would be maintained in the central computer and shared between various engineering units. Smaller computers capable of CAD design functions would be dispersed into the user departments. Engineers can develop proficiency on the system and innovate, without slowing response time or hindering functions needed by other users.

> **The issue is not a computing machine's physical location, but whether it helps business functions support a company's business goals.**

Because computer hardware can be placed anywhere it's needed, the most important task is dispersing the application software. The first and most important step is to determine the needs of departments and their users. The tendency is to recreate a massive data base, which stimulates the business technology people to think about larger processors, capacity planning, and the usual centralized scheme of things. It is far better to plan the applications in three stages:
1. What belongs in the central data base.
2. What works best at the departmental level.
3. What works best at the personal, or ad hoc, level.

A manufacturing company felt it should replicate almost 70% of the data in the corporate data base for planning and scheduling. My company found that what seemed to be a high quantity of data was really a high flowthrough; that is, material had to be tracked, but it moved through the plant very quickly. And, only 17% of this data needed to be stored in the corporate data base. Departments needed a relatively simple relational data base, accessed with a fourth-generation language, to produce all the computer power they needed.

EXHIBIT 2.3 *(continued)*

Dispersed technical expertise

Computers are not the only resource shared in a dispersed environment. The staff of the business technology department should also be dispersed. A group of CAD engineers wants to innovate, but needs system development assistance. The business technology department can transfer or assign some of its talent to the CAD group for developing new applications. They can also help train users. Two things are accomplished simultaneously:

- The business technology professionals feel like members of user departments responsible for helping the department become more productive.
- Rapport is created between the users and the technologists, dispelling misunderstanding—Both feel more productive.

We often forget that a business technology department, regardless of its shortcomings, is one of a company's greatest resources. It maintains the company's technical expertise; properly directed, it can be the driving force behind technological innovation. The business technology staff needs to be valued and nurtured. If they need to change the way they do things, management should help, support, and encourage the process. To help a company choose appropriate technologies, users and management must guide the business technology department. Senior management should be active in this process, guiding and shaping business technology's role to help the firm attain its goals. Without management's help, the business technology department's culture may never change.

Two kinds of innovations

After the computers and technical expertise are dispersed, innovation can begin. There are two kinds of innovation at work when it comes to computer technology:

- Technological innovation related to the computer system itself.
- Organizational innovation and its implications.

A common misconception is that innovation and productivity are antithetical. Technological innovation inspires employees to find better, faster ways to do their work. Both can occur simultaneously without diminishing the other; the two can be complementary if allowed.

The business technology department is traditionally responsible for technological innovation. There is no reason that cannot continue under dispersed computing, but there are three caveats:

- Innovation must benefit the users—Business technology is not the sole beneficiary of new techniques, machines, and improvements in computer services. Innovations, like other corporate resources, must be planned with and approved by user groups.
- Innovation must be carried out with senior management's involvement and approval—Employees must discuss how computer resources are managed and implemented in order to assure that those resources support the company's business goals and missions. Technology for technology's sake is out.
- Innovation should occur in a dispersed manner—Computers should be seen as an expendable resource. Prices have fallen dramatically, and in many cases it is cheaper to toss out an entire computer system and buy a new one than convert the old computer's software.

> ### Technology for technology's sake is out.

In his essay "Of Innovations," Sir Francis Bacon wrote: "He that will not apply new remedies must expect new evils; for time is the greatest innovator." Significant innovation no longer takes place on the mainframes that reside in centralized business technology departments, but as far from the central computer as possible. If there is any doubt about this, consider the software industry. Mainframe software companies have watched their annual growth decline from more than 30% to less than 10%. Microcomputer software companies are strong because microcomputers inspire innovation.

Organizational innovation is less straightforward, but no less important. How and where does it occur? It is difficult to say, but I can assure you that the more centralized the computing facility, the less innovation there will be. Innovation is

EXHIBIT 2.3 *(continued)*

greatest at the most dispersed end of the computing spectrum. Employees must have the opportunity to work with the computer on their own terms. There is a payback for the business technology department as well: the users may have useful suggestions for system improvement that would never occur to a member of the business technology staff who is removed from the centers of computer action.

Organizational innovation takes time and requires a major shift in thinking to enable creation of a new computing concept and culture, free from centralized control. In the new culture, employees don't care who is in control, as long as they have the computing resources they need.

A dispersed system should be implemented within a planned architecture. Although users may feel that computers are all over the company, willy-nilly, senior, departmental, and business technology management must orchestrate computer acquisition and dispersion through a sensible plan. If dispersed computing is not well planned, decentralized computing is often the result.

Under the dispersed approach, about 20% of the users need to be tied to the mainframe. The remaining 80% rarely need to connect with another computer, including the mainframe. The challenge is how to disperse the computer power properly.

The financial cost

The cost of computers and their supporting staff in a centralized environment might appear to be lower. But adding the effect that poor computer performance has on a business—failure to respond to users' changing needs or the lost opportunities in meeting business objectives and goals—the cost pendulum swings in favor of dispersed computing.

For example, assume a central computer facility operates at 97% of capacity, and the purchasing department requests more functions. An analyst reports that this will consume an extra 5% of the CPU, and thus the computer system will be running at 102%, or over capacity. If the request is not approved, purchasing loses an opportunity to increase its productivity. If the application is

approved, business technology will need an additional CPU, which costs $3 million.

In a dispersed system, the purchasing department would simply acquire its own computer, at a cost of perhaps $120,000. Software might cost an additional $30,000, and the salaries of two people to operate and maintain the system might be another $100,000. That's $250,000 versus $3 million.

> ### The more centralized the computing facility, the less innovation there will be.

Now purchasing can draw data (e.g., material requirements) from the central computer's data base into its own computer. If this data is automatically entered into the departmental computer, purchasing activities, vendor analyses, and other functions can be handled locally. Scheduled delivery dates are passed to the central computer, where they can be shared with other departments. Moreover, new work can be off-loaded from the central processors, improving response time and productivity throughout the company. All other centralized costs drop proportionally.

Implications

Begin this dispersing process now. The hardware, software, and technology staff must be dispersed gradually. Keep the corporate data base and the accounting system where they are—where they should be. But give the users control over their own applications.

The most important point for management is to think differently about its companies' computer resources. Business practices have changed, and technology must support those changes to achieve as many productivity gains as possible. Think long and hard about this and plan carefully. A well-planned strategy is required for implementing a dispersed computer architecture; it must be managed properly, with respect for the people involved and with the company's business goals foremost. ▲

EXHIBIT 2.4

The JIA Management Group, Inc.

1299 OCEAN AVENUE • SUITE 333 • SANTA MONICA, CALIFORNIA   90401

———————————— (213) 451-3041 ————————————

Computers Need to Be Managed

As Printed in the
Business Section of the
Los Angeles Times

Business Not Prepared For
Onslaught Of Personal Computers

By JOSEPH E. IZZO

Personal computers are mushrooming in corporate offices these days, but, ironically, instead of improving the management of information, they are threatening to disrupt it.

This is not the fault of the computers, which can greatly enhance executive productivity and effectiveness. The problem is lack of corporate planning and control.

Business simply hasn't been prepared for the onslaught of personal computers and is not handling it well. This isn't surprising, considering how new these machines are. The personal computer industry is only 6 years old, and it has grown with amazing speed.

Revenues were $2 billion in 1981 and, according to industry forecasts, are expected to multiply to between $10 billion and $14 billion by 1985. Personal computers started popping up on executives' desks perhaps three years ago. IBM's entry into the market in 1981 fully legitimized their use in business (if, indeed, that was needed), and there has been no holding them since. A trickle has turned into a torrent.

Companies Are Perplexed

Industry reports and evidence of our own and other consulting practices indicate that more and more companies are perplexed by the microcomputers in their midst. The headaches they're causing include deterioration in information quality; muddled communication; conflict between general management and data-processing management (never an altogether comfortable relationship), as the data-processing people see microcomputers diminishing their own importance to the organization, and rising costs, as

companies pay for more and more personal computers.

The main problem with personal computers is that, although they simplify many business tasks, the information they generate frequently doesn't dovetail with overall corporate objectives. In that case, no matter how much it may be prized by its user, the computer becomes a hindrance to the corporation rather than the boon it can and should be.

Some illustrations:

—An engineering group of an aerospace manufacturer used a microcomputer's graphics capability to draw certain parts of an aircraft assembly for maintenance manuals. Putting together such computer-aided graphics is a precise and time-consuming task. In this case, however, it was unnecessary. The parts in question were already stored in graphics form in the company's mainframe computer. These engineers were, in effect, reinventing the wheel.

—A corporate planner used his computer to prepare a mathematical model that figured critically in the company's long-range business plan. Before the work was completed, the planner left the company.

Because this executive developed the program for his model in unique, idiosyncratic fashion, and prepared no supporting documentation, no one else could use it. His former colleagues had to reconstruct the model. (With a complex program, lack of documentation is likely to cause trouble, even for its author. Many a program has been rewritten because the writer could not remember how he or she developed the original.)

—A medium-sized company decides to inventory its personal computers for the first time. In addition to discovering more computers than it expected, it learns that five brands are represented, none of which is compatible with the others. The company realizes it will have maintenance and communication problems it didn't bargain for. Similarly, in our own firm, several of our consultants write reports and proposals on personal computers. Unfortunately, these machines are incompatible with the company's word processor, so all this material must be reentered to process it for client presentation.

—In a large company, highly paid managers fascinated with their personal computers were spending many hours writing programs for their machines that an entry-level programmer could have produced in no time. Their use of computers was actually decreasing their productivity.

Larger companies are the most likely to be troubled with the rise in microcomputers, since, because of their relatively modest cost for a sizable organization, these units can readily find a home in many offices and go virtually unnoticed by top management until problems emerge. But small companies are not immune.

A main danger for smaller concerns is trying to make personal computers do too much, or to perform tasks for which they are not equipped. For example, we have seen micros used to generate calcu-

EXHIBIT 2.4 *(continued)*

lations in hours that a larger machine could do in seconds. In our experience, such wasteful applications are rife. Most businesses with, say, more than $500,000 in sales cannot be managed with a personal computer, attractive as the idea might seem to the boss. Assuming that they can use microcomputers effectively, small companies probably will still require supplementary manual systems or the assistance of a service bureau.

Corporations are dealing with the growth of the personal computer in various ways. Most of these approaches are ineffective. One tactic is to strongly discourage use of microcomputers or to ban them outright. (This is like trying to hold back the tide.) Some companies have adopted a wait-and-see attitude, perhaps hoping either that the personal computer will go away or that the difficulties connected with it will clear up of their own accord.

Still others, incredibly, are not yet aware of either the benefits or the difficulties that these machines can bring with them.

Resistance, inaction or ignorance will not help a company handle its personal computer problems. What's required are firm policies. And these policies should be developed within an overall strategy that takes into account all the company's data-processing resources.

Ask Fundamental Questions

In formulating this strategy, a company must ask itself some fundamental questions: What information do we need to run our business? What alternatives should we consider to gather it, process it, communicate it? Do we need centralization of electronic data-processing facilities, decentralization, distributed processing? How do we organize to take advantage of, rather than be overtaken by, continuously de-

veloping technology?

Once a company's overall data-processing needs are determined, setting policy on personal computers in such matters as hardware and software, training, support and budgeting and approval levels will be a relatively easy task.

Personal computers were brought into corporations because executives perceived that they would help them do their jobs better and faster. They offer business a magnificent opportunity to increase the productivity not only of managers but of personnel at all levels. But, despite its small size, ease of handling and relatively low costs, the personal computer is still a computer. And computers must be managed, or they will manage us.

Joseph E. Izzo is president of JIA Management Group Inc., a firm of data-processing consultants based in Santa Monica.

Information Explosion May Create New Type Of Executive
The "Information Specialist"

Reprinted with Permission from The Evening Outlook

By ED MOOSBRUGGER
Evening Outlook Business Editor

SANTA MONICA — A new type of job may be developing because of the explosion of information available through computer systems.

Within 10 years, the top aide to chief executive officers will be a new kind of professional called an information specialist, according to Joseph Izzo, president of The JIA Management Group, a consulting firm which helps companies with their data processing problems.

The information specialist will take the mounds of information available through company and outside computers and put it in a form easier for the executive to use.

The specialists will be more business oriented than technically oriented, Izzo said. They will be adept at dissecting information needs and will know the high-level tools for getting access to information. They will format the information and get it to the executive fast without going through the data processing department.

They will becomes executives in their own right.

"He or she will probably have an MBA in business administra-

tion or finance, and will be adroit at getting and synthesizing information from data bases as well as from personal contacts," Izzo said.

A background in library science will be a plus, he said.

Among companies beginning to move in this direction are Lockheed-Georgia and Southern California Edison Co., Izzo said.

Too many reports from data processing departments are fixed in format while the needs of the users of the reports vary widely, Izzo said. Some of the reports have outgrown their usefulness — they were developed to meet a specific need but continued past the time it was solved, he said.

"Today reports from the data processing department are fixed in format and content, even though the needs of individual executives may vary greatly," Izzo said. "This new specialist will permit executives to get what they want, when they want it."

JIA works primarily with companies with annual sales of more than $20 million.

"When executives look at computers as technology they've been conned," said Izzo, a former vice

president of Computer Sciences Corp. and former director of data processing for the Rocketdyne Division of North American Aviation. He also was with System Development Corp., Santa Monica.

Some executives have abrogated their responsibility in the data processing area and accepted performance there that they would not tolerate from other departments, Izzo said.

"When you say you want something done and data processing says it will take six to eight months, something is wrong," Izzo said. "When you say to do it by July and it is not done by December, something is wrong."

"They won't accept that level of performance in any department but they accept it in data processing."

Izzo added that poor results are not always the fault of the data processing department. It may be other elements of management.

"Data processing is a business within a business" and needs guidance from executives on such things as setting priorities, Izzo said.

appeared in key newspapers across the country and, more importantly, reached the audience Revel was after—the mass market. As is the case with many publications that utilize articles, they allowed Revel to tag (end) each one with an offer. The offer cannot be self-serving (e.g., "send me $10 for my latest book on how to find the best business in your area"), and should be more of a public service announcement ("send for a free brochure on 'how to avoid being ripped off by business opportunity fraud peddlers'").

The latter offer provides the reader with something of benefit for nothing. It is a tag editors will consider. On the other hand, they seldom want a column ending with an offer that someone has to buy. If the reader purchases and is unhappy, they may blame the publication and it comes back to haunt the editor.

Examples of offers that usually are acceptable to editors include: A data processing consultant writing an article for a trade may offer a free brochure on "the Seven Key Ways to Evaluate a DP Consultant." A CPA penning an article for a trade that could be tagged with a free brochure on "Six Ways for Manufacturers to Handle the New Tax Laws and Profit from Them." Or, the marketing consultant could offer "Five Little-Known Ways to Increase Sales and Add to the Bottom Line."

Each brochure promises a benefit to the reader and answers a need at no cost. To generate response, offers should be targeted at the needs of prospective customers. Few will respond to an offer that says send for a free brochure on James Doe, the author of this article. Prospective clients are no different than most of us. Their motivation falls into two general categories: ego and greed.

The offer at the end of a column is there for one reason—to generate leads. Not every response will be a lead. There is a small percentage of people who will send for anything if it is free, but the vast majority of those who respond to an offer do so because they are interested.

In Revel's case, anyone who sent in for a brochure on how to find the right business, was a candidate for purchasing one of *Entrepreneur's* $55 manuals on a business. The data processing manufacturing executives may have internal problems, and their response is potential business for the DP consultants.

FREELANCE ARTICLE PAYOFF

There are other ways to utilize printed articles/columns aside from the tag. In fact, the greatest value of any article is in reprinting and sending it out to present, past, and prospective clients with a simple note:

> Dear _____,
>
> Thought you might be interested in seeing the recent article that ran in *Nation's Business*. I think it might give you some interesting ideas on where data processing is going and how your company might utilize it to the fullest.
> Hope you enjoy it.
>
> your signature

That's all it requires. The article's content does the rest. It sells for the consultant. And, once the article and note have been mailed, the consultant has a perfect "excuse" to make a follow-up call the next week.

Consultants do not have to be writers and authors, in order to take advantage of the credibility that media offers. Several of the consultants in this book have generated positive media coverage through their seminars and speeches.

One of the most successful cases of a consultant making news and media headlines belongs to Howard Vardel, who was, at the time (the 1970s) a struggling CPA.

The Vardel case illustrates two things. First, there are changes and events within every industry that are new but seldom talked about. Vardel was not the first CPA to stress the need for CPAs to become proactive, however, he was the first to use it in a speech and as the subject of a news release.

■ Case Study

On numerous occasions Howard Vardel had spoken to small, community groups and businesses on the new tax laws and how they would impact the local area. Vardel was a good speaker, and the talk frequently led to a new client. But, he was doing the same type of marketing that other CPAs were practicing. All of them were competing for the same speaking engagements, and none had made any significant impact in the community.

Vardel was at a loss until he spent time one afternoon with his brother-in-law, a local public relations consultant. Vardel's brother-in-law suggested restructuring the talk and making it more newsworthy. Put some new, contemporary idea into it that would intrigue the media; something that would apply to more than just CPAs and would have impact with every client.

That evening, Vardel went home, did a great deal of thinking and came up with an idea. The next day he revisited his brother-in-law, and outlined the approach. His brother-in-law validated Vardel's initial thinking—he had found a newsworthy topic, one that would set him apart from his competitors. His brother-in-law agreed to help if Vardel could get the speaking engagement.

That afternoon, Vardel visited the local CPA society and its program chairman. He outlined his idea for a talk, and the chairperson agreed it would be a topic with appeal to the group. Vardel knew the topic would be of great interest to the business media as well.

A date was set for the speech and Vardel went to work. The afternoon of his speech, Vardel's brother-in-law did a two-page capsule summary of the talk in the release. In it, Vardel's idea and the theme for the talk was outlined. The release was sent to local media as well as trade journals.

The thrust of Vardel's talk was to call for CPAs to get "more involved in their client's business . . . instead of just adding up numbers and letting clients know where they stand financially, the CPA of the future is going to have to do some forecasting, projecting, and advise clients what they should be doing with cash flow . . . they should be cautioning clients about the impact of the economy and how it could change their businesses."

As a result of the release, Vardel received page one exposure in the business section of the local newspaper, and two CPA journals also made his talk the subject of an editorial. His brother-in-law took the news release and also sent it out on Business Wire, a wire service that reaches newspapers, television, and radio stations across the country. (There is a fee for using the Wire.)

Vardel's practice was transformed overnight. From the local media story, he received more than a dozen calls from companies that were interested in talking to him. The editorials his speech generated, prompted calls from CEOs in four different industries, and the wire service story was picked up by dozens of newspapers and it, too, prompted calls from more than 20 additional companies.

Suddenly, Vardel had more business and prospects than he could handle. The topic of his speech was not revolutionary. It was, in fact, a service that many CPA consultants were already offering, however, there had been little written about it. Vardel was the first CPA to call attention to the need clients had for CPAs to be more than just accountants.

■

In every industry, consultants have the same opportunity. New techniques are being utilized that would fascinate clients and make news, too. The consultant who is the first—and not necessarily the originator—to point out the technique will obtain the media exposure, just as Vardel did.

To take advantage of the publicity and promotion potential in their industry, consultants must ask themselves these questions:

1. What am I doing that is different?
2. What are consultants in my industry doing differently?
3. How have client demands changed the way we are operating?
4. Is this technique newsworthy?
5. Could it become the subject of a speech or article? If so, who would I send it to? Where will I get the most mileage?

Successful speechmaking consultants recognize these opportunities. When they give a speech or talk, they inject some newsworthy topic; a topic that will generate media coverage and client interest. If that can be done—and it can in most cases—the consultant has an immense opportunity to expand their client base. That's exactly what Bill Coleman did.

■ Case Study

Bill Coleman is an attorney who struggled for years to build his own practice. He did every kind of legal work imaginable, from criminal to trusts. Still, Bill could never generate enough revenue to go beyond his one-person office and secretary.

Although his work encompassed every phase of the law profession, there were aspects of it that Bill disliked. Bill was good at tax and he liked working with families. Finally, he decided he was going to specialize in a phase of legal work that combined both elements, living trusts.

For months, he continued to struggle. Abandoning the other areas of law cost him financially, but he was determined to stick with living trusts. One evening, he and his wife were at a dinner party where they met one of the area's leading marketing consultants. Reluctantly, Bill began to discuss marketing with the consultant. Frankly, he told him, he did not understand it, but he realized he would have to do something if he was going to continue his practice.

The marketing consultant gave Bill a number of ideas, ranging from mailings to previous clients to establishing a newsletter. Then the consultant gave Bill the idea; the idea that turned Coleman's practice around.

Write a column. Write a column for the local newspaper and do it in a question-and-answer (Q&A) format on living trusts. Q&As were easy to put together. They take no special skills, since all the writer has to do is think of the most common questions asked and answer them.

Bill liked the approach. The next day, he approached the editor of the local newspaper and proposed writing a weekly column on living trusts, at no cost for the paper's business section. It would be a Q&A and readers could even send in questions which Bill would answer in future columns.

Coleman discovered that many local, smaller newspapers are open to this type of suggestion. They have small budgets and cannot afford the huge staff of writers that a major metropolitan publication may have. Yet, in many cases they compete with the metro.

The editor discussed the project with other staff members, and they decided to give Bill's column a try. They asked him to prepare four—in advance—and as a condition, they wanted Bill to always stay four weeks in advance.

The editor explained they had been approached by other professionals in the past, and although many of the subjects were of interest, none of those who proposed them could write and deliver them on time. Bill did.

Two weeks after the first column was printed, the marketing consultant called Bill and offered another piece of advice. Start using the columns. Reprint them and send them out with a note to present and potential clients. That's exactly what he did.

Coleman's newspaper column is now four years old, and Bill has the leading living trust legal practice in the entire county. He credits most of his success to the column, the marketing of it, and the leads he generated, not to mention the reputation he has garnered throughout the community as an expert in living trusts—because he writes on the subject.

■

The Coleman story is an example of aggressive marketing. In today's competitive marketplace, consultants cannot sit back and wait for business. They have to be proactive and take advantage of opportunities. Writing columns, giving speeches, publishing newsletters, and authoring books are not the only marketing tools at the consultant's disposal. Another is becoming a local or national spokesperson on the industry. Examples are all around. When there is an auto industry story, Lee Iaccoca or someone of similar stature is always called. When there is a major story on the economy, a leading economist is called.

In examining these, you will find that the media is always quoting three, four, or five people in the business. These people are considered authorities because they are quoted so frequently.

Notice how local stories are handled. In one revolving around the rise or fall in the stock market, a local economist, financial consultant, or banker may be included. In a story revolving around the economy and real estate activity, there is always a leading broker and/or lender quoted.

How are these people selected by the media? Why are they picked and not others in the same field? The answer: They communicate meaningful and newsworthy information on a regular basis to the press.

The key words are meaningful, newsworthy, and regular basis. Consultants who supply media with valuable information soon generate the confidence of the newspeople. Once the relationship is built, the media calls.

When the local paper is doing a trend piece, the confidence translates to a telephone call from the reporter, and an interview in which the consultant is quoted. That is how media relationships are built and why some consultants are quoted continuously while others never get exposure.

RISE OF "ADVERTORIALS"

Not every consultant has the time to search for newsworthy events and talk to the media about it. But some consultants have found other ways of generating positive media coverage. For instance, while Coleman generated free column space, others may buy the space and run their own Q&A column. It is actually a paid advertisement, but it does not look like a typical ad. At the top of the column (or bottom), the word advertising usually appears. Although most of these columns have the words "advertisement" written in small type across the top, few readers notice the printed disclaimer.

Perhaps, the best example of the impact of these "advertorials" (a combination of advertising and editorial material), is the campaign that *Entrepreneur Magazine* ran for more than four years in promoting its business expos.

The business expos ran Friday-Sunday in a major city, and the Sunday prior to the opening, the company would run six-page advertorials in the city's major newspaper. The results were astounding. The first supplement generated nearly $100,000 in advance orders for tape programs, and more than $150,000 in seminar reservations. The advertorial, which was the company's only advertising expenditure, helped draw a record-breaking, three-day attendance of more than 38,000 to the Los Angeles Convention Center.

Why? Credibility. Even though the six-pager was branded "advertisement," it generated credibility because it looked like the rest of the newspaper (editorial format).

The same is true of television and the rise of so-called "infommercials," which a number of consultants are utilizing. An infommercial runs a half-hour to an hour and airs on a cable channel or a local independent. Instead of just hearing 30 minutes of hard sell on why you should buy this product or service, the infommercials persuade with endorsements, evidence, and education. There is no hard-sell. Viewers see a body of evidence for the product/service and are given an opportunity to respond, usually through a tollfree 800 number.

Infommercials are advertisements, but the fact that they appear in editorial format enhances their credibility. The variety of formats range from panels discussing the product/service to audience participation, where testimonials are given by those attending. Although this approach has been abused by some, it has proven to be quite effective for products/services that utilize the correct approach: facts, figures, education, and no hype.

The advertorial approach goes beyond television and newspapers. For example, *Entrepreneur Magazine* and Bantam Books took the concept one step farther. Revel wrote the book *182 Businesses You Can Start for Low Cost* and Bantam distributed it. In the book, each of the 182 businesses was briefly explained. If a reader wanted to know more, there was an order blank that readers could utilize to purchase in-depth information.

The Bantam publication was nothing more than a mailorder catalog, a way for Bantam and *Entrepreneur* to generate revenues, which they split. But, it was written like a book and looked just the same as any other nonfiction paperback. It retained its credibility.

The potency that the media can bring to a consultant and their practice can be best illustrated by the following case.

■ **Case Study**

> A number of years ago, the *Los Angeles Times* did a story on *Entrepreneur Magazine* and its publisher, Chase Revel. It told the rags to riches tale of how he had founded the publication. It also told how astute Revel was at forecasting trends and determining which businesses would be hot in the coming years.
>
> At the time, *Entrepreneur* generated most of its income from mailorder sales. Each month it mailed a catalog—complete with manuals on different businesses—to opportunity seekers. Some months, as many as one million catalogs hit the post office.
>
> Typically, the catalog generated about a 1 percent return and an average order in the $18 to $20 range. When the *Times'* story appeared, Revel cut it out, pasted it up, and put it on the back cover of the catalog. He continued mailing the same lists he always had. Within weeks there was a dramatic change. The response rate jumped to 1.5 percent and the average order more than doubled, from $20 to $44.

■

FINDING A NICHE

Every consultant mentioned in this book has utilized the media to help build their practice. They have done one other thing, too. They have found their niche; their specialty. Consultants in the 1990s cannot be all things to all clients.

Companies expect and demand expertise. As McCuistion explains, "When you are working for someone, it is advantageous to have a multitude of skills. That way, you can prove your value in more than one position. But, for consultants to really thrive in today's market, I believe they have to specialize. The generalist may be able to find more business, but the specialist is going to be able to command a higher price."

Kracke agrees with the assessment and he practices it. Consequently, he is not only paid three times more by clients than he was a decade ago, but he also has earned the tag of the "Red Adair of licensing."

Van Den Berg stresses specialization, too. "There are many more ins and outs to the financial industry today than there were a decade ago. For a money manager, who is compensated by the size of the portfolio and not the amount of trading, it is imperative that they specialize and know one field extremely well. I have studied the stock market for 25 years, and it still takes constant monitoring to stay ahead of it. It would be almost impossible for someone to be a generalist in the financial arena and still be competent."

Holbert takes it one step farther. "If someone wants to be an authority in an industry, they should spend time working in it before they ever become a consultant." Holbert spent years as a real estate agent before he became a real estate attorney. He has one specialty—real estate.

Moore put in years in her industry before specializing in marketing within the industry. Alessandra taught sales and marketing at Georgia State University for a number of years, before entering the field full-time. Tony, incidentally, did what many prospective consultants would love to do—practice consulting part-time while holding down a regular full-time job. In fact, Tony practically entered the field accidentally. While at the University, local merchants would call and ask for help—some might be having a problem with sales, others merchandising, and others advertising. Before long, Alessandra found himself immersed in the consulting field. That was nearly 20 years ago, and he has been independent since that time.

McCuistion spent 20 years in the banking business and was even CEO of a small bank in Irving, Texas, before entering the consulting field. When he left the bank in 1977, he actually had two clients—one was a local bank.

The bottom line for every one of these consultants is experience, specialization, and knowledge of their industry. There are no overnight success stories. Those who do well usually have "paid their dues."

Experience and industry knowledge, however, do not necessarily generate business for fledgling consultants. Pennington insists consultants must be "marketing oriented. Marketing is everything and everything is marketing," he says, quoting marketing guru Regis McKenna from the Harvard *Business Review* of several years ago.

"I learned, if you cannot sell, you cannot survive in this business. You need marketing skills to get started. Sure, later, it is the referrals that build the business, but initially you need to be able to sell."

Perception is everything, says Qubein. "People want to deal with someone who they believe knows the answers. Someone who is ethical. Someone who can work with those in their company. That position is established in the client's mind long before the consultant ever walks in the door. It is built through marketing and past performance. To succeed, a consultant has to excel in both."

In the next chapter, we'll examine what these consultants do once they sell their services and pique the interest of a prospective client. What does it take to write a proposal? What should be in it? And how do you close the deal?

CHAPTER 3

Writing the Winning Proposal

Going in, there was little chance that the pair of marketing consultants would win the contract. At best, they were a longshot. After all, the client was the second largest builder in the state and the project was one of the biggest the developer had ever constructed. He was looking for a firm that could handle the marketing for a 1,400 residential development that would be built over a five-year period. Every aspect of the project seemed to call for a large, highly experienced firm that knew real estate marketing.

To everyone's surprise, the smaller firm was selected. They won because of three reasons:

1. They had studied the project and knew it and the challenges of the area well.
2. Their marketing approach was unique, creative, and innovative.
3. They understood the client's needs.

Those ingredients are the keys to writing and presenting any winning proposal. Perhaps the most difficult step to understand and master for any consultant is item two—how creative do you get in a presentation, and can't someone steal your ideas?

Don Kracke says there is one sure way to protect your ideas, "Lock them in a drawer and throw the key away. That way, you can be sure no one will ever steal them."

Kracke's point is well-taken. When a consultant comes into a competitive situation, the element that separates one company from another is their ideas. In the case of the builder, the consultants made a daring proposal. Instead of spending 5 percent (or more) of the project's total budget on advertising, they would not spend anything on ads. Instead, they would invest a fraction of that amount in public relations (or free publicity) and sell the project through it.

"They gave the builder an excellent idea," explains Kracke, "but they did not tell him how they were going to execute it. That's the difference and how you protect ideas. Say what you are going to do, but don't tell the client the specifics."

McCuistion does something similar. "There's always a problem as to how much you put in a proposal. The fear is someone will take the ideas and run. It is a genuine concern. I get around it by being general, not specific."

In consulting, the Kracke approach is called "selling the sizzle." That is, the consultant presents unique, curiosity-stirring ideas that the client knows will meet the company's objectives, but the implementation is not detailed. Aside from leaving the idea open to "theft," if the execution is spelled out, there is no mystique left in the proposal. Clients can make an immediate judgment as to whether they think the idea will work or not.

For instance, in the case of the 1,400 unit development, the consultants stirred the company president's interest when they said they would sell the entire project without taking any ads. The first question asked was how? Instead of revealing a step-by-step publicity approach, the two consultants provided the company president with the results of some research they had done.

The area, one of the consultant's explained, is one of the most in-demand residential markets in the entire county. "The last residential project built sold within four months, and its pricing was significantly higher than the cost of these homes.

"With that demand, a publicity campaign that stimulates demand and informs customers at the same time, will enable us to sell out—without advertising."

The consultants gave the CEO additional information. First, they had studied the area and similar projects. They knew the supply-demand situation, and that was why they had proposed the daring nonadvertising approach.

ANSWERING NEEDS

Second, they knew the community. They displayed their knowledge by citing previous statistics and providing a history of other projects.

Third, they answered the client's needs in a rational, logical manner. *Every builder* would like to construct a development and sell it without advertising. But, it is difficult to believe it can be done. They allayed any fears the client had by citing previous history and statistics. There was no emotion, just facts.

Proposals that adequately enumerate those three categories—knowledge, creativity, and satisfying the customer's needs—seldom lose.

CHANGE IN PROPOSALS

To provide those three elements in a written form does not take reams of copy. That's the good news and the big change in proposal writing during the past few years. Aside from Request for Proposals (RFPs), which the government or public entities require, proposal making has been simplified.

RFPs can go on for pages merely detailing the consultant's qualifications before they ever get to the creative side of the project. In today's environment, where public funds are minimal, many consultants are steering away from RFPs and the paperwork. "It is too bureaucratic for us," says Izzo.

Much of the credit for the shortening belongs to downsizing. There are less people in the corporate hierarchy, consequently there is less time to read. Prospective clients do not want to go through pages of qualifications about the firm, nor do they want to see detailed information about the principals of the consulting firm. Everything has been shortened and simplified.

"Once you develop a reputation," says Bill Johnson, "the need for lengthy, detailed proposals diminishes. We find the prospect who calls knows you are capable of doing the job. They are not interested in written dialog as much as they are in what you can do; what you explain to them verbally."

"Reputation sells," says Holbert. "After this many years in the business, the people who call are familiar with our background and accomplishments."

Moore agrees with Holbert. "When you're known, there is not a great need for a proposal. Most of the things you are going to be doing are written in the letter of agreement. There usually is not a separate proposal."

Pennington, who deals on a national level, says that "if a client calls and asks for a proposal and they are located several thousand miles away, I send one. I generate most of the information via telephone." Pennington says, however, it is difficult to write and submit a proposal with thousands of miles between the client and consultant.

"My first and preferred strategy is to talk to the prospect, get a feel for the job and see if we have rapport before I ever write a proposal. Then, when I do write one, it usually runs no longer than a page to page and a half." If they insist on a proposal, Pennington says he "asks them to help me write it!"

Alessandra is not an advocate of long proposals. He believes most people prefer something short, to the point. The type of material that traditionally can be found in a letter of agreement.

Johnson's proposals are nearly all verbal. To answer client questions, Johnson will bring up other similar cases that his firm has handled. He will go into these other cases and show the prospect the parallel. Once Johnson is hired, he sends an engagement letter (see next chapter), which outlines what his firm will do. That is the closest he comes to presenting a proposal.

One exception to the need for proposals is Izzo. "We still do lengthy, detailed proposals for clients. I think many of the larger firms—which are our clientele—almost expect it."

When his company puts one together, it is professionally packaged and usually written on a computer with graphics. "If you are going for any substantial clientele, you need desktop. Otherwise, you cannot compete with some of the high quality proposals they see."

While proposals have changed, research has not. If a consultant is going to do the best job possible, research is critical. Clients expect a consultant to know everything about their company. The initial step is interviewing people within the prospect's company and getting them to talk. This was difficult in the 1980s because employees viewed consultants with suspicion. The consultant was someone who could cost them their job.

In the 1990s, trust in the corporation has not grown, but employees are more willing to talk because they see the consultant as someone who is going to help with the workload, not replace them.

The most important person to question is the CEO or decision maker. It is the decision maker who outlines the client's needs. The consultant who operates with only the CEO's input may not be getting the entire story. Ultimately, an outside firm has to solve problems and this takes more than just input from the CEO or decision maker. CEOs have their perspective. Other executives and employees may provide input that can be quite enlightening, especially when compared to the decision maker's and/or CEO's thoughts.

A word of caution: Access to the CEO and other senior managers does not automatically solve all the information-gathering problems. Other lower level managers may have valuable input. If they are bypassed, the consultant may not only miss a key point, but they may also find themselves with a potent adversary. Sometimes, lower level managers have influence with the CEO or decision maker.

Another potential problem: Management is in a hurry. They need the proposal today, and the project started tomorrow. This happens because companies do not react to problems until they become a crisis. They expect the consultant to do the same thing.

Consultants advise their counterparts to avoid rushing, regardless of the problem. "You might say to yourself," says Izzo, "'If I write this proposal now, I might have this new client tomorrow instead of next month.' In doing that you can blow the entire project."

Rushed proposals come back to haunt consultants. They demonstrate the consultant has not done a thorough study. If management needs something immediately, a consultant can present preliminary data, but it should be presented as only that—preliminary data. A simple statement preceding the presentation ("based upon our limited information these are some of our initial thoughts") should be made.

In gathering information, it is important for the consulting firm to structure questions that will help determine the needs of the company. Without an adequate needs assessment, recommended action is never going to be accurate. Nor will it satisfy management. Questions to be asked:

1. What are we after?
2. Who will we interview?
3. How deep does the problem go?

4. What kind of personality does the company have?

5. Who are the decision makers?

6. Does there seem to be differences of opinion within the firm?

7. Have we faced similar situations in the past?

8. Who are our competitors? What are their strengths?

9. Is there a planned budget?

10. Will this take the time of the principals of our company or will staff be able to accomplish the task?

11. Will the prospect's management be satisfied with staff? If not, how do we approach them?

ROLE OF SUMMARY

Whether the proposal is written, abbreviated, or oral, there are certain elements required. Even if a presentation is oral, there should be a written summary that outlines the problem, steps, timetable and solution. It should also give a background on the consulting firm, the qualifications of the consultants involved.

Do not mistake informality (for example, management's suggestion that a verbal presentation will suffice), for a reason to eliminate the written portion of the proposal. You can do things within the written presentation that cannot be done orally.

For example, you can include an in-depth biographical sketch (or profile) of your company and its abilities. This can be much more potent in writing than if given orally. You can insert reprints of newspaper articles that were written about your firm or principals.

Written presentations should be thorough, but not verbose. They can also contain references.

The following lists the steps in preparing a presentation for a prospective client:

1. Determine needs
   a. Interview client
   b. Get idea of client's true needs
2. Research industry
   a. Call industry trade associations
   b. Research competitors
   c. Check library for industry information
3. Research company
   a. Annual reports/10K/clippings
   b. Trade journals
   c. Newspaper articles/morgue in newspaper
   d. Check library
   e. Check chamber of commerce
   f. Check company vendors
   g. Get company brochures
4. Research presentation area
   a. Determine how many will be in room
   b. Where the room will be
   c. What type a/v and other equipment will be available
5. Begin presentation preparation
6. Divide presentation
   a. Your company's expertise
   b. Your background in field
   c. Your knowledge of potential client and industry
   d. Creative ideas
   e. A time frame for proposal project (if feasible)
   f. Design questions to bring out client involvement
7. Prepare approach
   a. Find your unique selling proposition (USP) to present to client

8. Prepare visuals

    a. Use slides, reprints, other visuals

9. Prepare portfolio

10. Prepare presentation kit to leave with client

    a. Insert your company brochure and background

TWO TYPES OF PRESENTATIONS

There are two types of presentations: First, the in-depth document that lays out ideas (without execution); the second is more conceptual. It does not go into detail. It may only cover one or two pages.

The in-depth document is usually presented by the consultant to a prospective client who has spoken to several different firms and wants to see what kind of ideas each has to offer.

Whether the document is in-depth or conceptual, the consultant will need to supply the data for the 10 steps. Every consultant, whether preparing a formal proposal or not, needs these questions answered and data supplied.

The most important information comes from the decision maker. Interestingly, the odds of getting the business "drop by about 40 percent if you cannot get the decision maker involved in the information gathering process," says Izzo.

Izzo's presentations, which are formal and detailed, involve two presentations. First, preliminary information is presented. Izzo broadly outlines how he sees the situation. This first session can be a problem. The purpose is to get feedback from management on the consultant's initial findings.

Izzo and other consultants do not want to have their firms branded as ones that jump to incorrect conclusions. To avoid misunderstandings, the meeting is frequently prefaced by a statement from the consultant similar to, "these are our thoughts and ideas, and some of our interpretations that we would like to share with you. They are based solely on our initial session and the information we gathered at it."

The meeting is to generate additional information and determine what turns management on and off. It is a low-risk, feeling out situation. The ideas are presented as being only "initial thoughts" that can be modified.

This probing session can reveal quite a bit about the company and those in it. If the prospect asks a great many questions, they may be confused as to what, exactly, the consulting firm should be doing. Executives may know their industry and company, but few know the inner workings of a consulting firm, what it could and should be doing.

Consultants should remember that the CEO or executives in the meeting are not familiar with consulting jargon. Acronyms and buzzwords should be forgotten. Everything should be explained in a practical, how-to manner.

During this session, astute consultants watch for reactions. What interests the prospect? This is a time for questioning and listening to feedback. The sessions should not be one-sided lectures.

Note-taking is critical. No one remembers everything. An important thought expressed by management can be lost before the proposal is written, if notes are not available. Accuracy is also paramount. Once the proposal is written and presented, it is too late to change anything. If you have an incorrect statement or inaccuracy in it, you may blow the entire account.

THE "SKUNK WORKS" APPROACH

Aside from interviewing executives and employees for information gathering, Izzo likes what is commonly called the "skunk works" approach. The term stems from idea-generating sessions that Lockheed Aircraft used years ago. The company put its brightest engineers together in one room, and lets them throw out as many creative thoughts as possible.

It was called "skunk" because no one within the company wanted to get near the engineers during these creative sessions. A skunk works session can be valuable for a consultant, especially if the company supports openness among its employees. Problems will surface that no one has mentioned, and many may be critical in preparing the proposal.

■ Case Study

In researching a company, consultants may come up with information that can be embarrassing. Don Kracke ran into exactly that kind of situation. Kracke spends days, sometimes weeks, researching and doing his homework when it comes to consulting with companies insofar as licensing opportunities are concerned.

He was called by a major soft drink company and asked if he was interested in submitting a proposal to handle its licensing. The soft drink manufacturer, well-known to consumers in the United States, had a proprietary trademark that many companies had expressed an interest in licensing.

The company had spent years establishing its trademark, and it was of considerable value to licensees who could use it on t-shirts, cups, glasses, and a variety of other products. Although Kracke usually only licenses his own designs, the account was substantial and it intrigued him.

Kracke delved into the firm and the industry. He studied trade papers, spent hours talking to executives within the soft drink company, he interviewed competitors and spent countless hours talking to existing licensees who already had agreements with the soft drink company.

When the research was completed, Kracke turned in a proposal that got an immediate response from the firm. The reaction came quickly because of one line in it that read, "What your licensees think about you is that you are not the licensor but the rippor, and the licensees the rippees."

The statement brought home the thought to the soft drink company executives, that their licensees suspected they were getting absolutely nothing for their licensing fees. It was a bold statement for a consultant to make to a prospective client. ■

Sources of Proposal Information

1. Decision maker, CEO, senior managers, other executives

2. Employees

3. Annual reports/10ks

4. Company brochures/sales literature

5. Local bankers, CPAs, other businesspeople

6. Suppliers/vendors

7. Local library, clipping file

8. Local newspaper "morgue" where microfilmed stories are kept and cataloged.

Did Kracke do the right thing? Should he have just stuck to the value of the firm's licensing and forgotten the complaints?

Kracke did not get the account, however, he is convinced that when senior managers at the soft drink company read the report they said "he is right."

The approach can be hazardous, but "it can set your proposal apart from everyone else's," Kracke says. It can also earn the respect of the client. That is, if the consultant is sure the statement is correct.

While the Kracke illustration may not be typical, it is not unusual for a consultant to find that the decision maker is off-base as far as the company's problem is concerned. Their opinion may differ substantially from everyone else's in the company.

The consultant can play it safe and reiterate the decision maker's concerns and base its plan of action on the executive's input. It may get them business, but it may never solve the problem. In the end the consultant loses because he or she lacked honesty and the problem was never solved. That failure may not only cost the consultant the client, but it can also hurt with referrals and future business.

Not all decision makers take kindly to the blunt, Kracke approach, however, there is a growing trend in U.S. industry to "straight talk." Major companies, realizing that they are not only in a battle for market share but existence as well, are beginning to call for it. With a downsized workforce, companies cannot afford to ignore straight talk.

The Proposal Personality

Kracke says proposals do more than outline what a firm can do. Well-written proposals give the consulting firm personality. "It enables you to stand out from the crowd. I take risks in writing them because of that. In the long run, you will win more than you lose."

Proposals need not be dry and boring. When the decision maker selects one, they base part of the selection on the tone of the proposal. Did it excite and motivate them? Did they get a feel for the consultant's company?

In the end, proposals are vehicles for one person to talk to another. Too many are dry with stiff, formal language. To win, consultants need their proposals to come "alive." "In today's market, no one wants b.s.," says Kracke. "People buy honesty. If they do not, you're better off without the business."

HANDLING SOPHISTICATED CLIENTS

In writing, be specific and avoid generalizations. When someone picks a consultant it is a subjective judgment. Be straightforward—so they have a concrete reason to select your firm—but be entertaining. People like to work with people they can relate to—the straight, colorless proposal can cost you even if it is honest. Put a little language into the proposal. Get the thesaurus out. And don't sound like a college professor. Write plain English.

When a company buys a proposal, whether it is verbal or written, they are going for the personality as well as the content. It's the same as hiring a new employee. The hiring manager goes for someone with whom they have rapport. Colorful language does not mean going overboard with superlatives. Beware of how you describe your firm and its qualifications. Do not overuse adjectives; they can cast doubt as to the firm's ability and your credibility. Facts help sell. Success stories have impact. If your firm represented clients in the same industry, say so. If there were special accomplishments for those clients, state them.

Tone is important in the proposal. Be positive. "We can" versus "We will try" connotes two different messages to a client. Clients seek outsiders because they want the expertise. They do not want someone who will merely "try." They want a firm that is convinced it "can." Positive tone demonstrates a "knowledge-based confidence" to the prospect. If a firm has done the job for others, it can do it for the prospect's company. Cite examples, mention names.

Need-Based Proposals

For better insight into a company's problems, consultants should put themselves in the place of the client. Imagine who is going to read the proposal. Who is going to make the decision. What things are of concern? What does the company need? Does the proposal answer those needs?

Need-based proposals are keys to success. In some cases, determining needs may be easier than others. Many needs are straightforward, while others are not. The company that has trouble getting timely information from its data processing department may or may not have a computer (hardware) problem. It could be a time management problem.

Suppose the head of the department may not want to distribute the information until he or she has seen and analyzed it. Or, suppose the department head is afraid to share too much for fear it will undermine the importance of his or her position. The proposal company that does sufficient research will know the problem exists before the proposal is written. Often, the consultant is as much a psychologist as consultant.

Every firm must have a unique selling proposition (USP). A USP sets one consulting firm apart from another. In Johnson's case, his consultants offer restructuring and reorganization specialists to assist firms that are having difficulty coping with today's economy. Moore's USP is that she is a marketing specialist who concentrates on a particular industry, real estate. McCuistion is an experienced veteran of a troubled industry.

USPs set consultants apart from competitors. They are the hooks or angles by which most firms sell their products and services. Every successful firm has a USP. In the beer industry, a USP for one brand might be that it is made with "mountain spring water." In the automobile industry, it may be a car's mileage potential, the price, or luxurious interior. Cadillac sells luxury and status, but Hyundai sells low price. Each has its own USP. It can be a particular service or way of doing business. It may even be one of the principals in the consulting firm who is noted for a specialized expertise, for example, Kracke.

The USP may be present in the approach that two rival consultants utilize, however, one may bring it out and use it as a selling point, while the second bypasses it.

USPs do not guarantee the contract, but they give the firm something unique they can stress and market to prospects. It helps set them apart.

Stumbling Blocks

Not every situation involves research and presentation. Some are more complex. For instance, suppose there is already a consulting company in place and management wants to switch. The consultant and proposal writer have a complex chore. They not only have to analyze the job to be done, but they also must determine why the present firm failed. Why is management displeased with the current vendor? What errors were made?

Clients who have a consultant in place, do not decide to change overnight. The need for change has been brewing. Why? Has the previous consultant failed to deliver? Or, is this a company that plays musical chairs with outside consultants?

In some industries such as advertising, changing firms frequently is commonplace. An automobile manufacturer, for instance, has the opportunity to compare his ad agency's work with that of others in the industry. Others with mass-marketed products have the same comparison opportunity.

The CEO of a company may be unhappy with his CPA consultants because he "dislikes the way they did the audit." In reality, he may be disturbed with the lack of attention they gave to his company. Or, it could be that the head of the proposal team sold the CEO on the services, and the company never saw the team leader again. Izzo's point of knowing how much service—and by whom—the client is going to demand, becomes important.

Some consulting firms utilize super salespeople to present the proposal and nail down the account. The client is sold as much by personality as content. When the deal is closed and the salesperson or principal is gone, the client is disappointed.

One way to avoid this misunderstanding is to make sure that everyone on the proposal team is listed in the proposal, along with their fees. Then, if a client is sold on an individual or partner, he can also see that he may be paying a premium for that person's services.

Who Makes Decisions?

Many consulting firms are perplexed when they have to make a presentation to someone other than the decision maker. It is desirable and preferable to sit down with the decision maker and let them hear and see the proposal. At times, however, that does not happen. A firm may find itself stymied by a lower management employee who insists that he or she hear the proposal first.

What do you do? Consultants should remember that bypassing a lower echelon manager can be a mistake. You never know who has the ear of the decision maker. If the decision maker has asked the lower level manager to see and hear the proposal, the consultant should be sure they do. Bypass them and you invite problems.

Kracke is perfectly content to work his way up the ladder with the proposal. Remember, even if the proposal is presented at the lower management, nondecision-making level, that person is going to have an opinion; an opinion that can influence the decision maker. It is important to have rapport with everyone you deal with at a prospect's company, and not just the decision maker.

"Don't bypass those down the line who are supposed to see the proposal," says Izzo, "but make sure the decision maker sees the document."

Rapport can be everything. Most people would rather deal with people they like, rather than those they do not know. The proposal may be great, but if the client does not like the consultant(s), there will never be an agreement.

Astute firms realize that unless there is chemistry between the client and consultant, there will be no business dealings between the two. Any long-term relationship requires the cooperation of all management within a client firm, not just the decision maker. When Johnson deals with prospective clients, he urges the owners/executives—or whomever brought him in—to include those in management who will be involved in the proposal sessions.

"Clients," says Izzo, "either love or hate you. If they don't have emotions about you and your firm, you will not get the contract." Before someone gets the contract, feelings will emerge. It is up to the consultant to make sure he or she is not abrasive or irritating. You do not want to give the client or decision maker a reason to dislike you or your firm.

Emotions become apparent early-on. When the proposal writer does research and begins to interface with management, they quickly discover if management is cooperative. Do they open doors? Do they give researchers the time required? If researchers run into a stone wall, it is a sign the company (and decision maker) do not want to cooperate. They may not like the researcher, or the questions being asked.

Usually, there is one person on the proposal team or in the consulting firm who has the best rapport with the client. This person should be the main contact and the on-going go-between. Occasionally, a consulting firm will find the client problems untenable, regardless of the rapport they have with the client. The following case is a good example of what can happen.

■ Case Study

It was one of the world's largest airport food, beverage, and merchandise companies, and it provided service to most of the major airports in the United States. Chances were if you were in any of the major metropolitan airport terminals in this country, the drinks, food, books, jewelry, or magazines you purchased were provided by this firm.

The founder was noted for his hip-shooting, straight talk. He was a blunt but likable man who treated his employees as he would have liked to be treated. As time went on, however, the founder stepped aside and let younger managers run the firm. The founder became chairman of the board, but had little to do with the running of the company. The further he was removed from the day-to-day running, the more the company's personality changed.

Within a year after the founder had moved to the chairman's spot, new rules came down from management. Executives were housed on the second floor of the two-story building, and clerks and others were on the first. One of the first changes was the company's coffee policy. Those on the first floor would have to pay for their coffee, while the executives on the second floor would be given it gratis.

An entire series of restrictive rules and regulations were put in place, and within a short period of time the company's morale was at a low ebb. Productivity began to suffer and costs rose. Shareholders began to grumble and demanded to know what was wrong. In an effort to appease the stockholders, management agreed to bring in an outside productivity consultant who would evaluate policy and procedures.

Management interviewed three firms for the assignment, and asked each to bring back a written proposal. The companies were provided with an executive liaison to help them gather information. Each had an initial meeting with senior managers, where input was provided on the company and its history. Nearly every one of the senior managers had a theory as to why the company's profits were declining. They ranged from rising costs and higher airport rentals to theft.

Although two of the three consulting firms took the information provided by the liaison and went back to write a proposal, the third firm asked for additional input. The proposal writer and researcher wanted to talk to a broader cross-section of employees for additional input. As a result, they spent an extra afternoon talking to employees on the first floor. What they found out clarified the problems and the cause.

When the proposals were presented, management was surprised to find that there were only two firms submitting them. The third, the company that had talked to employees on the first floor, withdrew.

Why did the productivity firm back-off? It did not take the consultants long to compare notes once they had talked to employees on the first floor. They discovered a company whose managers had fostered the separation of employees. Senior managers had actually been responsible for the destruction of the company's feeling of teamwork.

The consulting firm had to make a decision. Based upon its research, would this be a viable client? There were immediate problems. There was not one or two, but a half-dozen senior managers and none recognized the problems that existed on the first floor. None realized the causes, either. None even suggested talking to the other employees, because they felt the input would not be of value.

For the consulting firm selected, this could be an insurmountable obstacle. If senior managers were made aware of the problem, would they change? Would they be willing to revert to old customs and policies? Perhaps one or two would, but how about the rest? Would they all vote for the necessary changes?

The firm that declined to bid decided so because it felt strongly there was no way to change the behavior patterns of all management. Even with straight talk.

The consulting firm that accepted the challenge was unable to effect the needed changes, productivity was not impacted, costs continued to rise, and management was dissatisfied.

Kracke agreed with the decision to pass on the contract. Every consultant has to "sit down and evaluate all the stuff they have gathered. They have to look at the company objectively. Whether or not we like it, not everyone needs our services. I learned that through the years and when I finish my research, if I find we are not needed, or cannot make a difference, I tell the prospect."

10 STEPS IN WRITING EFFECTIVE PROPOSALS

Once the firm is analyzed and the consultant(s) decide to bid on the project, the following proposal steps should be carefully considered:

1. *Research.* Not a word can be written until the problem and/or company is researched. In some cases, this may involve interviewing key executives and employees. It may require library research, the compiling of industry data. Needs cannot be accurately determined without sufficient research.

2. *Objective writing.* Watch out for the hyperbole and exaggerations when putting the proposal together. It comes off as self-serving. Let the facts speak for themselves.

3. *Creative ideas.* Do not be afraid to lay out ideas and solutions. Be careful to generalize (do not get into specific solutions). Present situations can be compared with previous ones that the consulting firm handled for other companies. Ideas are a must. They show the prospect that the consulting firm has a direction and has studied the situation. As long as the idea is generalized and the exact method of implementation is not outlined, the idea is relatively "theft-proof."

4. *USP.* Every firm needs one. It represents the consultant's specialty; their prime expertise. It sets them apart from competitors.

5. *Language.* Don't make the proposal a legal document. Make it reader friendly. Avoid acronyms, $64 words, and complex jargon. Don't ramble. Use colorful terms and write in a practical, how to manner so that anyone can understand.

6. *Addressing competition.* Don't ever put down the competitors. This technique does not make your firm look better. A way to handle competitors is to play up the strengths you have in areas where you know they are weak. For example, if the client needs someone who has great expertise in reorganization—and your firm does but the competitor does not—stress the reorganization ability of your company. It puts a thought in the client's mind; a thought that may turn into the prospective client asking your competitor about their ability in the area.

7. *Summary.* The key selling points of your proposal are reiterated and outlined at the beginning of the proposal. This portion of the proposal contains all the important information so that managers who read the proposal can simply study the summary and have a good idea of what your approach will be.

8. *Strategizing.* You must have a strategy. What should be stressed? Who are the influencers in the client company? How do you address them? Whom should your firm be talking to? Who will the competition be? Who has the ultimate say?

9. *Proper organization.* Make sure the proposal is clearly structured with a beginning, middle, and end. At the beginning, a summary; between the summary and the end, a statement of the problem, your solutions. Both should evidence that your firm has a good grasp on the problem. Leave your background for the end of the proposal.

10. *Determine budget/costs.* Is there a budget or does the client want the consulting firm to come up with one. How much and for what?

IMPACT OF COST

When a consulting firm has studied the prospective client, carefully written the proposal and presented it, there is one more intangible that impacts the decision—money.

Regardless of the proposal, the bottom line is always money. Says Kracke, "Someone has to put it up. You have to convince management to open their wallets. Anytime anyone contemplates spending money, they want back-up, and plenty of it. I always keep that in mind when writing a proposal. I must convince this person to give me their money?"

The proposal is part of the selling process. It is not the end result of a series of client/agency meetings, but it is an integral part of an ongoing process. It is designed to reinforce the reasons the consultant gives to someone in order to get them to part with their funds. "Remember," Kracke cautions, "consultants are always considered an expense. Prospective clients are always going to ask, 'Do we really need it?'"

IMPACT OF REFERRALS

Signing clients becomes easier when it is a referral. Established consulting firms operate entirely on referrals. Those that have been around for several years and are still unable to operate via referral have probably made mistakes. They may have taken a client they knew they should have turned down. If "a customer goes away unhappy, forget it. If he goes away smiling, it will open the doors for all the business you can handle."

14-Step Flow Chart Process

1. Meet with management/decision maker(s).
2. Initial information gathering, determine other sources of information from management/decision makers/nature of the problem (e.g., the department or departments involved).
3. Structure questions based upon knowledge from initial interview with management.
4. Return to management with initial research thrust for problem. Generate feedback and determine if research is on the right track.
5. Determine any hidden needs.
6. Structure final questionnaire and begin research.
7. Talk to internal/external employees and nonemployees.
8. Continue research through outside sources such as library, newspaper, vendors, bankers, CPAs.
9. Compile research and summarize.
10. Go over summary with decision maker for accuracy. Determine, once again, any other hidden needs.
11. Determine client priorities.
12. Determine problems/causes of problems.
13. Brainstorm solutions.
14. Write proposal:
    Summary
    Research methodology and results
    Problems and solutions
    Recommendations, long- and short-term
    Background on consulting firm
    Addendum with fees

CHAPTER 4

Determining Fees—and Getting Them

A few years ago, when he first introduced the fee-setting concept to clients, Jay Abraham was looked upon by some as a naive, young businessman or by others as a consultant who knew something that they did not.

Jay's approach was to base his services entirely on a percentage; a percentage of the increase that he could generate for the client's business. In simple terms, Jay's approach, which has earned him more than $8 million in the past 10 years as a marketing consultant, works in the following manner.

VENTURE MARKETING

Called "venture marketing," Abraham is compensated strictly on a percentage of the increased sales of a client company. For example, suppose the company has $1 million in sales, and it has been averaging 10 percent growth each year. Based upon that input, the client can expect sales to reach $1.1 million during the next 12 months. If they retain Abraham, he will provide marketing services and implementation of the program. In return, he gets a percentage (anywhere from 25 to 70 percent) of the sales that are above the $1.1 million mark.

Thus, if the firm only does $1.1 million, Abraham gets nothing. If it does $1.2, he can earn anywhere from $25,000 to $70,000, depending upon the arrangement.

Before embarking on a venture marketing arrangement, a consultant must be sold on the potential for success. It can be extremely rewarding to consulting firms willing to take the risk. The approach can be applied to an increase in productivity, a decrease in absenteeism, a lowering of costs in the human resource area, or a more efficient engineering operation. The applications are endless, but the principles remain the same. The client does not have to invest any cash, but they agree to compensate the consultant on the basis of the increased profits, decreased costs, or some other related parameter.

Abraham's most noteworthy success was with a large, midwestern firm that specialized in selling collectibles. The items, which normally do well in high-inflationary times (consumers purchase art and other similar objects to keep up with inflation), were being marketed by a firm that began to experience a definite slide in earnings as inflation abated.

Abraham knew the company and saw the potential—even in noninflationary times—for a tremendous profit. His venture marketing proposal was appealing to the owners and they retained his services. Within weeks, Abraham had developed a number of unique programs that were working. Within months, the firm's sales were skyrocketing and eventually hit $500 million a year.

Tony Alessandra smiles when he recalls his early days in the business and his efforts to get someone—anyone—to go for a percentage arrangement. "I told people I was so sure I could increase their business that I was willing to accept a percentage, based solely upon the amount I actually brought into the company. No one ever accepted. I found the attitude most people had was that if I was so sure, why not pay him the fee. Bigger companies shied away from it, too. They had to answer to stockholders, and the arrangement could prove embarrassing."

Percentage packages are popular among clients today; however, they have pitfalls. The project has to be something that the consultant truly believes has growth potential. The consultant has to be willing to invest time and effort without compensation. The consultant has to be willing to wait for the payoff.

PERCENTAGE VARIATIONS

There is another pitfall that consultants face with this arrangement—they may be taking a "flyer" with the client, but their bills still have to be paid. If they take on a venture project and another client comes along—with cash—will the consultant's attention be diverted? If it is, the consultant runs the risk of not only failing with the venture client and seeing time and effort wasted, but he or she may also generate ill will and bad word-of-mouth from an unhappy venture client. The potential rewards are great but the consultant must be cognizant of the risks.

McCuistion has worked a variation of the percentage. He has taken a small percentage plus a smaller fee, but he has never waived the complete fee. "It's tough, especially when you have people working for you that you have to pay."

McCuistion points out that what makes sense is if the consultant can obtain a piece of the company or stock through performance. Strict performance, however, is something he tries to avoid.

THE "BURN RATE"

Somewhere in-between the client with sufficient funds and those with limited capital, is the billing concept called the "burn rate."

In the burn rate billing process, the consultant estimates the length of time it will take to do a project. For instance, suppose the consultant estimates it will take five months. He will bill the client $5,000 a month (the burn rate) for five months, and if it goes beyond that time period the consultant will split the billing (e.g., $2,500 comes from the consultant, out of his pocket, and $2,500 from the company).

The consultant is saying the job is worth $25,000 and will take five months to complete. The letter of agreement presented to the client does not contain a cutoff point. It starts at $5,000 a month, runs for five months and has a two-month extension during which time the monthly cost is reduced.

Suppose it goes 10 months. The company would be paying the initial $25,000 (first five months) and another $12,500 for the remaining five months. While some clients like this approach, others prefer the closed-end contract where there is a fixed price for the services, and a definite cut-off.

Problems can crop up with this arrangement. "Let's say," explains Izzo, "I have a burn rate agreement that runs five months with a $20,000 monthly fee. At the end of the five months, I discover I have at least another two months worth of work left. My billing is going to be halved. I'm going to be working for $10,000. Psychologically, this does not sit well with many consultants."

Some lose interest and give their attention to other, full-paying projects. The burn rate project drags on, the client grows unhappy, the consultant is unhappy because he is not being fully compensated, and the relationship can turn into a disaster.

There is sales appeal in the concept. The consultant is guaranteeing a completed project within the time frame (five months). If it goes beyond, the consultant suffers. The client knows the consultant had added incentive to live up to the timetable. It is another way of placating fears that many clients have—once they hire a consultant will the project end in a timely manner?

For experienced consultants, the burn rate can work well. As Qubein puts it: "If you've been there before, you know how long it will take to do a project."

FOUR BILLING FACTORS

All consultants, however, have to do more than just estimate time when deciding on billing. They should also look at four other factors:

1. Profitability. How profitable will it be? How many hours will I have to put into it?
2. Stability. Is the client stable?
3. Vulnerability. What if the CEO or decision maker changes? Will they want to bring in someone else?
4. Will this assignment lead to other assignments?

Before deciding on a billing rate, whether it be a percentage or burn rate, or some other billing variation, consultants evaluate those four areas. If the job is extremely profitable, it may pay to use a lower rate. If the client is unstable, the consultant may want to charge a higher fee, and if the company appears ready for a shake-up, should the consultant put in time, effort and a proposal when change is imminent? The last factor—referrals and additional business impacts fees as well. The greater the promise of additional business, the more lenient the consultant can be in his fee determination.

FIXED PRICE TECHNIQUES

Most clients still prefer the fixed price arrangement. The consultant agrees to do the project for $X and the client agrees to pay on a regular monthly basis. If the project goes beyond the initial estimation, the financial loss belongs to the consultant.

Consulting fees, however, can be deceiving. In contrast to a grocery store, parts house, or automobile dealer, when a customer purchases services from a consultant, he or she is buying a promise to deliver a nontangible piece of goods.

The purchaser often pays a portion (or all) of the fee in advance for something he or she will not receive for months. Establishing prices, perceiving the value of a consultant's services, and collecting the fees, must take into account the psychological impact upon the client.

Consumers have the ability to shop and compare when it comes to nonservice goods. The price of a bag of sugar can be easily compared by shoppers, and they know immediately if it is overpriced. There is no question when it comes to quality, either. The bag of sugar at one store has the same content as the bag of sugar at another.

But, what about the consultant's client? There is no guarantee of a fair price or quality service when the consultant is given the contract. There are references, a track record, and other intangibles, but the consultant's client is still "taking a chance." Consulting involves psychology as well as performance when it comes to pricing, collecting, and selling.

Although there are many pricing techniques in addition to venture marketing and the burn rate, one thing every consultant has to do before he or she determines price—have a clear idea of what the client needs, what resources it will take to meet those needs, and how long it will take.

But, even if a consultant has an idea as to what must be done and how long it will take, that does not guarantee that the price will guarantee a profit. Qubein says if "you have been there you probably know how long it will take to do the job. You also have to build in time, because you do not just go straight in and do the job. You'll spend time talking to the executives, decision makers, and other employees. It always takes longer than you figure."

Time can be misleading. Take, for instance, the case study on page 105.

Today, Holbert recalls those days with a smile. "I worked 60 hours and billed for 40. Like many beginners, I was anxious to do the job and the compensation was secondary. Certainly, you have to eat, but when a consultant opens his doors, he is concerned with getting the job. I was thrilled with the work; I enjoyed it immensely."

■ Case Study

After four years of law school and countless years of studying his industry, Hugh Holbert was anxious to open his law office. His specialty was real estate law and, thankfully, there were not many consultants who specialized in the area. Thus, almost from the day he opened his doors, clients were waiting.

Still, Holbert had to decide what he would charge. Like many consultants, he took the survey route. He made a few calls and found out what other attorneys in the area were charging. Some billed as much as $100 an hour, while others were as low as $60. Since he was a newcomer, Holbert decided on the latter rate. Besides, it was a dollar amount that could easily be divided into 60 minutes ($1 a minute), so he could even break down hourly fees.

What happened in the next few months surprised Holbert and taught him an important lesson about fees. At $60 an hour, he found himself working 17 hours a day and on weekends.

Why the high demand? Holbert was a specialist and a bargain. He was one of the few attorneys who specialized in real estate law. He understood the profession and the technical jargon, and anyone comparable would cost the client twice as much.

In his desire to be fair, Holbert underpriced his services and joined the long list of other consultants who opened their doors and found it difficult to decide on the correct billing fee.

■

HOURLY RATES

Holbert has become one of the highest paid legal consultants in the field. His hourly rate is $300 an hour and he will charge clients for a fraction of an hour if they call and take more than four or five minutes on the telephone with him.

"Knowing they have to pay if they spend too much time on the telephone makes a client more cognizant of time and its value. I always take their calls and talk to them, but if it turns into a problem-solving session that runs more than four or five minutes, I bill them."

McCuistion received a great deal of advice when he opened his practice. "Some of the best advice was do not bill yourself on a time basis." At first he did, but he switched quickly. Today, he operates on a monthly retainer or fee for the entire project. The average length of a project may run from a few days to years. Whatever the length, McCuistion dislikes hourly rates and time billing. He has found the recordkeeping is difficult and he theorizes there is a "perverse incentive." That is, if the consultant needs additional revenue, he can always mark down another hour or two.

"I found I was busy with my retainer clients, and ignored those on the hourly basis. As long as I did not charge them (the hourly clients), why worry?"

Additionally, many hourly clients hesitate when it comes to contacting the consultant. They know the minute the telephone is answered, the meter begins ticking. Regardless of how the client was billed, McCuistion says a must is to spell it out in the engagement letter.

"Spell out the fees and the scope of the work. It may not be called a contract, but it is just as important."

The letter of agreement is binding but McCuistion and others have an open door policy. If, at any time, the client feels the fee is too high, he encourages them to say something. At the same time, if he feels the fee is too low, he will say something as well.

People do not mind paying the top rate as long as the service is there. "As long as you do the job," Holbert says, "pricing becomes secondary. Only when a consultant fails to perform do they run into pricing complaints."

QUESTIONS TO ASK WHEN SETTING FEES

How does a consultant arrive at fees? First, there is a 7-step check-list of questions:

1. How long will the job take?
2. Can I do the job myself, or will it take additional help? If I do it myself, how many hours of my time will it take?
3. If it takes additional help, how many people will it take?
4. How much will I have to pay each person who assists on the job?
5. Will there be expenses? If so, should the client approve all of them, or just those over a certain amount?
6. Should I allow extra hours for the unexpected? (Yes)
7. How will this job fit into my overhead calculations and profit-making goals?

Suppose it takes 100 hours to do the job. If, for instance, it costs the consultant $3,000 in overhead and help, and he or she intends to make $3,000, the fee would be $6,000 divided by 100 hours, or $60 an hour.

EXPLAINING ESTIMATES AND FEES

Consultants should explain estimates, the time it will take for inter-viewing; the time to analyze the results; time for reinterviewing; the hours involved in compiling a summary of the problem, analyz-ing it, and proposing a solution. There may also be X hours in-volved for the consulting firm if it has to implement the proposed solution.

Each area should be itemized so clients do not believe the fig-ures were pulled out of the air. The consultant should link his or her past experience with similar clients and problems, and the time these projects took. The client should feel that the fees and costs were put together in a tangible, logical manner.

By itemizing the job into understandable units, the time and fees become reasonable and acceptable. The mistake occasionally made when asked about fees, is for the consultant to say "Well, I estimate it will take 100 hours, and at $100 an hour that means $10,000."

In their minds, clients are asking, how did you arrive at the 100 hours? How do you see tackling the job? Are you sure it is exactly 100 hours? Isn't that an inordinate amount of time for a job of this type? Is the $10,000 figure something you had in your head all along, and you are now trying to justify it?

Remember, clients are not specialists in consulting. Everything has to be spelled out, especially in an intangible field such as consulting. Imagine an audience viewing a motion picture before it was edited, or a play before it reaches the dress rehearsal stage. People have a difficult time conceptualizing. Without thorough explanation, 100 hours does not give anyone insight into what is involved. The burden rests with the consultant to justify the hours and the fees.

If the reasons for the fee are not justified, the relationship can go downhill—fast. Even consultants who work on monthly retainers should supply a breakdown for the client. Let clients see how many hours of time they are getting and for what purpose.

Even if a client shrugs his shoulders and does not press for a detailed breakdown, supply it. Usually, if a client is sold on a consultant's service, he will not object to the price, unless it is too high (meaning not affordable) or cannot be explained. Problems develop when consultants do a poor job of communicating what they are going to do and how they are going to do it.

Importance of Fee Communication

Always communicate the obvious. For a consultant, the work is understandable. But it may be a mystery to the client. Clients may lack marketing background. Explain the procedure. Never take a client's knowledge for granted.

In setting and justifying fees, never make it seem simple. The job may be simple—to the consultant—because it is their business. They have experience and know what has to be done.

Do not undersell your efforts. Never say "it's a piece of cake . . . we'll solve it in no time." That diminishes the importance of the job and the consultant's role. Consultants are called to solve problems, and problems take time, knowledge, and effort. That's what the client is paying for.

On the other hand, there is nothing wrong with a consultant commenting on the fact the job may be difficult, but "thanks to experience and background, I'm confident we'll solve it in a timely manner." Clients want to feel that they are getting their money's worth. If they believe the job is too easy, they will question whether or not they should retain the consultant's services.

6-Point Fee Communication Checklist

1. Communicate the obvious. Do not assume the client knows anything about the job or what getting it done entails.

2. Explain everything, regardless of how simple and mundane it may seem.

3. Never announce to the client that the job is easy. This may lead to the client believing the fee should be lower.

4. Display confidence in your ability to do the job. Clients hire consultants for their expertise. If a consultant does not appear confident, the client will detect the attitude. Attitude is critical.

5. Cite other similar jobs which you have done that have turned out well. Make the comparison whenever possible.

6. Explain fees and rates carefully. Never assume that the client understands rates. Take time to walk the client through the firm's procedures, so he or she understands how time consuming the project may be.

BILLING METHODS

How much should a consultant make? Successful consultants generate fees which earn them gross profits of 10 to 50 percent before taxes. The profit is usually after the consultant has paid themselves a salary and taken fringe benefits (e.g., auto, insurance). To earn a gross profit in this range, there are several pricing procedures that can be followed.

Market Average Billing

The simplest is *market average billing*. A consultant simply surveys competitors, finds out their fees, and prices services accordingly. Laurie Moore talked to other people who were doing similar kinds of consulting. She got a sense of the rates, the length of time (and knowledge) they had, and based upon her experience and demand came up with a reasonable rate. "It wasn't the top nor the bottom."

She priced her services on a package basis. A flat rate for a project, which was discounted if she was able to get the entire job. She would estimate the number of days, and she knew her overhead and the profit she wanted to make. If a client hired her for a day or two, she charged a normal day rate. If she was retained for a lengthy period of time, she would discount it 10 percent from her day rate.

The best way to compile competitive data and get an idea of what is being charged:

1. Make a few telephone calls. For example, if the consultant is an attorney, call a few others and ask about their hourly rates.
2. If rates average $100 an hour, with a low of $80 and a high of $120, set fees accordingly.
3. Hourly rates can be divided into minutes and minimums. If a consultant spends a minute on the telephone with a client,

should they charge $1.50 (if the billing rate is $75 an hour). Some consultants automatically charge a minimum, which means once the telephone rings they bill the client for 15 minutes (or $18.75). They charge the minimum whether they spend five minutes or 15. The consultant has to make this decision. Other consultants do not charge a minimum unless the conversation goes on and on.

Fee setting and billing involves judgment and common sense. The client may be calling to clarify some work or instructions. Some consultants have a practice of not charging if a client calls and asks about a past issue. The breaking (or charge) point arrives if the client brings up a new issue or problem. In this case, the meter can start ticking.

If a current or potential client calls and asks about fees for a particular job, does the consultant charge? The consultant cannot charge the questioner if they are not a client. If they do become a client, the time spent initially on the telephone can be built into the overall fee. It is impractical to bill a potential client for business you have not been given, unless the prospect clearly understands there is an initial consultation fee for nonclients. (In many cases, consultants who prepare proposals do not charge for the presentation. If they sign the client, they build the cost of the presentation into the fee. In other cases, consultants do charge, whether they get the job or not.)

What about brain-picking? What do you do if a potential client calls and tries to get all the answers during the conversation? Judgment is important. A consultant can allow the client five or even ten minutes, however, should it go beyond that period, businesspeople understand the concept of "minimum compensation."

Many consultants avoid this conflict by supplying clients with telephone or office consulting guidelines. The outline explains that services, for example, on the telephone are free for the first five (or ten) minutes. After that there is a fee. The same rules may apply to office visits.

Regardless of policies, it is advisable to set a minimum if a client spends more than X minutes on the telephone or X minutes in the office. Without minimums, clients may spend countless hours on the telephone and visiting the consultant, with no real purpose. The minimum makes a client think; they know before they pick up the telephone it can cost. Thus, they become more selective when they call, and the call usually has a definite point to it.

Equally as important, the minimum maintains the business relationship between the consultant and the client, which is the foundation of a solid consulting practice. A client selects a consultant partially on the basis of rapport, however, clients understand (and consultants must reinforce) the fact that it is the consultant's skill, knowledge, and experience that is being retained.

For market average billing, follow these steps:

1. Call competitors to determine hourly, daily rates.
2. Be sure to call enough to get a good cross-section.
3. Determine where you want to be on the scale—that is, high, low, or average.
4. Break the rates into hourly fees.
5. Break the rates into minutes.
6. Develop a rough outline of potential rates.
7. Multiply the hourly rates by the number of workable hours in a month (160).
8. Subtract a percentage of the workable hours to allow for marketing or sales activities, which are not compensated by the client. Marketing hours for a new business can total 20 percent (32 hours) or more for a new business per month.
9. Subtract the hourly and get a new hourly base (128).
10. Determine monthly gross via this method.
11. Determine monthly overhead.
12. Determine the profit (before taxes) you want to make.

13. Does the monthly gross allow for the profit and overhead desired?

14. If the monthly gross is too low, readjust salary, cut overhead, or examine the fee structure once again.

An important billing question that enters into a consultant's business is travel time. Do you charge for it? A standard is charging for travel when it takes the consultant out of town on behalf of the client. If there is out-of-town travel, make sure it is included in the cost of the consulting contract, and not presented to the client as a billing afterthought.

If a consultant drives from his or her office to the client, travel time is usually not included. However, if traveling time (even local) is a major consideration in the project, it should be addressed at the contract stage, and included before contract finalization.

Overhead Plus Profit Billing

With this method, consultants determine their yearly overhead and desired profit. This is divided into yearly workable hours and hourly rates are established.

For example, if overhead is $3,500 per month, and the consultant wants to gross $6,000 per month after overhead, the total needs are $9,500 per month. If the consultant wants to take home $6,000, the total amount has to be higher to allow for taxes.

Overhead items include:

1. Rent.

2. Utilities (if not included in rent).

3. Cleaning service.

4. Telephone/fax/other communications equipment.

5. Postage.

6. Equipment rental/leases.

7. Insurance/workmen's compensation.

8. Auto (if company paying for it).

9. Letterhead/stationery.

10. Secretary/other employees/part-timers.

11. Taxes (social security, disability, business, etc.).

How to Determine Hourly Rates with Overhead/Profit Method

There are approximately four working weeks in a month, or 160 hours (40 hours per week). One hundred sixty divided into $9,500 means the hourly rate should be approximately $60 per hour.

$$40 \times 4 = 160 \text{ (Total working hours/Month)}$$
$$160 \text{ divided into } \$9,500 = \$60 \text{ per hour}$$

There are other considerations for consultants. Not all working time produces income. Some time might be spent on marketing, bookkeeping, or even volunteer work. Consultants can subtract these hours from the total working hours and revise rates accordingly.

Suppose, for instance, 15 hours per month is spent on marketing and five on bookkeeping. Take the 20 hours from the 160 (140) and divide the 140 into $9,500 = $67 (plus) per hour or $68 (rounded off) is the new consulting rate.

Use of Hourly Multipliers

When consultants utilize workers within their company for a project, they bill the client for the worker, and use a multiplier (of the employee's salary) to determine the rate.

If, for instance, an employee makes $35,000 per year (or $16.80 per hour) based upon 2,080 workable hours (52 × 40) per year, there should be a multiplier of approximately three used to cover salary, overhead, and profit. The employee's total hourly billing rate (to the client) would be $50.40.

The multiplier is an excellent tool to determine how much the consultant/owner should be billing for his or her time.

Consultants forget that their time, too, should be marked up in order to cover overhead and profit. Utilizing this formula, the consultant will usually show a profit of around 20 percent (before taxes). Some consultants increase the multiplier, and some have it higher for certain levels of employees while others have it lower.

Johnson bills at three or three-and-a-half times hourly rate because it covers his cost, provides a profit, and makes the firm competitive. Johnson, who will bill around $3 million this year (two-thirds from consulting), reserves the highest rate (3.5) for the consultant(s) who do the most work with the client.

"Usually that is the middle manager," he says. "Clients do not resent paying a higher multiple for people who are doing the work. They do resent paying a high multiple for someone they never see."

If the consultant who has the most contact is earning $30 an hour, Johnson will bill his hours at $105. "Remember, too, that clients resent the top billing (3.5) multiplier being used for the consultants with the highest rate. They resent the top billing multiplier for someone at the bottom because usually that person has the least skills and is contributing less than anyone else on the team."

Johnson does one other thing unique to the business. He has created a network of 30 to 40 other people (nonemployees) he can call upon. They come into the client's business, and charge and bill their own rates—and report to Johnson. Most of these people supply routine accounting services that are infrequently needed. Utilizing the outsider, Johnson does not have to carry "excess" CPAs who only perform standard services. It is a unique technique that other consultants can use to supply a full line of services without carrying additional employee overhead.

Johnson's specialty is accounting, but he has found a profitable (and wide open) niche in reorganization counseling. His

26-member staff are all CPAs, but each has specialties. Some have expertise in acquisition, others in estate planning, business valuations, and litigation support. He never uses them for the customary financial statements and audits. Johnson leaves these duties to the "outside" staff.

Don Kracke tackles fees from another perspective. He looks at his total, yearly overhead and what it costs to keep his doors open (with a profit). Last year, it was $2 million, which means "I have to earn $1,000 an hour (2,000 hours approximately) or $16.67 per minute." Kracke is able to generate that fee because of the unique position he has in the market. There are few—if any—licensing consultants with his experience. Most of the time when he is called in for his expertise, the company has a major licensing problem.

The fee never is a question. "After all," he explains, "if you're dying you do not negotiate with the brain surgeon when he comes in the room. If I can construct a program for a company, the fee is inconsequential. The arrangement may vary. Sometimes it is a straight fee, others it may be a percentage."

Pennington has worked out several different fee methods. Typically, he bills his services on a day rate. He arrived at the fees by simply "studying the market and knowing what other productivity consultants charge." Pennington, who works out of Dallas but does consulting on a national basis, will charge less if the job is at home. "Fees," he explains, "are a subjective call. For the larger clients, it is less important, but for the smaller ones it can be a major consideration." Pennington is aware of the fee concern and if he detects there is a financial problem he tells the client "don't worry, we'll work it out."

Pennington adds that if everything is based upon a fee decision, the project may be extremely difficult. The company is going to evaluate all efforts based upon one thing—how much they have to pay for it.

"That's not a good situation. The most important thing—long before fee—is do you (the client) and I get along. Do both of us understand the problem and what I can do about it. Let's first decide if we can do business together."

If they can, Pennington will bend fees. If, for instance, they need him for three days but can only afford two, he will make special arrangements to work nights during those two days in order for the company to obtain its objectives. "Fees are important," he says, "but they should not be the determining factor for a client."

Tony Alessandra did what many consultants do—he looked at the competition, saw what they charged, and asked for the same thing. He does, however, point out an interesting psychological impact of fees on consultants. "If you ask for the fee in an apologetic way, you're too high. You have to feel comfortable."

Holbert followed the same surveying technique that other consultants practiced, but he did additional research which enabled him to get a better grasp on pricing. How much, he wondered, would it cost a client to hire an employee with my skills full-time? Could they save money by doing so?

"In most cases," he says, "if a company has a continuing need for consulting services and they can hire a full-time person, they probably will—if they can save money. But, if the consultant is a 'better bargain,' they will stay with the outside service."

Unlike consultants who earn their fees by performing a specific service, money managers, such as Arnold Van Den Berg, are compensated on the amount of money they manage. Typically, the fee is anywhere from 1 to 1.5 percent of the client's portfolio. On the surface, it may sound as if the consultant cannot lose, however, there are few clients who would allow a money manager to continue with the account if the value of the portfolio dropped. Thus, Van Den Berg's challenge is not in setting the correct fee, but in knowing enough about the stock market (his specialty) to ensure that his client's portfolios will grow.

Dennis McCuistion's approach to fee setting differs, too. When he entered the consulting field he studied the market to see what others were billing. He received a great deal of advice as well. "Some people said bill on an hourly basis, others on a project basis, others monthly."

McCuistion points out several other disadvantages of the hourly arrangement. For example, many clients in that category would not call, because they knew as soon as they did the meter would be turned on. McCuistion found it to be a hindrance. It stifled communication and he is convinced that retainers are a better road.

THE RETAINER

Working on a monthly retainer, however, requires consulting skill. The consultant not only has to ensure that the client feels they are getting their money's worth, but he or she also has to make sure that the fee is not too low. McCuistion bases retainer fee-setting on several elements.

For example, how much can the company afford? "You cannot charge $5,000 a month to a company that is doing $1 million a year in sales. With retainers, you have to evaluate what services you can provide and what the company can afford."

Each client is different. "Regardless of who it is, the consultant on retainer has to carefully outline exactly what they are going to do for the fee."

CHAPTER 5

Contracts and Letters of Agreement

The two had known each other for more than five years and had become the best of friends. At least once a week they had lunch together, and on two occasions they had even taken vacations together. One was an up-and-coming accountant with a growing practice and the other a well-known marketing consultant. They probably would still be friends if it was not for a chance happening. The CPA found himself part-owner of a small product company. He also found he needed help, especially with marketing. Naturally, he turned to his long-time friend.

The marketing consultant carefully studied the young company and its product line. It was one of the most promising enterprises he had seen in years. Excitedly, he sat down with the CPA and went through a marketing plan he had put together the day before. The smiling CPA was extremely pleased with the approach. It would take some funding, but he was sure it would pay off in the long run. The CPA agreed on the fee, shook hands with his friend, and the two parted company.

Five months later, the pair were shouting and screaming at each other in court. Each had hired an expensive attorney, and each pointed an accusing "breach of contract" finger at the other. The problem: There never was a contract. Both businessmen had embarked on a venture without signing any agreement or contract. Each accused the other of making unfulfilled verbal promises.

The judge studied the two, shook his head, and gave up. He was stymied. Without any written agreement, there was no way for him to tell who was right. The judge dismissed the case and the two former friends angrily went their own separate ways. Another friendship had been destroyed by an ill-fated business venture.

The case is true and it is only one of thousands because someone failed to put something in writing. Regardless of how friendly businesspeople are, there is no reason for them to not have an agreement. Unfortunately, some businesspeople—and consultants—feel if you insist that someone sign an agreement, you are displaying a lack of trust. On the contrary, a signed contract shows that each side has faith that the other will live up to their promises.

Signed agreements are a must in the consulting field. Remember, consulting is a business and contracts are part of business. No client should refuse to sign an agreement. Agreements prevent confusion and conflict. They spell out the obligations of each party and if the consultant and client ever have a difference of opinion, the agreement is there to clarify the arrangement.

One problem that is frequently encountered is that the consultant and client start out knowing each other as friends. One says to the other "we can do this with a handshake." But handshakes fall apart when disagreements arise. And, if there is not a contract to clarify the differences, arguments and court are usually the end result.

SIMPLIFIED AGREEMENTS

In today's environment, there has been a definite push to simplify agreements and contracts. Bill Johnson says the contracts have become more commonplace. "They may be shorter, but there are more of them. It is just good business practice to put things in writing."

As to complexity, Johnson feels the agreements are still fairly "generic, but they have to address more types of services. For example, years ago CPAs were primarily concerned with financial statements and audits. Today, we are doing everything from business valuation to reorganization."

Joseph Izzo points out the biggest change in agreements is the detailing of how charges are arrived at, what each phase of the job will cost, and when the payments are due. "This has to be spelled out beforehand. If the client does not like what he sees, they can change it before the job begins. In the past, the billing and charges were frequently left up in the air. The client had a good idea of what the job would cost, but there were not definite parameters spelled out."

Part of the desire for explicitness may be due to the tightening of budgets and the accountability that many executives face. They want the consulting job done, but they do not want there to be grey areas, especially when it comes to billing.

PHASE CONTRACTS

Kracke handles agreements with similar care. He provides clients with a written estimate of what the fee will be and then he provides a written estimate per phase. If, for instance, he explores the licensing validity of a company's trademark, he might call that Phase I and quote the client a fee. If he goes beyond and intends to outline a product line and possible customers for the client, he may call that Phase II—and spell out a fee, as well.

"The biggest change," says Pennington, "is measurement of results. Today's consultant not only talks about results, but helps the client set things up so results can be tracked and measured." Contracts not only have to spell out what is expected, but they also have to have a mechanism for tracking and measuring results.

LETTERS OF AGREEMENT

Astute consultants usually visit an attorney only once—when they get their first client and need a letter that can be enforced in court. They have a standard letter of agreement or contract written and use it—with some revisions—with all future clients.

Some consultants prefer to avoid attorneys. They say the business has to be built on trust and too many agreements that are drawn by attorneys are written in legalese making them difficult to understand. Kracke is blunt when he discusses the attorney's role in the client/consultant's relationship.

"More deals are messed up by attorneys than any other group I know. That," he says, "comes from a guy whose son is an attorney and who retains four different attorneys. I have a lot of respect for them, but I do not want them negotiating contracts and agreements. I'll do that. They should just stick to putting the language together—per my instructions—when the negotiations are completed."

Kracke, and most consultants operate with a simple letter—often no more than two to three pages. Kracke, who deals with many Fortune 500 companies, has a simple 2-page letter. Typical letters outline the duties the consultant has to perform, cover the responsibilities, and include payment due dates.

With businesses trying to save costs, expensive, drawn-out contracts between consultant and client have become a thing of the past.

THE GOVERNMENT CONTRACT

Most government entities have not changed the manner in which they deal with private consultants. There can be pages ranging from the requirements a consultant must fulfill in their hiring practices, to the duties of the particular project. Any consultant who wins a Request for Proposal (RFP) contest can look forward to a lengthy, government document that must be signed before the project can be launched.

THE PERCENTAGE-BASED CONTRACT

Regardless of length, letters of agreement/contracts should not be taken lightly. Jay Abraham, a marketing/direct mail consultant, operates on the basis of collecting a percentage of the increased business he can generate for a client. In one case, he increased a client's business several thousand percent, and the corporation found itself paying Abraham in excess of $50,000 a month. That high of a fee can gnaw and irritate a client.

"Unquestionably," says Abraham, "a client will not pay high fees for long before they begin to feel as if they are being 'robbed.' It's an interesting phenomena. When I started with the client, they could not afford a direct mail consultant. Profits were virtually nonexistent. When we developed several pieces that began to bring revenues in by the carload, resentment emerged. The client began to think that maybe it was not our efforts that brought in the money. Maybe it was just fate, luck, or whatever. Either way, they eventually made it so difficult to deal with them that we resigned the account."

Abraham's example is well-taken. A consultant may generate a fee that is predicated on a sliding scale. As fees mount, the consultant—in the client's view—is getting rich.

When feelings of this type emerge, the consultant has to make a decision: (1) should they continue to bill in the manner prescribed in the contract or (2) should they approach the client and readjust the method upon which the fee is predicated? The decision is up to the consultant and it is a difficult call. It is almost as touchy as getting a fee raised when the project suddenly begins to demand more hours than the consultant initially estimated. But consultants must face facts. They operate in a highly competitive, volatile environment. If a client resents fees, they will eventually do something if the consultant does not. The consultant's goal should be to be fair. If the fee has an escalation clause or profitability stipulation that sends the fee skyrocketing, the consultant should ask himself, "Is the fee fair?" If not, never be afraid to lower or readjust it.

Alessandra gives a piece of advice related to fees and rapport. "If the client does not like you and, for some reason, resentment emerges, get out. Resign the account. There is no reason to stay if one party cannot get along with the other. If one wants to change something and the other does not, there is obvious mistrust and the arrangement is not going to last long."

ADJUSTING CONTRACTS

Adjusting contracts is a two-way street. Sometimes the consultant finds himself in a position where he is putting in far more hours than he estimated. The job has become unprofitable. What happens then?

Consultants find that most clients—if they are getting the service and the job is being done—are understanding. If the consultant explains different aspects of the job to the client, why his estimates were off, and where the job demands are far exceeding previous estimates, in many cases the client will adjust the fee or terms. Clients want to keep a good consultant just as a consultant wants to keep a good client. Consulting is a business, and if one side is not getting a fair deal there are ways of readjusting the terms and compensation.

LETTER OF AGREEMENT VS. CONTRACT

Regardless of terms, consultants do better when they present a letter of agreement rather than a contract. "The term contract," explains Moore, "can be intimidating. That's why you find car salespeople using the term 'agreement' rather than contract.

Contract says to the client that everything is final, done. It can also bring out buyer's remorse and additional questions."

It is wise to get them to sign an agreement as soon as possible. "We're still in the sales business," explains Moore, "and even though the success of the account depends a great deal upon the consultant and client rapport, you'd be amazed at how much that rapport improves once the agreement is signed. The signature removes all doubts."

The cardinal rule is to be as specific as possible. Put everything into writing. There is less room for confusion and questions. The client and consultant know exactly what is expected. The specific agreement frequently helps avoid differences between client and consultant, while the general one fosters it.

Some typical letters of agreement follow. All are actual contracts utilized by consultants, however, the name of the company and client have been removed for confidentiality.

Exhibit 5.1 is a simple letter of agreement. (All letters of agreement or contracts should be on a company letterhead.) Exhibit 5.1 is commonly known as a monthly retainer contract, and usually applies where the consultant will be doing work on an ongoing basis. The set fee precludes the billing of individual hours. Many clients prefer the retainer to the hourly billing, especially if they foresee an inordinate amount of time to do the job. It is, of course, up to the consultant to surmise which is better—hourly or retainer.

If the client/consultant agree on the retainer, it is critical for the consultant to judge, as accurately as possible, how many hours per month the job will take. Those hours can then be converted (by the consultant) into a fair monthly retainer.

Exhibit 5.2 spells out fees for individual services and also has an escalating clause in it. This type agreement is utilized by a client who hires a consultant for a specific project, but expects the revenues to initially lag and build as time goes on. It gives the client "breathing" room and does not put undue pressure on the customer's capital and/or initial cash flow.

EXHIBIT 5.1
Letter of Agreement—Monthly Retainer

[Name of client] hereby retains [consulting firm] for [type of services] commencing [date] and continuing monthly thereafter, until [date]. Either party hereto may terminate this agreement earlier by tendering a 30-day written notice of termination.

For these services, [client] agrees to pay a monthly fee of _____ dollars [$_____], plus expenses. The monthly fee shall be due and payable in advance and in the following manner:

- The first month's fee shall be due and payable upon the signing of this agreement and a like amount on the same day of each subsequent month thereafter.

- Expenses shall be billed by invoice and shall be due and payable within fifteen days of the invoice date. No expense in excess of _____ dollars [$_____] shall be incurred by [consultant] on the client's behalf without the client's prior approval.

- In the event that any legal action is required to enforce this agreement or any portion thereof, the prevailing party of such legal action shall be entitled to recover from the other party the reasonable attorney's fees and legal costs thereof.

By _____ [Consulting firm] _____   _____ [Client] _____

Date _____   Date _____

EXHIBIT 5.2
Letter of Agreement

["Client"] hereby retains [Consultant] for marketing services for its [Name of project] commencing [date] and continuing until either party hereto terminates this agreement by tendering a 30-day written notice of cancellation.

For these services, the Client agrees to pay a monthly retainer of _____ dollars [$_____], from the effective date of this contract through [date]. The retainer will be increased to [amount] dollars [$_____] effective [date] and will remain at that level through [date]. On [date], the retainer shall be increased to _____ dollars [$_____] per month and will remain at that level until [date].

For the retainer, the Agency will provide to the Client account services, meeting time, conceptual time, public relations services, clerical time (in preparing conference reports, ad schedules, marketing plans). The client will be billed separately for art design, art production and creative copywriting time. The fees for these services shall be:

Creative copywriting	$_____	per hour
Art design	$_____	per hour
Art production	$_____	per hour

The agency's responsibilities will be to provide the client with a marketing plan, media mix and breakdown, brochure design, copywriting, display design, arrange for any photography, ad placement, promotion and publicity.

The agency will provide all ad placements and buyouts and will be entitled to a [_____%] advertising commission on all media and a [_____%] mark-up on all buy-outs. The client will be billed on a monthly basis with the retainer due the first of the month. For all brochure and display work, one-half of the cost will be due upon the client's approval and one-half upon delivery and/or installation.

For ads, one-half will be due upon final approval of ad and one half due upon invoice billing following publication. All brochures and display work will be put out on a competitive bid with three bids for all work.

EXHIBIT 5.2 *(continued)*

Expenses, creative copywriting, art design, and art production fees shall be billed monthly by invoice and shall be due and payable within 15 days of the invoice date.

In the event that any legal action is required to enforce this agreement or any portion thereof, the prevailing party of such legal action shall be entitled to recover from the other party the reasonable attorney's fees and legal costs thereof.

[Name of Company/Client]	[Name of Company/Agency]
By _____ [signature] _____	By _____ [signature] _____
Date _____	Date _____

Implicit in this contract is trust between the client and consultant. Notice how the billing (for hours) does not state prior approval by the client. There is no maximum for any of the services, consequently the monthly retainer can turn out to be minuscule compared to the hourly fees. That's why trust is critical to the success of this relationship.

PERFORMANCE-BASED CONTRACT

The next agreement is based entirely on performance. There is no retainer and the consultant only gets paid when services are actually performed (Exhibit 5.3).

The performance-based contract spells out exactly what the consultant has to do in order to earn the fee. A proposal accompanies this agreement, and the proposal is in the form of a plan. From a consultant's standpoint, the weakness in this agreement is that the services may be performed but the consultant might not be able to generate the type of coverage spelled out in the agreement and proposal.

The consultant—in this case—is a public relations (PR) specialist and PR coverage is impossible to guarantee. Even if the idea for the story is good, there is no way to ensure that the editor will decide to do the story. Thus, the consultant can spend countless hours selling the editor and/or media and never receive anything for it.

This is an agreement that demands the consultant have a definite idea of what can and cannot be done. From the client's standpoint, there is an additional weakness. In order to make this contract viable and worthwhile for the consultant, the client usually offers significant fees for individual accomplishments. Should the consultant be extremely successful, the client frequently gets upset because of the inordinate amount of money it is costing. The performance-based contract has grown in popularity, but it may work better in consulting areas that are not as intangible as public relations and promotion.

EXHIBIT 5.3
Letter of Agreement

[Client] agrees to retain [Consultant] for [Type of services] as outlined in a letter from [Consultant] to [Client] on March 19, 19XX. The effective date of this agreement will be when [Consultant] presents an acceptable plan and/or outline for [Type of services] for [Client], and that plan and this contract is signed by all parties.

During the tenure of this agreement, [Consultant] will be compensated on the basis of performance. The compensation shall be in the form of a _____ dollar [$_____] retainer that will be paid monthly on the condition that [Consultant] secures for [Client] one of the following three types of coverage during each 30-day period.

A. National story and/or TV

B. TV or radio exposure on a top station in a major market

C. Major editorial (print) coverage in top market

Top or major markets shall be agreed to beforehand by the client and agency. Initial markets will be spelled out in the plan.

The fee shall also cover all normal expenses. Mass mailings requiring photo duplication shall be billed separately.

This agreement may be terminated by either party with a written XX-day notice.

In the event any legal action is taken to enforce this agreement or any portion thereof, the party which prevails in that suit shall be entitled to recover, from the other, its attorney's fees, in a reasonable amount, plus cost of said suit.

[Signature]	[Signature]
[Name of Company]	[Name of Company]
[Date]	[Date]

The next agreement (Exhibit 5.4) is another performance-based contract.

In the consulting field, retainers are normally paid in advance. That is, for July services, the client pays on July 1. The agreement in Exhibit 5.5 recognizes that the client does not want to start the relationship in that manner (possibly because of cash flow problems) and prefers to move the billing cycle up one week each month until monies are due and payable one month in advance.

The contract also reflects credit that the client is getting for fees that were paid for previous services. This frequently comes about if the consultant (1) bills for the proposal and credits the client with the fee if they are retained or (2) the client used the services of the consultant previously and is getting a discount or credit because the consultant is being hired for a longer term.

THE STANDARD RETAINER AGREEMENT

The next agreement is a standard retainer, however, the client is a politician and the payment is being made by a political group. Typically, agreements with politicians almost always require payment in advance of services.

Some agreements can cover a multitude of duties, however, they remain relatively easy to understand. (See Exhibit 5.6.) Exhibit 5.6 spells out specific duties and payments. This approach can be used by a multitude of consultants who perform specific duties for clients with each falling into a different classification.

Exhibit 5.7 is a lengthy, seemingly complex letter of agreement between a developer and engineering firm, however, when it is examined closely there is little that a layman would not understand. Both sides have requirements in the contract along with time parameters.

Several things of interest are in this agreement. First, construction is a tenuous business, and the 30-day cancellation clause is almost a must for the Developer since his financing could run

EXHIBIT 5.4
Letter of Agreement

[Client] agrees to retain [Consultant] for [Type service] commencing January 14, 19XX, and continuing until either party terminates this agreement by tendering a 30-day written notice of cancellation.

During the tenure of this agreement, [Consultant] will be compensated on the basis of performance. The compensation shall be in the form of a _____ dollars [$_____] fee for each feature story that is published on [Name of company] and his marketing skills.

These stories will be targeted at various industries through trade publications. The industries shall be proposed by [Client] and approved by [Client].

The performance fee shall be payable in the following manner: One half [$_____] shall be due and payable upon acceptance of the publication of a feature and/or interview on [Client]. The second half [$_____] shall be due and payable upon publication of the article.

Any expenses incurred in the form of long distance telephone calls or special mailings shall also be paid by [Client]. These expenses shall be approved in advance by the client and will be due and payable upon billing.

In the event any legal action is taken to enforce this agreement or any portion thereof, the party which prevails in that suit shall be entitled to recover, from the other, its attorney's fees, in a reasonable amount, plus cost of said suit.

Agreed to:

[Name of company]   [Name of company]

[Date]   [Date]

EXHIBIT 5.5
Letter of Agreement

[Client] agrees to retain [Name of company] for [Type of services] commencing July 12, 19XX, and continuing until either party hereto terminates this agreement by tendering a 30-day written notice of cancellation.

During the length of this agreement, [Consultant] will perform [Type of services] for [Client] as outlined in a letter of June 19, 19XX. For these services, [Client] agrees to pay a monthly retainer of _____ dollars [$_____], plus expenses. No expense in excess of _____ dollars [$_____] shall be incurred without client's prior approval.

The fee shall be payable in the following manner: The first month's fee shall be due and payable four weeks after the signing of this agreement. The first month's fee shall be _____ dollars [$_____], which is a reduction of _____ dollars [$_____] reflecting credit for the client's previous payment for consulting services. Subsequent retainers will be _____ dollars [$_____] and will be due and payable upon invoicing. Each subsequent billing cycle shall be moved up one week a month until such time as the retainer is payable in advance. Expenses shall be billed by invoice and shall be due and payable within fifteen (15) days of the invoice date.

In the event any legal action is taken to enforce this agreement or any portion thereof, the party which prevails in that suit shall be entitled to recover, from the other, its attorney's fees, in a reasonable amount, plus cost of said suit.

[Signature]	[Signature]
[Name of Company]	[Name of Company]
[Date]	[Date]

EXHIBIT 5.6
Letter of Agreement

[Name of company] a registered [Name of state] political committee agrees to retain [Company] for [Type of services] commencing January 1, 19XX and continuing until either party hereto terminates this agreement by tendering a 30-day written notice of cancellation.

During the length of this agreement, [Consultant] will perform [type of] services for [Client] as outlined in a letter of [Month, day, year]. For those services, [Client] agrees to pay a monthly retainer of _____ dollars [$_____], plus expenses. No expense in excess of _____ dollars [$_____] shall be incurred without client's prior approval.

The fee shall be payable in the following manner: Upon signing of this agreement, the first month's fee shall be due and payable, and every thirty (30) days thereafter an additional monthly fee, plus expenses incurred shall be due and payable until such time as the services are no longer required.

In the event any legal action is taken to enforce this contract or any portion thereof, the party which prevails in the suit shall be entitled to recover from the other its attorney's fees, in a reasonable amount, plus cost of said suit.

AGREED TO:

[Client] _____   [Consultant] _____

[Date] _____   [Date] _____

EXHIBIT 5.7
Agreement between Developer and Engineer

Section 1: Engineer agrees to furnish and perform the various professional services hereinafter listed. Further it is the intent of this agreement that a complete professional engineering job shall be done, and to that extent the scope of work is not necessarily limited to the services hereinafter listed:

Office:

1. Prepare preliminary land planning studies of property.
2. Attend meetings as required with developer [client] and [City] and other public agencies.
3. Prepare formal tract maps and perform all work required for recordation.
4. Prepare street improvement plans for construction purposes, effect corrections, and obtain approval by [City].
5. Prepare domestic water and sanitary sewer plans for construction purposes, effect corrections and obtain approval by [City].
6. Prepare storm drain plans for construction purposes, effect corrections, and obtain approvals by [City] and any other involved agencies.
7. Prepare rough grading plans and obtain approval of [City].
8. Prepare 20-foot scale plot plan in accordance with the mylar system; prepare composite plot and grading plan; prepare 20-scale master utility plan.
9. Prepare sales map.
10. Perform necessary coordination work with utility companies.
11. Furnish three (3) sets of quantity and cost estimates:
    a. A preliminary estimate from tentative map.
    b. A preliminary estimate from unsigned plans.
    c. A final estimate from signed plans.
12. Prepare legal description and plot for each recorded unit.
13. Perform normal inspection of site improvements, required certifications and prepare "as-built" plans.

EXHIBIT 5.7 *(continued)*

Fields:

1. Prepare necessary grade sheets for inspectors, developers, and so on.
2. Furnish one set of stakes for rough grading of lots and streets.
3. Furnish one set of "blue top" stakes for finish grading as required.
4. After the rough grading has been completed, engineer shall verify that streets, pads, slopes, and so on, have been graded in accordance with the approved plans. It shall be the responsibility of the grading contractor to protect the stakes until all verification work has been completed.
5. Furnish one set of stakes for sanitary sewer construction.
6. Furnish one set of stakes for storm drain construction, drainage terraces and other drainage facilities as shown on the approved plans.
7. Furnish one set of stakes defining building locations.
8. Furnish one set of stakes for underground electrical and telephone utilities.
9. Furnish one set of stakes for curb and gutter construction, cross gutters and any other improvements required to complete the street construction.
10. After completion of improvements and landscaping, set final lot corners, tract boundary monuments, street centerline monuments and other survey controls as shown on the record map and required by the County of [_____] and [City].
11. Prepare tie notes for street centerline monuments and furnish copies to the County of [_____].
12. Prepare "as built" plans.

SECTION 2. [Developer] agrees to pay Engineer as compensation for the above-named professional services as set forth in Section 1 a fee of:

$_____ per dwelling unit.

EXHIBIT 5.7 *(continued)*

SECTION 3. [Developer] agrees to pay [Engineer] interim compensation for work performed on the "percentage-of-compensation" method. The attached Schedule "A" per unit cost estimate, based on an estimated [_____] units, shall be used as a guide in determining the percentage of work completed by [Engineer]. The contract shall be adjusted for any changes in the number or recorded residential units. Progress billings will be made monthly by [Engineer] on forms supplied by [Developer].

SECTION 4. Revisions, variances, or change orders needed to meet the requirements of the various jurisdictional agencies or good engineering practices, shall not be deemed extra work. Only revisions, variances of change orders requested by [Developer] after completion of the plans to the satisfaction of said jurisdictional agencies, legal descriptions not called for in the scope of the work, and plans for pumping stations, bridges, and similar construction, shall be considered extra work. It shall be the responsibility of [Engineer] to work with [Developer] and apprise him of solutions to engineering problems and the general details, approach or technique to be used in preparing final approvement plans. In any event, all orders for extra work shall be authorized in writing by [Developer] and acknowledged by [Engineer]. With respect to extra work authorized by [Developer] as provided above, [Engineer] shall be entitled to charge for his services the following rates:

Office Technical Personnel	$_____	per hour
Three-Person Survey Party	$_____	per hour
Two-Person Party	$_____	per hour

SECTION 5. On [Month, day, year], and as appropriate thereafter, the "per unit fee" as set forth in Section 2 and the rate for "extra work" as set forth in Section 4 shall be increased by 80 percent of the percentage of wage and/or other employee benefits granted surveyors under the Master Agreement between the [State] Council of Civil Engineers and Land Surveyors and the International Union of Operating Engineers Local No. 12, AFL-CIO. These increases shall apply only to the finished work as of the date of increase.

EXHIBIT 5.7 *(continued)*

SECTION 6. [Engineer] shall coordinate the planning of all structures, utilities, and other facilities which will affect the tract and the subdivision development, including existing as well as proposed facilities and regardless of whether plans for said facilities are prepared by [Engineer] of third parties.

SECTION 7. All sketches, tracings, drawings, computations, details, and other original documents and plans are and shall become and/or required to be filed with a governmental agency and become public property, in which case [Engineer] is to furnish duplicates to [Developer] upon its request.

SECTION 8. [Developer] reserves right to terminate this agreement upon 30 days written notice to [Engineer]. In such event, for completed stages of the work, [Engineer] shall receive that percentage of the fee set forth in the Schedule A; and in the case of partially completed stage of work, [Engineer] shall receive an appropriately prorated percentage of the fee.

SECTION 9. [Developer] shall pay the cost of all fees, permits, bond premium, and title company charges not specifically covered by the terms of this agreement. All blueprinting and Xerox costs will be included in the per unit cost as outlined in Schedule A attached hereto.

SECTION 10. [Engineer] and [Developer] each binds himself, his partners, executors, and administrators of such other party in respect to all covenants of this Agreement. Neither party shall assign, sublet, or transfer his interest in this Agreement without the written consent of the other party hereto.

SECTION 11. Progress billings will be made monthly by [Engineer] in accordance with rates set forth in Section 3 and Section 4. [Developer] will pay these billings within ten (10) days after receipt.

[Engineer] _____   [Developer] _____

By: _____   By: _____

Date: _____   Date: _____

into trouble. At the same time, the Engineer is protected because his fees are prorated in the event of cancellation.

Additionally, notice in Section 11 the payment requirement— within 10 days. This stipulation is in there for two reasons. First, the engineering firm may find itself putting out a significant amount of cash because of the labor-intensiveness of the business. Second, because financing and development companies (especially in the 1990s) are shaky "partnerships," the funding may not always be there. The Engineer wants to make sure that his firm does not get in too deep in the event the funding is cutoff or reduced, hence the 10-day requirement. The short time frame enables the engineering firm to constantly monitor the Developer's payment ability without letting much time go by.

Exhibit 5.8 is typical of a contract that is currently popular. It combines the elements of a contract with the commitment of the proposal.

This letter/agreement/contract is widely used because it spells out exactly what the consulting firm has to do, reiterates conversations at previous meetings, proposal guidelines, and payment schedules. Notice, too, that signing a "letter" (although binding) is not as threatening as putting a signature on a legal looking (and sounding) document.

Another example is shown in Exhibit 5.9. Although much of the document sounds formal, the letter format allows the consulting firm end it with a paragraph that would not typically be found in a contract.

As is the case with most letter/proposal/contracts, there are two copies usually sent to the client. One is for the client's files, the other is signed and returned to the consultant.

Another letter of agreement—this one involving a data processing firm—is shown in Exhibit 5.10.

Letter agreements combine the elements of a proposal along with those of a contract. Every one has the same characteristic. There are several other trademarks that are universal in these letter agreements:

1. Exact duties and responsibilities are spelled out.
2. Fees are never mentioned at the beginning of the letter. Rather, they are left for the closing section—after the consulting firm has had a chance to articulate exactly what it will be doing for their money.
3. Most letter agreements have the same format:
   a. The opening, which may refer to a previous conversation or proposal.
   b. This is followed by a laundry list of duties that the consulting firm will perform.
   c. This may be followed by another section, or paragraph, in which the client's responsibility, insofar as supplying help, records, and so on, is clearly spelled out.
   d. The next section usually lists the type personnel (from the consulting firm) who will be working on the project.
   e. Fees are spelled out.
   f. A close, which is usually in a friendly tone, can always be found.
   g. Specific action steps on the part of the client are detailed, that is, "please sign both copies of the contract, keep one for your records, and return the other to us."

At times, the letter may include a rate schedule (Exhibit 5.11).

Litigation Clauses

Some letter agreements have a closing paragraph involving litigation if there is a disagreement between the client and consulting firm. The inclusion of this paragraph gets mixed reaction from many consultants.

Some feel that including the statement automatically complicates the job and brings a company's legal department into the negotiations. Others feel that the paragraph is easy-to-understand and straight-forward and that there should be no objection to its use in a letter or contract.

EXHIBIT 5.8
The Letter Proposal Contract

Dear _____

Based upon our discussion of [Date], [Consultant] submits the following proposal to assist [Client] in developing an office automation/business data service strategy and long-range plan. [Consultant] proposes to work with the established [Client] steering committee and its members in accomplishing the above goal.

The objectives of the plan are to:

- Identify and document the office automation and business data system needs of the [Client].
- Determine the impact of the LOMM architecture on these needs, and identify the items that will be developed and supported by [Consultant].
- Develop a long-term office automation/business data services strategy and plan to support [Company] current and future business requirements. This will include a strategy and plan for the following:

—Business applications

—Office automation applications

—Business data services organization

—Computer hardware and software

The plan will also identify personnel resource requirements, costs of the program, and the financial impact on [Client] in the near-term, as well as over the long term.

The approach recommended for the study was identified during our previous discussions and [Consultant's] presentation to you on [Month, day, year] (Attachment I). The key ingredient in that presentation was a description of the proposed working relationship between [Consultant] and members of the committee and their staff: [Consultant's] role in the project is to assist the committee in developing the future strategy, not to develop a [Consultant] recommended strategy for [Client] which will then be presented to the committee.

EXHIBIT 5.8 *(continued)*

The implication of this approach is that the committee members must maintain significant involvement in all aspects of the study. This does not necessarily imply a significant time commitment; it does though require that the members provide the project with guidance and ideas. A key element in this is the "three-day strategy session" where the fundamental [Client] office automation/business data services strategy will emerge and be agreed to.

Attachment II identifies study plan activities and schedule. We estimate the effort to take approximately [_____] weeks. Two and one quarter [Consultant] staff members will be involved in the study. The schedule was developed assuming the availability of the committee members and their staff, including the possible involvement of a new [Client] hire who will be included as part of the study team.

The estimated cost for professional services is [$_____] based on the attached rate schedule (Attachment III). Expenses for necessary travel, living and document preparation will be charged as incurred. Invoices for professional services and expenses will be billed at the end of each month. Payment is expected within 15 days after receipt of invoice.

We look forward to the opportunity to work with you and the committee on this important engagement.

Sincerely,

[Consultant]

JEI/en

Attachments

Approved: _____

Date: _____

EXHIBIT 5.9
Letter of Agreement

Dear Mr. _____:

This letter is to confirm the arrangements we discussed for you retaining our firm as the independent certified public accountants for [Client]. As we informed you, our acceptance of this engagement is subject to the results of our firm's investigatory and approval procedures.

We will examine the consolidated balance sheet of [Client], and subsidiaries as of [Month, day, year], and the related statements of income, retained earnings, and changes in financial position for the year then ended.

Our examination will be in accordance with generally accepted auditing standards and will include such tests of the accounting records and such auditing procedures as we consider necessary in the circumstances.

Our examination will be for the purpose of expressing an opinion on the consolidated balance sheet as of [Month, day, year], and on the related statements of income, retained earnings, and changes in financial position for the year then ended. Since we were not the company's auditors for the previous year, we will have to extend our procedures to satisfy ourselves as to the opening balances for the current year, and the consistency of application of accounting principles and methods in the current year with those of the preceding year.

We are not considering a detailed examination of all transactions nor do we expect that we will necessarily discover fraud, should any exist. We will, however, inform you of findings that appear to be unusual or abnormal.

Your accounting department personnel will assist us to the extent practical in completing our engagement. They will provide us with the detailed trial balances and supporting schedules we deem necessary. A list of such schedules will be furnished you shortly after we begin the engagement.

We will also be available to assist you, either in person or by telephone, with accounting, business or tax problems, and with planning. We will prepare the 19XX federal and state income tax returns for the company, and its subsidiaries.

EXHIBIT 5.9 *(continued)*

Since this is our first examination of the company, you requested that we review the company's accounting system and procedures in detail and submit a separate report, including our evaluation, comments and recommendations. We will also review copies of the company's income tax returns for the preceding three years and submit to you any comments we feel appropriate.

Fees for these services are at our standard rates and will be billed to you, plus out-of-pocket costs, monthly. These invoices are payable upon presentation.

If this letter correctly expresses your understanding, please sign the enclosed copy where indicated and return it to us.

Thank you for the confidence you have placed in us by engaging us as your independent certified public accountants. We hope this proves to be the beginning of a long and mutually beneficial association.

Sincerely,

[Name]

Approved By: _____

Date: _____

EXHIBIT 5.10
Letter of Agreement

Dear _____:

To evaluate the effectiveness of [Client] MIS group, [Consultant] will perform the tasks listed below. The objectives of the study are to:

- Assess the capability of the MIS group to support the business, both for the short-term and for the next several years. This is critical because of rapid business growth.
- Determine ways of improving communication between MIS and executive and user management to enhance the effectiveness of directing and controlling the MIS function at [Client].

Approach

After a brief orientation to acquaint study team members with the operations and system environment, these activities will be undertaken:

- Interview the 10 to 12 key users of MIS services in order to understand their perception of the quality of service being delivered.
- Conduct an MIS administration review to include planning and budgeting processes, project approval, and priority assignment procedures, use of standards and product quality reviews, and management reporting.
- Conduct an MIS operations review to examine service delivery; problem identification, tracking, and resolution; production scheduling; library controls; production documentation and change control procedures; computer utilization, performance, capacity analysis, and reporting.
- Perform communication network performance analysis, including system availability, response time, network monitoring capability, growth plans, and use of available hardware and software tools to enhance network performance.
- Perform a systems and programming review, encompass staff capability, performance, turnover, and compensation; project management processes, and workload management; use of standard system development methods; use of productivity tools; and the quality of installed applications.

EXHIBIT 5.10 *(continued)*

- Assess factors that are causing difficulties in MIS's ability to support the business and perform to the expectations of the company. These may include:
  —Communication with senior management
  —Management of the MIS resource
  —Organization of the MIS function
  —Staff quality and quantity
  —Equipment
- Identify short-term actions that should be taken to improve communications between MIS and executive and user management, and improve the quality of direction given to MIS.
- Develop a one-year plan to address network performance, organization, procedures, and management control issues.
- Prepare and present a management report of findings and recommendations.

Study Plan and Cost

Project activities and their duration are shown on the following chart. The estimated charge for professional services is [$_____]. There will be additional charges for any travel, living and document preparation. Charges will be billed monthly.

We look forward to working with [name of company] on this assignment.

Sincerely

[Name]

Approved: _____

Date: _____

EXHIBIT 5.11
Letter with Rate Schedule

Dear _____:

Based on previous discussions with you and [Names] the following outlines our approach for assisting [Client] in migrating the computing activities of the [Client] into the [Client] computer center. The [Consultant] will accomplish this in two phases:

> Phase I —Review current environment and migration plan.
>
> Phase II—Direction of the west coast computer facility in achieving the migration goals.

This letter proposal only addresses Phase I. The approach and degree of involvement of [Consultant] related to Phase II will be determined at the conclusion of the Phase I activity. The review of the current environment and migration plan will be designed to accomplish the following objectives:

- Gain an understanding of existing environments at both [Client] and [Client] computer centers.
- Review the overall migration plan to determine the role that [Consultant] can best perform in achieving migration objectives.
- Identify areas of vulnerability that may exist related to the [Client] company computer center close-down or the migration process.
- Develop an implementation for Phase II.

The accomplishment of the above will require review of current activities, plans, and computer centers in [Name] and [Name]. The cost of Phase I will not exceed [$_____] in professional services, and will be billed per the attached rate schedule. Additional costs for travel, living and report preparation will be billed as accrued.

EXHIBIT 5.11 *(continued)*

We look forward to working with you and [Client] on this important endeavor.

Sincerely,

[Name]

Accepted:

_____

_____

Date _____

Name of Consulting Firm

Rate Schedule

Managing Partner	$ _____ per hour
Managing Principal	$ _____ per hour
Principal Consultant	$ _____ per hour
Consultant	$ _____ per hour

Exhibit 5.12 is an engagement letter from a CPA firm to a prospective client. It not only spells out what the accountancy corporation is going to do, but it also says what the firm limits of the firm's services happen to be. This is done for legal protection, and any consulting organization that is licensed (money and financial managers, accountants, attorneys) has to be particularly careful with agreements. Whereas, many marketing and sales consultants sometimes put extravagant prognostications in a letter, the licensed consultant must be extremely careful to deliver exactly what is promised, lest a regulatory agency get involved and threaten the consultant's license.

Part of the reason for these precautionary statements is the potential liability a professional firm, such as an accountancy or legal corporation, runs when dealing with a client. A growing trend has been to sue the auditors or file a malpractice suit against the attorney if something goes wrong. Spelling out exact responsibilities was designed to try and cut down the number of these suits and, at the same time, achieve a reduction in practice liability policies.

Exhibit 5.13 is from an attorney and it spells out his fees and the client's personal responsibility for the billing.

One of the interesting aspects of this agreement is the clause which spells out a "minimum fee" for telephone conversations. Consultants frequently find that clients will call, state their problem, get an answer and hang up—and never expect to be billed because, in their mind, they did not take up the consultant's office time.

Billing for every call, however, can be cumbersome and annoying to the client. A good policy is when the person becomes a client, the telephone billing policy is spelled out. If, for instance, the client simply calls and spends less than five minutes on the telephone verifying something or getting a clarification about something that was said (by the consultant) previously, it does not behoove the consultant to bill the call. Only when the client begins to take advantage of the telephone and spend excessive time on it, should billing be put into motion.

EXHIBIT 5.12
Engagement Letter

Dear Mr. _____:

This letter is to confirm our understanding of the terms and objectives of our engagement and the nature and limitations of the services we will provide.

We will perform the following services:

1. We will compile, from information you provide, the annual balance sheet and related statements of income, retained earnings, and changes in financial position of [name of company] for the year 19XX. We will not audit or review the financial statements. Our report on the annual financial statements of the company is presently expected to read as follows:

   > We have compiled the accompanying balance sheet of the company as of [Month, day, year], and the related statements of income, retained earnings, and changes in financial position for the year then ended, in accordance with standards established by the American Institute of Certified Public Accountants.
   >
   > A compilation is limited to presenting in the form of financial statements information that is the representation of management. We have not audited or reviewed the accompanying financial statements and, accordingly, do not express an opinion or any other form of assurance on them.

Our engagement cannot be relied upon to disclose errors, irregularities, or illegal acts, including fraud or defalcations, that may exist; however, we will inform you of any such matters that come to our attention.

Our fees for these services will be computed at our standard hourly rates. Billings will not be submitted monthly and are payable when due.

EXHIBIT 5.12 *(continued)*

We would be pleased to discuss this letter with you at any time. If the foregoing is in accordance with your understanding, please sign the copy of this letter in the space provided and return it to us.

Sincerely,

[Name]

APPROVED:

Company

_____

President

_____

Date

_____

EXHIBIT 5.13
Fee Agreement

I understand that your fee for professional services is [$_____] per hour and that your minimum fee for any service rendered, including each telephone conversation, is [$_____].

I understand that I will be billed monthly for services rendered and costs advanced on my behalf during the month. I understand that your statement must be paid in full within thirty (30) days of your billing date. In the event that I fail to pay the balance of my account in full when due, I further understand that I will incur a monthly administrative charge of 2 percent of the unpaid balance or [$_____] whichever is greater, and that you reserve the right to withhold rendering additional services until my account is current.

I understand that a retainer or security for payment of your fees will be required prior to commencement of services beyond the initial interview where the services to be rendered are estimated to exceed [$_____].

I understand you may find it necessary to increase your hourly rates and that any such increase will apply in my case. I will, however, be notified at least sixty (60) days in advance of such change and will, at that time, have the option to retain other counsel.

I understand that by signing this agreement, I accept personal responsibility for all legal fees and costs billed to my account regardless of the fact that a third party may ultimately agree or be ordered to pay some portion of said fees and costs. I agree to pay reasonable attorney's fees and costs in the event that litigation becomes necessary to collect any amounts pursuant to this agreement.

I am aware that you have the right to associate any other attorney of your choice in the handling of my legal matter at your discretion. I further understand that your firm does not render advice pertaining to state or federal taxation and that you recommend only that such advice be obtained from a Certified Public Accountant.

I understand that modification of this agreement must be in writing.

Dated: _____   _____
                                        Signature

FEE LIMIT AGREEMENT

The next agreement (Exhibit 5.14) spells out the fee but also puts a limitation on it. In many cases, the client requests the limit because of budgetary constraints or company policy that may require additional approval if more than [$_____] is spent for a service. If the consultant exceeds the amount, the client has to go back to an executive committee, group of senior managers or board of directors and explain the reason for the request for additional funds.

SPECIFIC ASSIGNMENT AGREEMENT

With business becoming more complex and specialized each day, some consultants opt for a letter of agreement/contract that is written to cover a specific assignment. The following are the Engagement Letters that Bill Johnson's accountancy corporation has on hand. They range from compilation and review to audit and management advisory services.

Engagement Letters

1. **Compilation Engagements**

   Annual compilation, corporation, accrual basis

   Annual and interim compilations, corporation, accrual

   Personal financial statements

   Combination—compilation and tax returns

   Prospective financial statements—see Chapter 14, PPC

2. **Review Engagements**

   Annual review engagement, corporation

   Combination—review and tax returns

   Personal financial statements

EXHIBIT 5.14
Fee Limit Agreement

Dear _____:

This letter will confirm our understanding of the nature and limitations of the accounting and review services we are to render to [Client], as we previously discussed.

We will review the balance sheet of [Client] as of June [Month, day, year] and the related statements of income, retained earnings, and changes in financial position for the year then ended, in accordance with the standards established by the American Institute of Certified Public Accountants. We will not perform an audit of such financial statements, the objective of which is the expression of an opinion regarding the financial statements taken as a whole and, accordingly, we will not express such an opinion on them. Our report on the financial statements is presently expected to read as follows:

> We have reviewed the accompanying balance sheet of [Name of company] as of [Month, day, year], and the related statements of income, retained earnings, and changes in financial position for the year then ended in accordance with standards established by the American Institute of Certified Public Accountants. All information included in the financial statements is the representation of the management of [Client].

> A review consists principally of inquiries of company personnel and analytical procedures applied to financial data. It is substantially less in scope than an examination in accordance with generally accepted auditing standards, the objective of which is the expression of an opinion regarding the financial statements taken as a whole. Accordingly, we do not express such opinion.

> Based on our review, we are not aware of any material modifications that should be made to the accompanying financial statements in order for them to be in conformity with generally accepted accounting principles.

If, for any reason, we are unable to complete our review of your financial statements, we will not issue a report on such statements as a result of this engagement.

EXHIBIT 5.14 *(continued)*

We will provide your chief accountant with such consultation on accounting matters as he or she may require in adjusting and closing the books of account and in drafting financial statements for our review. Your chief accountant also will provide us with a detailed trial balance and any supporting schedules we require.

We will also prepare the federal and state income tax returns for [Client] for the fiscal year ended June 30, 19XX.

Our engagement cannot be relied upon to disclose errors, irregularities, or illegal acts, including fraud or defalcations, that may exist. However, we will inform you of any such matters that come to our attention.

Our fees for these services will be based on our regular hourly rates and we will bill you monthly as work progresses. It is understood that the fee for our services will not exceed [$_____]. Our invoices are due and payable upon presentation.

If these arrangements meet with your understanding and approval, please sign the duplicate copy of this letter in the space provided and return it to us.

Yours Very Truly,

[Name]

Approved:

[Client]

By: _____

Date: _____

3. Audit Engagements

Audit engagement letter

Audit engagement letter—nonprofit organization

Audit engagement letter—HUD project

4. Management Advisory Services

Review of accounting and financial control systems

Computer system analysis and installations

Business valuations

Management Representation Letters

1. Review engagements

2. Audit engagements

3. Compilation of personal financial statements

The following engagement letters, prepared by Johnson's firm, can easily be adapted to other industries. Notice in the first letter (Exhibit 5.15), the caveat Johnson has prepared in the second to last paragraph on page 1, if the client decides not to submit all the disclosures. With law suits more prevalent in every industry, consultants must be extremely careful in the liability they assume and the delivery they promise. Any exceptions should be noted in the agreement.

A similar paragraph is in the next agreement (Exhibit 5.16), which is meant for a board of directors.

Although letters of agreement are not nearly as complex as the legalese in a contract, growing litigation has caused some consultants to begin to structure their letters more like a contract. In Exhibit 5.17, legal terminology and specific duties of the consultant (which they will and will not be responsible for) can be found throughout.

Exhibit 5.18 is a short, to-the-point engagement letter, however, it, too, has caveats. Notice the next to last paragraph on page one and its reference to "defalcations."

EXHIBIT 5.15
Engagement Letter

_____(Date)

_____(Company)
_____(Address)
_____(Address)

Dear _____(Company):

This letter is to confirm our understanding of the terms and objectives of our engagement and the nature and limitations of the services we will provide.

We will perform the following services:

1. We will compile from information you provide, the annual and interim balance sheets and related statements of income, retained earnings and cash flows of ____
    _____(Company) for the year ended _____(Date). We will not audit or review such financial statements. Our report on the annual financial statements of _____(Company) is presently expected to read as follows:

    > We have compiled the accompanying balance sheet of _____
    > _____(Company) as of _____(Date)
    > and the related statements of income, retained earnings and
    > cash flows for the year _____(Period) then ended, in
    > accordance with standards established by the American Institute
    > of Certified Public Accountants.

    > A compilation is limited to presenting in the form of financial
    > statements information that is the representation of
    > management. We have not audited or reviewed the
    > accompanying financial statement and, accordingly, do not
    > express an opinion or any other form of assurance on them.

    If management elects to omit substantially all of the disclosures from the financial statements, we will include an additional paragraph that will read as follows:

    > Management has elected to omit substantially all of the
    > disclosures required by generally accepted accounting principles.
    > If the omitted disclosures were included in the financial
    > statements, they might influence the user's conclusions about
    > the Company's financial position, results of operations, and cash
    > flows. Accordingly, these financial statements are not designed
    > for those who are not informed about such matters.

EXHIBIT 5.15 *(continued)*

_____(Company)
_____(Date)
Page Two

If, for any reason, we are unable to complete the compilation of your financial statements, we will not issue a report on such statements as a result of this engagement.

2.   We will prepare your federal and state corporate income tax returns from timely information provided to us by you.

We will furnish you with questionnaires and/or worksheets to guide you in gathering the necessary information. If you believe there is any additional information available which might be applicable to any of the areas either listed or discussed during our conferences, please advise us of it so we may consider it.

We will not audit or verify the data you submit, although we may ask you to explain it or to furnish us with additional data.

Your returns may be processed by an outside computer service.

By your signature below, you are confirming to us that unless we are otherwise advised, your travel, entertainment, gifts and related expenses are supported by the necessary records required under the Internal Revenue Code.

You are also confirming to us that your business use of joint-use property, such as computers, car phones or vehicles, is substantiated by a log of such use so as to preclude the deduction of any personal expenses which may be related to such property. If you have any questions as to the type of records required, please ask us for advice in that regard.

You are also confirming to us that you will furnish us with all information required for the timely preparation of your tax returns or, in the event extensions of time for filing are necessary, such information as may be required to enable us to reasonably estimate the tax payable with the extension request.

We will use our professional judgment in preparing your tax returns. Whenever we are aware that applicable tax is unclear or that there are conflicting interpretations of the law by authorities (e.g. tax agencies and courts), we will discuss with you our knowledge and understanding of the possible positions which may be taken on your return. We are not attorneys, however, and cannot provide you with legal opinions or analyses of these positions.

EXHIBIT 5.15 *(continued)*

_____(Company)
_____(Date)
Page Three

We will adopt whatever position you request on your return so long as it is consistent with our professional standards and ethics. If you desire a legal opinion before choosing between alternative tax positions, then you should retain legal counsel for this purpose. We will work with you and your chosen legal counsel to the best of our abilities in providing whatever information we have that may assist in your decision.

If the Internal Revenue Service should later contest the position(s) taken and included in your tax returns, there may be an assessment of additional tax liability plus interest and possible penalties. We assume no liability for any such additional assessments.

As we have previously outlined for you in our bulletins, the provisions of Section 6661 call for penalties against taxpayers for substantial understatement of tax (more than 10% of the tax shown on the return). This penalty will be assessed unless the taxpayer can show that there was "substantial authority" for any position that was ultimately disallowed or that there was "adequate disclosure" in the return of any conflict between an IRS position and that taken by the taxpayer.

You agree to advise us if you wish such disclosure to be made in your returns or if you desire us to identify or perform further research with respect to any material tax issues for any material tax issues for the purpose of ascertaining whether, in our opinion, there is "substantial authority" for the position proposed to be taken on such issues in your returns.

With respect to positions taken on your return regarding "tax shelter" issues, in addition to the "substantial authority" test, "the taxpayer must reasonably believe that the tax treatment of such item was more likely than not the proper treatment." Furthermore, as to the shelter issues, "adequate disclosure" will not prevent the assertion of the penalty.

After filing, your returns are subject to review by the taxing authorities. Any items which may be resolved against you by the examining agent are subject to certain rights of appeal. In the event of any tax examinations, we will be available upon request to represent you at all administrative levels, not in court, and will render additional invoices for such services.

At any time, if requested, we will consult with you regarding the income tax aspects of proposed or completed transactions, compile income tax projections and engage in research in connection with such matters. Similarly since the annual returns we prepare for you will be predicated upon the current tax law as we understand it to be, we do not consider ourselves responsible for future changes in the law which affect the returns we have already prepared. Such changes may require the amendment of prior-filed tax returns. We will render additional invoices for all such services at our customary billing rates.

EXHIBIT 5.15 *(continued)*

_____(Company)
_____(Date)
Page Four

Our engagement cannot be relied upon to disclose errors, irregularities, or illegal acts, including fraud or defalcations that may exist. However, we will inform you of any such matters that come to our attention unless they are clearly inconsequential.

The fees for these services will be based on the actual time spent at our standard hourly rates, plus out-of-pocket costs. The standard hourly rates vary according to the degree of responsibility involved and the experience level of the personnel assigned to the engagement. The invoices for these fees will be rendered each month as work progresses and are payable upon presentation.

We appreciate the opportunity to be of service to you and believe this letter accurately summarizes the significant terms of our engagement. If you have any questions, please let us know. If you agree with the terms of this engagement as described in this letter, please sign the enclosed copy and return it in the envelope provided.

Very truly yours,

JOHNSON & *Associates*
AN ACCOUNTANCY CORPORATION

ACKNOWLEDGMENT:

_____
Officer signature

_____
Title

_____
Date

g:\users\...\engagemn.ltr\compilat.tax

EXHIBIT 5.16
Engagement Letter

_____(Date)

To the Board of Directors
_____(Company)
_____(Address)
_____(Address)

Dear _____:(Name)

This letter is to confirm our understanding of the terms and objectives of our engagement and the nature and limitations of the services we will provide.

We will compile, from information you provide, the annual balance sheet and the related statements of income, retained earnings, and cash flows of _____ (Company) for the year ended _____.(Date) We will not audit or review such financial statements. Our report on the annual financial statement of _____ _____(Company) is presently expected to read as follows:

> We have compiled the accompanying balance sheet of _____ (Company) as of _____, (Date) and the related statements of income, retained earnings, and cash flows for the year then ended, in accordance with standards established by the American Institute of Certified Public Accountants.

> A compilation is limited to presenting in the form of financial statements information that is the representation of management. We have not audited or reviewed the accompanying financial statements and, accordingly, do not express an opinion or any other form of assurance on them.

If management elects to omit substantially all disclosures from the financial statements, we will include an additional paragraph that will read as follows:

> Management has elected to omit substantially all of the disclosures required by generally accepted accounting principles. If the omitted disclosures were included in the financial statements, they might influence the user's conclusions about the Company's financial position, results of operations, and cash flows. Accordingly, these financial statements are not designed for those who are not informed about such matters.

If, for any reason, we are unable to complete the compilation of your financial statements, we will not issue a report on such statements as a result of this engagement.

EXHIBIT 5.16 *(continued)*

_____Company
_____Date
Page Two

Our engagement cannot be relied upon to disclose errors, irregularities, or illegal acts, including fraud or defalcations, that may exist. However, we will inform you of any such matters that come to our attention unless they are clearly inconsequential.

The fees for these services will be based on the actual time spent at our standard hourly rates, plus out-of-pocket costs. The standard hourly rates vary according to the degree of responsibility involved and the experience level of the personnel assigned to the engagement. The invoices for these fees will be rendered each month as work progresses and are payable upon presentation.

We appreciate the opportunity to be of service to you and believe this letter accurately summarizes the significant terms of our engagement. If you have any questions, please let us know. If you agree with the terms of this engagement as described in this letter, please sign the enclosed copy and return it in the envelope provided.

Very truly yours,

JOHNSON & *Associates*
AN ACCOUNTANCY CORPORATION

ACKNOWLEDGMENT:

_____
Officer signature

_____
Title

_____
Date

g:\users\...\engagemn.ltr\compilat

EXHIBIT 5.17
Engagement Letter

Date

_____
_____
_____

Dear _____

We appreciate working with your company, and providing marketing advice to your organization. In order to ensure an understanding of your firm's and our responsibilities, we have listed the following duties, which we would like you to confirm on page two of this letter.

Our firm agrees to conduct a national market research study on your company's behalf. The study is designed to determine if _____ company's proposed new _____ audio/visual instructional sales program has validity in the marketplace.

The product will be deemed valid and marketable if more than _____% of buyers express an interest in purchasing at least 24 dozen units during the next 12 months.

Our firm will talk to no less than 20 purchasing agents for 32 of your accounts. In turn, your company will supply us with a complete list of companies and buyers. Your firm will also prepare a letter to be sent out seven to ten days in advance of our survey. This letter will introduce our firm, the project we are conducting, and the fact we will be contacting purchasing agents.

Our firm will segment these accounts into three categories, based upon each firm's dollar volume. We will then calculate the total distribution penetration of the surveyed firms. Our company will be obligated to survey purchasing agents/firms that cover a minimum of 50 percent of the market. If this percentage is not reached, the survey will be deemed invalid. Our firm will have four months from the date of signing of this agreement to complete the survey.

Our firm will report every thirty (30) days on the progress of this survey. We will submit this report in writing, and it will contain names of surveyed companies and agents, plus a capsule summary of their remarks.

EXHIBIT 5.17 *(continued)*

For these services, you agree to pay us an upfront advance of $_____$. Additionally, we will bill your firm every thirty (30) days for expenses incurred on your behalf. These expense monies, which are separate from the advance monies and fees, will be due and payable within two weeks after the billing date.

Upon completion of the survey, a final report will be due to your company within 60 days. This final report will also contain all expenses and additional fees due. The additional fees shall be predicated upon our agreed amount of $_____$, and will include the monies advanced to us.

Should there be any extraneous expenses incurred that are not covered in this agreement, we agree to discuss them with your company prior to incurring them.

We sincerely appreciate the opportunity to work with your company on this project, and believe that this agreement summarizes the key terms of the project.

If you have any questions, let us know. If you agree with the terms of this agreement as described above, please sign the enclosed original and copies, and return the original to us.

Very truly yours,

_____

_____

EXHIBIT 5.18
Engagement Letter

Date

_____
_____
_____

Dear _____

We appreciate the opportunity of working with you and advising you regarding your income tax. The Internal Revenue Service imposes penalties upon taxpayers, and upon us as return preparers, for failure to observe due care in reporting for income tax returns. In order to ensure an understanding of our mutual responsibilities, we ask all clients for whom we prepare tax returns to confirm the following arrangements.

We will prepare your 199____ federal and requested state income tax returns from information which you will furnish to us. We will make no audit or other verification of the data you submit, although we may need to ask you for clarification of some of the information. We will furnish you with questionnaires and/or worksheets to guide you in gathering the necessary information for us. Your use of such forms will assist us in keeping our fee to a minimum.

It is your responsibility to provide us with all the information required for the preparation of complete and accurate returns. You should retain all the documents, canceled checks and other data that form the basis of income and deductions. These may be necessary to prove the accuracy and completeness of the returns to a taxing authority. You have the final responsibility for the income tax returns and, therefore, you should review them carefully before you sign them.

Our work in connection with the preparation of your income tax returns does not include any procedures designed to discover defalcations or other irregularities, should any exist. We will render such accounting and bookkeeping assistance as we find necessary for preparation of the income tax returns.

We will use our judgment in resolving questions where the tax law is unclear, or where there may be conflicts between the taxing authorities' interpretations of the law and other supportable positions. Unless otherwise instructed by you, we will resolve such questions in your favor whenever possible.

EXHIBIT 5.18 *(continued)*

Name
Date
Page Two

The law provides various penalties that may be imposed when taxpayers understate their tax liability. If you would like information on the amount or circumstances of these penalties, please contact us.

Your returns may be selected for review by the taxing authorities. Any proposed adjustments by the examining agent are subject to certain rights of appeal. In the event of such government tax examination, we will be available upon request to represent you and will render additional invoices for the time and expenses incurred.

Our fee for these services will be based upon the amount of time required at our standard billing rates, plus out-of-pocket expenses. All invoices are due and payable upon presentation.

If the foregoing fairly sets forth your understanding, please sign the enclosed copy of this letter in the space indicated and return it to our office.

We want to express our appreciation for this opportunity to work with you.

Very truly yours,

JOHNSON & *Associates*
AN ACCOUNTANCY CORPORATION

ACKNOWLEDGMENT:

_____
Name

_____
Name

_____
Date

2/92 indtax.el

Exhibit 5.19 covers many routine accounting services. Once again, the letter spells out the responsibilities of the consultant.

The next letter of agreement (Exhibit 5.20) contains another growing trend among consultants—charging interest for account balances.

SERVICE CHARGES AND FEES

For years, many clients put off paying service fees because there usually was not an interest charge associated with the billing. On the other hand, any bankcard, mortgage or loan payment that is paid late will almost always earn a penalty fee for the debtor. As a result of the non-interest bearing bill, consultants usually found themselves at the end of the line when it came to settlement. Thus, there is a growing trend in the industry to insert a penalty clause. Although most consultants do not make it a practice to collect the penalty—if the principle is paid—the mere fact it is in the agreement letter often gets clients to think about it and, perhaps, pay in a more timely manner. Exhibit 5.20, from an attorney, is typical of how penalty and interest payments are written into agreements.

The next letter of agreement (Exhibit 5.21) outlines one specific project (audit) that the consultant will conduct, and it also goes into the fees.

To ensure a client's understanding of billing and what the consultant will be doing for their fees, some practitioners send an "informational" letter that precedes the letter of agreement. Exhibit 5.22 spells out everything from the billing rate and the engagement letter to the billing procedure.

Regardless of how they pay, or what a letter of agreement says, consultants will find that payment, a lasting relationship, and binding agreements are built around one factor: the trust and faith that a client has in the consultant and his or her firm.

EXHIBIT 5.19
Engagement Letter

April 20, 1992

_____(Name)
_____(Address)
_____(City, State, Zip)

Dear _____(Name):

This letter will serve to confirm our understanding of the terms of our engagement and the service we will provide.

None of these services can be relied on to detect fraud or defalcations that may exist. However, we will inform you of any such matters that come to our attention.

<u>Bookkeeping Services</u>

Record journals
Post general ledger
Post other ledgers (specify)
Reconcile bank statements
Post earnings record
Prepare payroll tax returns
Prepare W-2s
Prepare trial balance
Other services (specify)

Our fees for the above services will be based on the time expended at our standard rates and will be billed to you monthly, payable upon receipt.

Please indicate your acceptance of the above understanding by signing below. A copy is enclosed for your records. If your needs change during the year, the nature of our service can be adjusted appropriately. Likewise, if you have special projects with which we can assist, please let us know.

JOHNSON *& Associates*
AN ACCOUNTANCY CORPORATION

ACKNOWLEDGMENT:

_____
Name

_____
Title

_____
Date

g:\users\...\engagemn.ltr\undi stnd.el

EXHIBIT 5.20

HUGH W. HOLBERT
ATTORNEY AT LAW
4721 CALLE CARGA
CAMARILLO, CA 93012
(805) 482-6778

FEE AGREEMENT

I understand that your fee for professional services is $300.00 per hour and that your minimum fee for any service rendered, including each telephone conversation, is $50.00.

I understand that your firm limits the practice of law to matters involving real estate and that your firm is a consulting firm only and does not accept matters involving litigation.

I understand that I will be sent an itemized statement on a monthly basis for services rendered and costs advanced on my behalf for the period covered. I understand that your statement must be paid in full within thirty (30) days of your billing date. In the event that I fail to pay the balance of my account in full when due, I further understand that I will incur a monthly administrative charge of two (2) percent of the outstanding balance or $25.00, which ever is greater, and that you reserve the right to withhold rendering additional services until my account is current.

I understand that a retainer or security for payment of your fees may be required prior to the commencement of services beyond the initial interview where the services to be rendered are estimated to exceed $1,000.

I understand that you may find it necessary to increase your hourly rate and that any such increase will apply to my case. I will be notified in writing at least sixty (60) days in advance of such change and will have the option to retain other counsel.

I understand that by signing this Agreement I accept direct personal responsibility for all legal fees and costs billed to my account regardless of the fact that a third party may ultimately agree or be ordered to pay some portion of said fees and costs. I agree to pay reasonable attorney's fees and costs in the event that litigation becomes necessary to collect any amounts pursuant to this Agreement.

I am aware that you have the right to associate any other attorney of your choice in the handling of my legal matter at your discretion. I further understand that your firm does not render advice pertaining to state or federal taxation matters and that you recommend that such advice be obtained only from a Certified Public Accountant or an attorney who is Certified as a Tax Specialist by the State Bar of California.

I understand that any modification of this Agreement must be in writing.

_____   _____
SIGNATURE   DATE

EXHIBIT 5.21

_____Date

_____Client
_____Address
_____Address

Dear_____: Client

We are pleased to confirm our understanding of the services we are to provide for _____
_____(Client) for the _____(Period) ended _____(Date).

We will audit the balance sheet of _____(Client) as of _____
(Period or Year end) and the related statements of income, retained earnings, and cash
flows for the _____(Period or year) then ended. (Also, the document we submit
to you will include the following additional information that will (will not) be subjected to
the auditing procedures applied in our audit of the financial statements:)

1. _____

2. _____

3. _____

Our audit will be conducted in accordance with generally accepted auditing standards and
will include tests of your accounting records and other procedures we consider necessary to
enable us to express an unqualified opinion that your financial statements are fairly
presented, in all material respects, in conformity with generally accepted accounting
principles. If our opinion is other than unqualified, we will fully discuss the reasons with you
in advance.

Our procedures will include tests of documentary evidence supporting the transactions
recorded in the accounts, tests of the physical existence of inventories, and direct
confirmation of receivables and certain other assets and liabilities by correspondence with
selected customers, creditors, and banks. We will request written representations from your
attorneys as part of the engagement, and they may bill you for responding to this inquiry.
At the conclusion of our audit, we will also request certain written representations from you
about the financial statements and related matters.

EXHIBIT 5.21 *(continued)*

_____(Client)
_____(Date)
Page Two

An audit includes examining, on a test basis, evidence supporting the amounts and disclosures in the financial statements; therefore, our audit will involve judgment about the number of transactions to be examined and the areas to be tested. Also, we will plan and perform the audit to obtain reasonable assurance about whether the financial statements are free of material misstatement. However, because of the concept of reasonable assurance and because we will not perform a detailed examination of all transactions, there is a risk that material errors, irregularities, illegal acts, including fraud or defalcations, may exist and not be detected by us. We will advise you, however, of any matters of that nature that come to our attention. Our responsibility as auditors is limited to the period covered by our audit and does not extend to any later periods for which we are not engaged as auditors.

We understand that you will provide us with the basic information required for our audit and that you are responsible for the accuracy and completeness of that information. We will advise you about appropriate accounting principles and their application and will assist in the preparation of your financial statements, but the responsibility for the financial statements remains with you. This responsibility includes the maintenance of adequate records and related internal control structure, the selection and application of accounting principles, and the safeguarding of assets.

It is anticipated that prior to the start of our engagement, you will provide us with various workpaper schedules and other supporting documentation which we will require as detailed on the attached listing.

OPTIONAL: We understand that your employees will type all cash, accounts receivable, accounts payable, and other confirmations we request and will locate any invoices selected by us for testing.

Our audit is not specifically designed and cannot be relied upon to disclose reportable conditions, that is, significant deficiencies in the design or operation of the internal control structure. However, during the audit, if we become aware of such reportable conditions or ways that we believe management practices can be improved, we will communicate that to you in a separate letter.

OPTIONAL: As part of our engagement, we will also prepare the federal and state income tax returns for your company for the _____(Period) ended _____.(Date)

OPTIONAL: We expect to begin our audit on approximately _____(Date) and to complete your tax returns and issue our report no later than _____.(Date) We will observe the counting of inventories on _____.(Date)

EXHIBIT 5.21 *(continued)*

_____(Client)
_____(Date)
Page Three

Our fees for these services will be based on the actual time spent at our standard hourly rates, plus travel and other out-of-pocket costs such as report production, typing, postage, etc. Our standard hourly rates vary according to the degree of responsibility involved and the experience level of the personnel assigned to your audit. Our invoices for these fees will be rendered each month as work progresses and are payable on presentation. In accordance with our firm policies, work may be suspended if your account become _____ days or more overdue and will not be resumed until your account is paid in full. Based on our preliminary estimates, the fee should approximate $_____ for the audit and $_____for the tax return. This estimate is based on anticipated cooperation from your personnel and the assumption that unexpected circumstances will not be encountered during the audit. If significant additional time is necessary, we will discuss it with you and arrive at a new fee estimate before we incur the additional costs.

We appreciate the opportunity to be of service to you and believe this letter accurately summarizes the significant terms of our engagement. If you have any questions, please let us know. If you agree with the terms of our engagement as described in this letter, please sign the enclosed copy and return it to us, and this letter will continue in effect until canceled by either party.

Very truly yours,

JOHNSON *& Associates*
AN ACCOUNTANCY CORPORATION

ACKNOWLEDGMENT:

_____
Client

_____
Title

_____
Date

g:\users\...\engagemn.ltr\audit

EXHIBIT 5.22

<u>Information Regarding Fees For</u>
<u>Professional Services</u>

Dear Client:

Thank you for selecting Johnson & Associates as your CPA's. We are pleased to have you as a client. Experience has shown us that the client/CPA relationship is enhanced when there is a mutual understanding about the nature of fees and expectations regarding payment of them. This letter contains general information regarding fees and billing practices which we hope you will find informative.

<u>Fees and Rates</u>
Our fees are based on the professional and staff time which your matter requires and the sophistication, complexity and creativity of the work to be performed. Usually our fees are determined by the number of hours actually spent on your work. Hourly fees for CPA's time range from $65 per hour to $190 per hour, depending on the experience of the CPA. The amount of time which may be spent on any given matter is inherently unpredictable, and, accordingly, "estimates"of fees are only that and not a guaranty or limitation. In some cases, our professional services are provided on a fixed-fee basis.

<u>Engagement Letter</u>
When practical, prior to beginning work on your matter, we will give you an engagement letter specifying what services will be performed for you (i.e., accounting, tax, audit, computer, etc.) and the terms of payment.

<u>Understanding Your Bill</u>
We try to have our bills accurately reflect time and charges. Often, however, time expended by our staff is not "visible"to the client. This can sometimes cause misunderstanding with respect to billing.

Therefore, if you have any questions about the services delineated on a particular bill, please contact the CPA assigned to the matter.

EXHIBIT 5.22 *(continued)*

Information Regarding Fees
  For Professional Services
Page Two

Billing Procedure/Payment of Fees
Our bills are prepared monthly and will be sent to you on approximately the first of each
month, and will be dated the end of the prior month. Generally, the amount owing is
due and payable upon receipt of the bill. Unless special arrangements are made, if an
account remains delinquent for longer than 60 days, we may discontinue work for you
and will take appropriate steps to collect amounts owing on the account.

We desire to have a long and mutually beneficial business relationship with you. Please
do not hesitate to call if you should at any time have questions.

Very truly yours,

Johnson & Associates,
An Accountancy Corporation

CHAPTER 6

Billing and Communication

This story has become a legend, but it is illustrative of two things—how wrong a client can be and how important service is in today's market. It started a few years ago, when an irate consumer barged into a well-known department store demanding a refund for a set of tires he said was defective. The ranting, middle-aged customer never gave the salesperson a chance to say anything. All he did was demand a refund for the "crummy set of tires the store had the nerve to sell him."

Quizzically, the salesperson studied the consumer and then the tires. It was obvious the ragged, worn set of wheels had seen thousands of miles of wear. Unquestionably, the tires were not new, not even close. Looking them over, the salesperson guessed they had at least 10,000—maybe even 20,000 miles—of tough wear on them.

Still, he did what he had been taught by store management: Never question or argue with a customer. Give them what they need—without arguing—and send them happily on their way.

Remember, one displeased customer can cost you more business than one hundred satisfied clients. Disgruntled clients have a way of spreading the word, while happy clients, for whatever the reason, are seldom vocal.

Cognizant of this, the salesperson wrote a receipt, took the customer's name, address, and he recorded the date the man pur chased the tires. Without hesitation, he rang up a debit on the regis- ter and handed the man the funds he demanded.

The entire transaction took less than five minutes. Even the irate consumer seemed pleased, although his smile was barely visi- ble as he left the store with his tires stacked next to the cash regis- ter. The department manager picked up the telephone, called his supervisor and told him about the refund. Everyone in the depart- ment could hear the manager's supervisor laugh over the telephone as he hung up.

Unfortunately, he could not answer the manager's question as to "what should I do with the tires?" The manager and supervisor both had the same problem. Neither knew what to do with the aging tires, and for one simple reason. The store did not—nor did it ever—carry automobile tires!

Why, then, would the manager refund cash to a customer, knowing that the outlet did not even carry the goods? The answer: Store policy.

Nordstrom's—one of the fastest-growing, best-known depart- ment stores in the country—has always followed the same proce- dure. If a customer has a complaint or problem, refund the money, without question. That's exactly what the manager of the depart- ment did. Through the years, Nordstrom's has built a reputation on the premise of superior service and never arguing with a customer. The customer is always right.

Of course, customers are not always right. In many instances, particularly in the consulting industry, when suggestions are made, when bills are presented, and when problems are discussed, the customer/client is frequently wrong. Clients come to consultants because they need help. They do not have the answers.

Still, do you tell the client they are wrong? Yes . . . but not in so many words—especially if you want to keep them. Just as

Nordstrom's considers the client always right, successful consultants use tact. They show clients—usually through examples or facts—they may be mistaken. But, they never tell them in so many words. Clients have egos. Telling them they are wrong, mistaken, or foolish to do it "that way" can lead to an end to the relationship.

That does not mean that consultants should lie to clients. On the contrary, hiding the truth eventually destroys the client/consultant relationship. In fact, if there is one Golden Rule of consulting it is to be honest . . . but don't be brutal. Smart consultants can illustrate to a client that they are mistaken by citing other "similar" cases, but they never tell the client "you are dead wrong . . ."

THE DECISION PROCESS

The consultant walks a fine line. They must be honest and truthful yet, they cannot be abrasive and hardnosed. "Consultants," says Nido Qubein, "frequently feel that all they have to do is market their services and they will get the client. There's much more to it. Today's consultant has to be a salesperson as well as a marketer. Good salespeople understand the buyer likes to be involved in the process. They want to make the decision."

If Qubein feels the client may make the wrong choice, he will give the customer/decision maker three different choices. "None of them is wrong," he explains, "but each has a different cost attached to it. In the end, it does not matter which approach the client has selected. They are all correct. Thus, the client is never wrong, even though they make the decision."

At times, a consultant may find themselves with a project where the biggest obstacle is the client. That's when it becomes obvious that it takes tact and salesmanship—as well as knowledge—to be a consultant.

Diplomacy and selling skills are important but there is a limit. Bill Johnson says the "biggest mistake I ever made was trying to keep an unhappy person as a client. If a client is unhappy, he or she is going to stay that way and nothing you do is going to change that. If you try to keep the client, the only thing that happens is that you become the cause of their unhappiness. It has nothing to do with business, but it has everything to do with psychology."

■ Case Study

He was known as one of the most brilliant publishers in the industry, but one of the most stubborn as well. He did not follow a rule book and preferred to run his business by his own rules.

Bill Johnson remembers him well. One of Johnson's peers was called in to audit the company's books. To the astonishment of the auditor, the books were in complete disarray. Withholding taxes from employee checks had not been paid. Refunds to subscribers had not been made in six months, and creditors had not been paid for four months.

None of this shocked the owner. He had been away from the business for nearly a year, and when he returned he noticed a mounting stack of payables. Additionally, several of the accounting employees seized upon the opportunity to tell the owner that the firm was significantly in arrears on virtually every debt. The auditor was called in to verify the owner's suspicions. When he did, the owner took quick action. He fired the entire management team he had put in place the year before, and he took the company over once again.

Creditors, hearing that the managers had been fired, became concerned. They descended upon the owner demanding their payables. Within days, the owner had run into the IRS, which was demanding its overdue withholding monies, and the Federal Trade Commission, which was about to shut the doors of the magazine for failure to pay refunds.

Faced with mounting difficulties, and harassed by debtors on every side—debtors who not only disliked the owner because of his arrogance, but blamed him for the problems—the founder of the magazine took the company into Chapter 11 bankruptcy. It would enable him to reorganize and operate the firm, and raise the $3 million he needed to get the firm out of the hole.

With most companies the strategy would have worked, however, with this particular owner—an entrepreneur who was used to doing things his way—problems emerged. The bankruptcy court appointed a trustee, the creditors had an attorney, the accountants descended upon the company, and the board of directors was completely disorganized. Then the auditors found another discrepancy. It seems that on the side, the owner and one of his employees had formed a partnership. The business from the partnership was generated by the activities of the publishing company. And, in fact, it was the publishing company, under the owner's direction, that funneled the business and monies into the firm.

When the accountant found the problem, he took the owner aside and urged him to step down and appoint someone else to run the company until the debts were cleared and the creditors were out of the picture. If he did not, and the creditors got wind of the activities of this jointly owned firm, they could go to the bankruptcy court and demand the removal of the owner from the operation of the company.

The owner said no. The consultant argued in vain. The owner kept his position and during the next quarterly audit, an outraged group of creditors found out about the side venture. They immediately sent their attorney to court, and within days the owner was removed from the premises and along with it so was his authority.

Eventually, the company emerged from Chapter 11, however, the owner had been forced to accept numerous conditions put down by the creditors. In the end, he sold the publishing enterprise, one of the most promising in the country, for a fraction of what it was worth.

The lesson to Johnson was clear-cut: Some clients will not listen to consultants regardless of the situation. It behooves the consultant to try and determine if they have such a client. If they do, the consultant must make a choice. Do it the client's way—which may be wrong—and end up losing the account and being badmouthed by the client, or resign the account immediately and possibly avoid the disparaging comments.

■

Others echo Johnson's sentiments. Dennis McCuistion recalls more than one client who was willing to pay the fee, but not willing to listen. "Never take on a client who will not listen. If they absolutely refuse to hear what you are saying, the relationship will never work."

Determining who will listen and to what extent is never easy. When companies require consulting, they have a problem. If executives meet a consultant they like and believe can do the job, they may agree to many things they never intend to abide by. The consultant never finds this out until after the letter of agreement has been signed and the job is underway. When differences surface at this point, the relationship suffers.

Entrepreneurs, especially, can be difficult. They are used to doing things their way. If a consultant enters the picture, they may have every intention of listening, but many never do. Take, for example, the case study on pages 178–179.

FOLLOWING THE FINDINGS

McCuistion tries to avoid situations like the one described. If he has a doubt as to whether the client will listen, he will ask them upfront—"here's what I can do . . . let me ask you a question, are you going to do anything with it when I bring you the solutions?"

If he gets doubtful expressions, McCuistion will pass. The obvious question: Can any consultant afford to pass on a client, especially in today's tough economic environment?

McCuistion, Johnson, Hugh Holbert, and the others answer without hesitation—"yes!"

They point out the client who will not listen simply wastes the consultant's time. The unhappy client is also going to "bad mouth" the consultant. No one wants to be blamed for failure.

"It is not worth it," says Holbert. "If you think you are about to land a client that will not listen, consider passing regardless of the economic loss. In the long run it will be the best thing."

Alessandra says: "Stick to your guns. Recommend what is in the best interests of the client, even though they may not want to hear it. If you have that kind of business ethic, your reputation starts to build. It absolutely pays off in the long term."

Client rapport boils down to one thing, according to Moore—"the fact that you and the client are on the same wavelength." The chemistry has to be right and both client and consultant have to have a sense that they can both work together. If there is not a rapport, the client will never listen and the consultant will never hear what is being said.

To avoid misunderstandings, Izzo stresses the importance of the pre-proposal interview. Usually, he has at least two before presenting the client with a letter of agreement. "The time it takes to interview is well worth it. The first interview we gather a great deal of material, and in the second we feed much of it back. We use their words and vocabulary when we give them feedback. We'll say things like 'from what you said about this department, you expect . . . .' That way, there is no mistake."

THE QUESTION FACTOR

There is no sure way to avoid mistakes, but if you "ask questions . . . get input . . . and ask more questions," explains Izzo, "you can usually avoid a disaster." To communicate effectively, the consultant must know who the players are and who the decision-maker will be. Consultants should never underestimate the influence or input of a junior manager, either. Even though it appears as if the CEO is the last word, he or she may base decisions on input from junior managers.

Once a consultant generates a client-company, what should they do about communication? How frequently? How should it be done? Communication should not just come in the form of a monthly statement. Astute consultants read their clients, their needs and plan communication around those elements.

Johnson feels the most important communicator on his "consulting team" is the person who has the best rapport with the client. Almost always you will have someone in your firm who appears to have an excellent relationship with the client. He or she should be the point person, the communicator.

THE COMMUNICATION SCHEDULE

Johnson's firm frequently has several teams working on a project. There is usually one leader on each team who is the communicator. This person, too, should be the consultant with the greatest client rapport.

Alessandra believes in communicating as "often as possible. Just think about this," he explains. "The biggest reason for divorce is a lack of communication. A consulting/client relationship is similar to a marriage. If a lack of communication breaks a real marriage, it will break a consulting arrangement. Communicate frequently."

Kracke communicates at least "once a month or whenever there is something significant to tell the client." Often, he picks up the telephone just to "keep the communication channels open." He urges other consultants to do the same thing. "Let them know you have not forgotten them, even if nothing has been happening. If nothing has happened, explain why."

McCuistion communicates frequently, which he defines as several times a week. This is "especially important if you are working on a retainer. Be proactive." Do not wait for the client to call; initiate the contact. McCuistion suggests consultants have an agenda, too, when they call. "Have some things to discuss. Sit down and think about the call before it is made. There are always items to go over with the client."

Pennington is in constant contact with clients, and he suggests other consultants do the same. Pennington illustrates his point with a true story.

Three years ago, I was building a new home. I would leave a message for the builder, and sometimes three and four days would go by before I heard from him. By that time I was frantic. One day he told me I would have to understand that he was building 10 to 20 houses at any one time, and he did not always have the chance to get back to me. My response to him was "you have to remember that I am only building one—and to me it is the most important one."

For a consultant's client, it is the same. The consultant may have a dozen projects, but to each client his undertaking is not only the most important, but it may be—in his mind—the only one.

Moore is cognizant of that client fetish. Even if there is nothing to say, she will pick up the telephone and call to touch base with the client. To remind herself that every client needs constant contact, she even writes herself notes as a reminder that a call should be made. "I might just call to have them clarify something . . . and let them know I am around."

To Van Den Berg, there is no standard communication schedule. "It depends on the client. You have to read them. Some clients do not require telephone calls or meetings, while others want to come into the office and see what is going on."

Regardless of how often consultant's communicate, one thing is clear—in every case, communication is a must. Consulting is a service business; intangible, elusive. It takes nurturing and explanation. Clients are paying hefty hourly, monthly, or project retainers. They want to see something solid; they want to know something is being done. It is difficult to generate clients but easy to lose them if the consultant forgets the value of communication. Communication says the consultant cares. Communication says the consultant is thinking about the client and their problems.

PROTECTING ACCOUNTS

Some consultants assign the "contact" to a project chairperson or the consultant on the team who has the best client rapport. There is an obvious danger in this approach, however. If the principal allows team members to make the contact, is there a chance of losing the client—and the business?

Obviously, yes. In fact, the threat of having an employee (or so-called account executive) run off with a client has been the bane of the business. The best way to learn about consulting is to work for one, and for many the fastest-way to opening their own business is to walk off with a client.

In consulting—or any service business—losing clientele to employees happens. Nowhere is this better illustrated than in the advertising field. Agency principals may sell the client, but it is usually up to an account executive and other members of a team to work with the client, get to know them, and develop their advertising plans.

The advertising agency principals initially spend their time selling the client and reinforcing the sale, but in a short time they are gone, off to sell another client. Consultants in other fields have to do the same. Johnson may be the prime contact with a new accounting client, or Izzo with a company requiring data processing services, however, within a short time they have to move to another project; sell another company.

Clients can have the direct services of Johnson or Izzo, but their time is billed out at a premium. As Johnson says, it is usually the middle level consultant who ends up doing the work; the middle level consultant who maintains the client contact and establishes the rapport.

What can consultants/owners do? How can they prevent a subordinate from running off with the billing? In most cases, they cannot unless they plan to be the prime contact source. This approach may protect a few clients but in the long run it keeps the consulting firm from growing. The principals in a consulting firm should be off making contact with potential new clients.

Johnson is not afraid of an employee running off with an account. In fact, his attitude toward it is quite revealing. It shows one of the main reasons why his firm has gone, in about three years, from the newcomer on the block to one of the most successful accounting/consulting firms in the country.

"The fact someone would leave and take a client," says Johnson, "is okay. I wish them all the luck in the world. They will never hurt us by doing so. None of the original core of people who started this company with me have left. The few that have, usually end up being the best referral networks out there for us. They quickly discover they cannot handle some of the broad-based problems as we do. Consequently, when they run into a client who needs myriad services, they recommend us."

Johnson may wish his employees well if they leave, but he does everything possible to keep them by running a firm that has free and open discussion. His weekly staff meetings have open forums, and consultants are urged to get anything they want out on the table. He points out a factor in the business that few consultants think about.

"In our field, we are trained to be accountants. We are not trained to be managers. It is important for everyone within our company to learn how to be part of a team; how to solve problems with teamwork. It is not enough to just be a good CPA. That does not make you a good consultant."

The lesson: Consultants need as much management skill as they can if they are ever going to build a consulting company, and not just a small practice. Van Den Berg, an astute money manager, has invested as much time in mastering psychology and management as he has in the financial markets.

Perhaps Qubein puts it best: "I make sure that my staff has handsome, elegant surroundings in which they can work. If I provide that type atmosphere, my people are going to feel elegant and self-assured. They are going to feel successful and they will be. And, if they are successful, so will I be. That's why I maintain a class A office building even though few of my clients ever visit us.

"Remember, in the consulting business, or for that matter any business, an employee's mindset is not just a part of the whole. It can be everything. It reflects in every aspect of their work—from greeting and servicing the client to communicating with him later on."

10 RULES OF CLIENT COMMUNICATION

Aside from the frequency, every thriving consultant has developed a philosophy as to how and what they communicate. They can be condensed into 10 critical rules:

1. *Honesty.* From the very beginning, it is incumbent upon a consultant to use straight talk with a client. This does not mean blunt, abrasive talk, however, it does indicate that consultants should never avoid an issue that can manifest itself into a serious client/consultant problem.

2. *Never promise more than you can deliver and never deliver less than you promise.* In the frenzy and excitement of generating a new client, it is easy to make a rash, hasty commitment. Clients, however, never forget a promise and regardless of how much is delivered, if everything that was indicated has not been provided, the client is going to be disappointed.

3. *Remember chemistry.* If there is more than one consultant involved in the project, utilize the one who has the greatest rapport with the client as the "communicator."

4. *Timely communications.* Contact clients on a regular basis. Adhere to a schedule.

5. *Communications agenda.* When you call or visit clients, make sure you have an agenda that includes items of importance.

6. *Listen.* The most important attribute a consultant can have. The ability to listen to what a client is saying. This skill is a must when it comes to communication.

7. *Stay focused.* In client meetings, do not let your mind wander. Concentrate on the client and what is being said—and asked.

8. *Be yourself.* In meetings, do not take on the role of someone else. Be yourself.

9. *Confirm the facts.* Tell the client and then put it in writing. Always reinforce in writing.

10. *Be proactive.* Do not wait for the client to call before you provide information. Be aware of the client's situation.

These ten rules apply to written as well as verbal communication. In today's business environment, however, clients are not interested in an interim or final report loaded with con instead of content.

Every report should be straightforward and to-the-point. Consultants should avoid acronyms, slang, and reports that read like a runaway dictionary. Unfortunately, some consultants feel that to justify their fee, the report should be long. When a consultant takes that approach, the report may not only end up being excessive in length but cumbersome in language and irrelevant. There are few things that can be as damaging to a consultant's credibility as a report that was obviously manufactured with verbiage in mind instead of communication and information.

For instance, adjectives may be fitting in a fiction novel, but they are superfluous in a consultant's report. The same for excessive use of adverbs and needless descriptive passages.

The best and most effective reports are those that are written in practical, how-to terms; reports that are written in a language that anyone can understand, even if he or she does not know the details of the business.

Good report writers are akin to good newspaper reporters. Notice in a well-written news story, everything is explained—in plain, simple terms. If there is a technical term that is used, the reporter may use it but they also "translate" it so that anyone can read it.

The rule: Write your report (interim or final) so that anyone within the company can read or understand it. Even if the project involves a technical process, it behooves the consultant to write it in language that nontechnical people can understand.

Take the following scenario. A well-known high-tech firm called in a data processing analyst to evaluate the company's DP procedures. Much of the evaluation involved examining sophisticated computer equipment and software programs.

The analysis took several weeks, and when the consultant was finished, he honed a detailed report on the current situation, the problems within the department, why, the equipment, and recommendations for changes and why.

When the CEO was handed the report, he thanked the consultant and within five minutes—without ever examining it—he handed it to his secretary. Unbeknownst to the consultant, the CEO used his secretary as a sounding board. Before he read anything or made a decision, he usually described it to her and asked for her opinion.

Unusual? Not at all. There are thousands of CEOs and senior managers who utilize their secretaries or assistants as sounding boards. There is hardly an executive of a major corporation who does not use his or her secretary/assistant to "go over" correspondence before it is sent out.

In numerous cases, the senior manager will ask the secretary to draft the follow-up letter. There is one, well-known Fortune 500 CEO who pens a monthly column for his corporation's newsletter. He develops the ideas and approach, but never sees the column—until his secretary has created and written the first draft.

Seeking advice and opinions from others is a trademark of good executives. Thus, when the DP consultant came in with a report and recommendations, it was natural for the CEO to give it to his secretary for her reaction. Unfortunately, the report had been written in "dataease" and the secretary was unable to provide any input. The busy CEO put the report aside and did not pick it up for weeks. When he did, he discovered he was unable to decipher the results. It was too technical for him as well.

Suddenly, the CEO found himself in an awkward position. The report was written about the company's DP department. There was undoubtedly sections of it that would not be too complimentary of the area because of the problems it was encountering. Yet, because of the way it was written, it would take someone from DP to translate it.

As a result, the report languished on the executive's desk. He did not want to be put in a position of calling in an experienced DP manager to read the report, and then find that the manager was criticized. Thus, the report sat on the CEO's desk for months. The consultant, who was hoping to generate an additional contract through the recommendations in the report, was never called and never knew why. The only answer he ever received when he repeatedly telephoned the CEO, was that the executive had not had a chance to go through it, yet.

Aside from easy-to-understand English, reports should be organized in the following format:

1. *Executive summary.* Few executives have the time to read things in detail. They are looking for summaries; quick, one-page reports that give an overview of the contents, findings and recommendations.

2. *The process and problem.* Why the firm was called in and the approach it took. Details of any findings, studies.

3. *The problem.* What it was. How serious. A detailed analysis of it. Consequences if nothing is done about it. Data gathered.

4. *Recommendations.* What the consultant suggests. The time frame if it is done this way. Alternatives.

In the next chapter, we will examine some of the marketing tools that not only help consultants generate clients and keep them, but also help enhance the consultant's perceived value in the eyes of the client.

CHAPTER 7

Marketing Tools That Help Sell Fees, Contracts

U
p until 1990, he was an obscure officer in the U.S. Army, known primarily to the men who served under him. But, in one 30-day period, General Norman Schwarzkopf became a celebrity; a hero of Operation Desert Storm, and a speaker who was generating $70,000 for a 45-minute speech.

The same phenomena occurred nearly 15 years prior to Operation Desert Storm. This time, instead of it being a General, it was a magazine publisher. In the mid-to-late 1970s, this young writer and entrepreneur was making a modest living as editor of a creative and innovative publication that he had created.

Suddenly, in one 30-day period, his life was transformed, too. A business writer at the *Los Angeles Times* had picked up the magazine and was intrigued by the content. It seems the publisher had an uncanny knack of predicting what small businesses and trends would be "hot" in the coming months. The business writer called the publisher, did an interview, and shortly thereafter a page one feature appeared in the *Times* on the entrepreneur.

Within days, people were flooding the magazine's office with calls, asking for the publisher and trying to buy anywhere from fifteen minutes to an entire day of his time and advice. His consulting practice and the magazine took off. Within two years, his company had gone from $500,000 to a $2-million-a-year operation. Within four years, it was at $15 million and *Entrepreneur Magazine* and its founder/publisher, Chase Revel, had become nationally famous.

The careers and skills of General Schwarzkopf and Chase Revel are far apart, but both owe much of their fame and the financial success that followed to the recognition they received from the media. The credibility that the media gave to their names.

The media has done—and is doing—the same for many others. Syndicated columnists like Art Buchwald and Jim Murray; businessmen like Lee Iaccoca; authors like Tom Clancy and Tom Peters; and TV personalities such as Arsenio Hall and Pat Sajak. Every one of these people, regardless of their occupation, has been turned into a celebrity by the media. And every one of them can command thousands of dollars for a short speaking engagement or an hour of consulting time.

The key: They have had their names in print and they continue to generate notoriety. There are many consultants who have enhanced their notoriety—and value as a consultant—by doing the same thing. Media or print (TV and radio, too) generate credibility and inquiries for consultants. Certainly, not every consultant is a best-selling author, distinguished General or well-known magazine publisher. But, many have generated credibility, created a following and increased the demand for their services (and consequently the fees) by simply publishing newsletters or giving speeches that generated local or industry notoriety. Every one of these marketing activities leads to exposure and credibility.

NEWSLETTER APPROACH

How can one help increase the demand for a consultant's services and, of course, their fees? Well-done newsletters lead to a better image for the consultant, attract prospects, and end up generating more billing/fees. Good newsletters have common ingredients. They are targeted at specific industries and/or professions. In other words, the consultant's present and potential clients. They are not generic products that have a consultant's name and picture imprinted at the last minute. (Real estate salespeople are notorious for putting out this type of newsletter. Most customers immediately recognize that the publication has been put together by someone else, and the salesperson's picture was inserted at the last minute.)

This is not the case with effective newsletters. They look distinctive and have a message loaded with benefits for the reader. They are educational and informative, and contain information that the prospective client is so interested in that they may keep it around for weeks.

For example, suppose you are a personnel consultant specializing in some type of placement. Your audience is human resource directors. Those are the people who are in the market to retain your services. What kind of newsletter would appeal to them? Typical ingredients include:

1. News relating to the latest innovations in the human resource field. It could have a roundup on pending new laws, changes in labor relations, the growth in workmen's comp lawsuits, the latest developments in such areas as managing diversity.

2. A column and or interview with a panel of human resource experts covering a specific current problem (and solutions) in the field. It could be a Q&A session revolving around worker absenteeism, flexible work hours, drug abuse, productivity ideas. If you are in this field, you can probably name at least a dozen issues that impact human resource directors; issues they would be interested in reading about.

3. Success stories about placements. The stories would show how each has contributed to the company in which they were placed. It could contain quotes from the human resource people that the consultant was working with at the time of

placement. It might have hints or ideas that other human resource directors could adopt. It could have thoughts on why
the employee decided to go to work for the company; what
employment elements meant the most to him/her.

This approach works in other fields. A data processing
consultant could run a story centered around the redesign of a
system that was more productive. The newsletter could contain
hints on how to spot trouble areas within computer systems.
The audience—the same audience that the data processing
consultant is trying to reach—top management outside the DP
department as well as those within the DP department.

Effective newsletters should be constructed so that anyone can understand the content. Just because the newsletter is
geared, for instance, to DP problems does not mean that it
should be filled with complex jargon and terms. Keep it simple so that anyone, whether they are skilled in the field or not,
can understand. It broadens the audience. Instead of just the
department head being able to read it, the CEO can understand it as well. And, often, it is the CEO who does the hiring
of the consultant.

4. A column written by the consultant covering an area that
   would interest human resource (or DP, etc.) directors. It
   could, for instance revolve around the changing motivation of
   workers, downsizing's impact on morale and how to counter-
   act some of its effect. These are issues human resource people
   wrestle with daily and valuable insight is appreciated. It sets
   the consultant up as an authority, too.

All of these items would be of interest to the human resource
reader. The messages in a newsletter are multiple. They address the
needs of the reader, show them how to solve problems, educate and
inform, and position the consultant as an authority—without the
consultant ever saying they are one.

Nowhere does the newsletter contain a message from the consultant that says "hire me as a consultant." Rather it shows the

readers that the consultant/author is well-informed and wants to share information. Subliminally, it says "I am a well-informed consultant who wants to share information with you. If you like what you read, perhaps you may want to utilize my services."

Newsletters are a soft sell. They show knowledge but they do not twist the prospect's arm. They have both objective and subjective editorial ingredients. Objective elements would be in any news stories revolving around late breaking news. Subjective material could come from the consultant via their column. This facet of the newsletter contains opinions (supported by evidence) of things that will impact the customer (newsletter reader) and his company.

A critical element in newsletters is the value of the material. Recipes may be wonderful in *Good Housekeeping,* but they have no place in serious, informative, quality newsletters that are put together by professional consultants. The newsletter that does not have material that is value should not be printed. Ask yourself: "If I was in this business (human resources, data processing) would this content interest me?" If you have doubts, throw it out.

Make the newsletter easy to read. Pay attention to layout, headlines, typestyles, and use a glossy stock if you are going to put photographs in it. Glossy stock reproduces black-and-white photos much better than flat stock.

There should also be a photograph of you. Usually it is a head shot, and it belongs in your column. The photograph gives people a better idea of "what you are like." It also enhances your status as a professional. We all may be pessimistic about the media, and we may be aware that the consultant is paying for their newsletter, but the fact they are pictured in it; the fact it is widely distributed and in print all combine to not only promote the consultant, but give them credibility.

Radio, TV, and Print Exposure

Newsletters enhance an image and, more importantly, increase the perceived value of the consultant—as well as their expertise.

If the newsletter contains the correct elements, is informational, educational, and current it can provide incredible benefits for a consultant's practice. Laurie Moore, for instance, and her partner, Steve Murray (co-editors of *REAL Trends,* have built a following of more than 2,000 key industry people. The publication addresses current issues and does some forecasting as well. The co-editors feature themselves on the back page with each issue.

As a result, *REAL Trends* has become one of the most respected publications in the industry. Moore and Murray are both called upon by major companies for speaking engagements. The fact they are putting out a high-quality industry newsletter has done something else—it has given them entree to the decision makers in the business. They do interviews with many CEOs of major real estate firms. Those CEOs can "suggest" to other executives within their company that they use Moore or Murray for speaking and/or consulting.

Moore and Murray have taken it one step farther. Last year, they staged a program called "a gathering of Eagles" in which they invited (and charged) CEOs and top management executives in their industry, to a two-day conference that addressed current and critical issues in the business. They brought in a half-dozen speakers in different areas as well. As a result, more than 100 key decision makers attended. For two days, they were face-to-face with 100 potential clients.

Moore and Murray, however, are careful to keep the newsletter and their speaking and consulting engagements separate. If they are doing an interview with an industry CEO for the newsletter, they never bring up the subject of consulting or giving a talk. They stick to the business at hand and leave it up to the CEO—or whomever—to contact them. The consultant who is talking to a decision maker as part of a newsletter interview, makes a serious mistake if they try to sell their consulting and/or speaking services at the same time. The value of the newsletter (and the consultant) diminishes. It becomes apparent to the prospect that the consultant is merely in the newsletter business to hustle clientele. Never mix the two. Leave the subject of "hiring me as a speaker or consultant" up to the company executive.

It is a mistake to try wearing more than one hat at a time. Later, the company executive may contact the consultant/speaker for an engagement. Or, the consultant can contact the executive. But, when they do, it should be made clear that the purpose of the call is not the newsletter, but a problem the consultant saw that they might be able to assist the company in solving.

Keeping consulting/speaking and newsletter enterprises separate, enables consultants to enhance their credibility. It makes them more valuable in the prospect's eyes, whereas, trying to hustle business when you are interviewing for a story, diminishes the consultant's value.

Many consultants are not writers. That obstacle can be overcome. There are freelance writers who will write and supervise the newsletter. They must, however, understand the newsletter, the market and the editorial approach. Many can be found through newspapers, college journalism departments, advertising agencies and even the local chamber of commerce.

Newsletters, however, do take time. In fact, it can take up to a month or more to put one together. The sample timetable below provides an accurate guideline:

Assuming the consultant has already determined the audience, hired a writer/supervisor, developed a theme or concept for it and the format—with the aid of a printer—the following schedule can be looked upon as one that is fairly accurate.

Task	Days Needed
1. Begin interviews/writing	10
Develop lead story	
Develop consultants column	
Develop success stories/other material	
2. Copy set and proofread	3
3. Approvals obtained if necessary	2

   4. Layout, design mechanical boards   4–6
   5. Photography (if necessary)   3–4
       Arrange photos with subject
       Receive contact sheet from photog
       Select photos/order
   6. Deliver photos to printer with boards
   7. Decide on printing quantities
   8. Approve blueline/brownline   2
   9. Newsletters printed/folded   4–5
  10. Deliver newsletters to mailing house   2
       Affix labels
       Mail

Notice there are approximately 30 working days to complete a newsletter. This allows everyone time to do their job, and gives you an idea of how time-consuming a newsletter can be. That's one of the reasons some consultants purchase a "canned" or ready-made newsletter. The disadvantage of these publications is that they look canned. They cannot be targeted as well and do not set the consultant apart from competitors who may be doing similar things. If a consultant is going to get into the newsletter field, they should do it in professionally. Give it a unique, customized appearance, as in Exhibit 7.1.

BUSINESS GENERATING SPEECHES

A second technique that a growing number of consultants are utilizing in order to enhance their perceived value, is giving speeches in front of organizations. The key is that the speaker/consultant has (1) knowledge of the industry and/or subject and (2) has targeted an organization in which there are potential clients.

   Before she attempted to generate any marketing clients, Moore had more than a decade of experience in advertising and she

EXHIBIT 7.1

REAL *Trends*

Vol. IV- Number 7/July 1990

Trends, Events and Strategies
shaping tomorrow's Real Estate industry.

Hunneman Real Estate Targets Europe

New England firm to establish international real estate company with aid of Swiss corporate partner

Hunneman Real Estate Corporation, a Boston-based realty firm and Iten Immobilien Treuhand, a major Swiss real estate organization, have announced a letter of intent to establish an international real estate service company. As part of the agreement, Iten will purchase a significant minority interest in Hunneman. Stuart Pratt, President and CEO of Hunneman will be Chairman, President and CEO of the new company which plans offices in Frankfort, London and Paris.

The relationship joins two firms with combined real estate transactions in 1989 of $2.2 billion. Iten, which is headquartered near Zurich, is expected to attract up to $50 million of overseas capital to the Massachusetts real estate market between now and the end of 1991, with funds to be targeted primarily at commercial office and retail properties.

Deal eases entre into U.S. market

According to Iten President and CEO, Max Iten, the firm wanted to expand into the United States and considered several cities before

deciding on Boston. "We found Boston an ideal entrance into the United States real estate market because of the size of the city, financial community, and the institutional business base. Hunneman was a likely partner because they provide a broad scope of real estate services." (Hunneman and Company Realtors, Better Homes and Gardens, the residential brokerage division of Hunneman Real Estate Corporation was number 96 on the 1989 REAL Trends Big Broker Report's list of the Top 100 Brokers.) Iten is a full service real estate firm serving residential and commercial real estate markets and offering property leasing and sales, management, construction, development, appraisal and consulting services.

Dual benefits: investors and expansion

While Iten was contemplating the U.S. market, Pratt was eyeing foreign investor dollars and opportunities abroad. "We have been looking for overseas business and expansion opportunities for some time, and began talks with Iten last year in anticipation of Europe

1992," said Pratt. "The partnership opens up major new markets overseas to Hunneman, and provides access to new capital and financial leverage for local investment at a time when buying opportunities are significant."

Hunneman has four divisions including commercial brokerage, investment management, appraisal/ consulting, and the residential brokerage arm which is a franchise affiliate of Better Homes and Gardens. The firm is also affiliated with the commercial network New America and Sotheby's International.

Editors' Note

Watch for more real estate firms to go transnational. The major franchises have already turned their attention to developing franchise affiliates in other countries — with emphasis on Western Europe and the Pacific Rim. Individual firms, especially those located in markets which are attractive to foreign investors, will increasingly seek out marketing relationships with foreign real estate organizations. Some, such as Hunneman, may opt for equity relationships.

EXHIBIT 7.1 *(continued)*

Editors' Note

Laurie C. Moore
Editor
214-250-0633

Stephen H. Murray
Editor
303-740-6778

Wow! We've been overwhelmed with positive feedback on our last two issues. Both the Big Broker Report: Top 100 Residential Firms and our National Franchise Company Report have generated tremendous media response and lots of inquiries from brokers, state associations and industry vendors who want to purchase copies of the issues and want more information about our research reports.

Special offer to subscribers
At the end of the summer, "REAL Facts: The Information Sourcebook for the Real Estate In-

dustry" will be hot off the press. This new book will contain:
* More information about the 100 largest residential firms
* Additional valuable data on the national franchise firms and their market share
* Profiles of over 100 major players in the commercial brokerage business
* Information on the major referral networks
* Predictions for real estate brokerage in the 1990's
* Comments and opinions from major industry personalities

Don't miss this exciting resource book! It contains information not available anywhere else. If you liked the Big Broker and the Franchise Company reports, you'll want the complete data in the REAL Facts sourcebook.
Here's the good news. Designed to sell for $95, REAL Trends subscribers may, for a limited time, purchase this book for only $75 plus a small postage and handling fee. That's a pre-publication savings of over 20 percent! To reserve your copies of REAL Facts, return the coupon below with your check. This offer is limited! Order now.

continued from page 2
philosophy is that the first one to do something usually gets the maximum benefit, but he cautions brokers that this kind of program is harder to develop in a slow market. "A normal or strong market is a good time to begin because it gives newer people time to get established as strong producers," according to Scott.

How do John L. Scott's agents and managers view the firm's All Pro Team concept and commission plan? "They love it!" says Scott.

EDITORS' NOTE: One more suggestion to Scott's guidelines above: build in some sort of expected, automatic annual increase to your maximum company dollar figure. Peg it to CPI or some other index so that you can make a reasonable adjustment without having agents feel you are taking away what you've given.

had worked for a major real estate firm. At the real estate company, she created numerous marketing programs, and before long her ability in the area became known to others in the industry and they asked her to speak to their sales organizations. Laurie did, and soon she found herself with people asking her for in-depth programs—her consulting practice was underway.

"Speaking," she says, "sets you up as an authority, just as publishing your own newsletter. I think most of us have listened to speakers, and we never question their background. We assume they know what they are talking about. After all, if someone thought they were knowledgable enough to address this crowd, they must know what they are talking about."

SPEAKING AND CONSULTING

Hugh Holbert is another example of what speaking can do for a consultant's practice. He was one of the few attorneys who specialized in liability and malpractice, and it was not long before every sales organization in the industry was asking him to present a seminar on the subject. The more he spoke, the faster his practice grew. Initially, what he did for free—give seminars—he had to start charging for because of the demand on his time.

Tom Hopkins utilized the same technique to open the sales training doors. At first, Hopkins spoke to anyone, anywhere—and he did it for free. Slowly, his reputation built and today he is not only one of the most in-demand speakers in the country, but he has created tape programs and written books as well.

Dennis McCuistion is an excellent example of how speaking not only leads to other speaking engagements, but to consulting business as well. He does about 100 speaking engagements each year and reaches about 10,000 to 20,000 financial executives through those talks. He usually addresses strategic planning for banks and small business. "I was in California last year giving an address to bankers at their lending conference. One of the people who heard me said we are going to have a board retreat and hired me to do a session with the board. Then they referred me to another bank board. I met the directors of that second board, who said they have problems with management and they hired me as a consultant."

Alessandra was a consultant when he started speaking, and although he utilized the talks to help him build his practice, today he spends most of his time giving anywhere from 70 to 100 speeches a year, each paying somewhere around $7,000 an hour.

"Speaking initially fed my consulting business," he says, "but now most of my time goes into giving talks and for one simple reason—it is difficult to generate $7,000 an hour as a consultant. You can as a speaker."

Randy Pennington stresses the edge a consultant has if they can speak and combine consulting with it. He started as a training consultant and within a year he was doing some speaking. To get things moving, he began to submit proposals to associations and societies. "Most people typically start off by making a presentation to a local or regional association. Once you have done that, you can move up to national. The ideal engagement is one in which the audience is filled with people who can make decisions—the president, key executives, and so-on—as to whether they will retain you as a consultant. I always look at engagements and try to stick to the ones where I know the key decision makers will be."

Qubein, who charges from $6,000 to $10,000 a day for speaking, started his personal development consulting business through direct mail. He sold personal development/leadership materials via the mails, and soon found some of his buyers inviting him to conduct leadership seminars. From the seminars, his involvement with many companies expanded to the point where they would bring him in as a consultant.

THE EFFECTIVE BROCHURE

Another marketing approach many consultants utilize in order to enhance their value is a brochure. Consultants sometimes overlook the impact of a brochure, but it can be significant. In many cases, the first thing a prospective client sees is a mailing piece from the consultant. If the brochure is put together poorly, looks cheap, or unprofessional, the prospect has the same initial impression of the consultant. Once that thought is embedded, it is difficult to change.

It is the same as someone going in for a job interview. When the hiring manager sees the candidate, the first impression is not what comes out of the applicant's mouth, but how they look. Are they neat or sloppy; are their shoes shined or dull; is he clean shaven or is their a trace of a beard; is her dress neat and pressed, or wrinkled?

All those visual elements make the first impression, and the first impression, for most of us, is the one that shapes opinions.

Brochures do the same thing. Consequently, the consultants who send literature and brochures, make sure they are putting nothing but quality in the mail. Take McCuistion. On the cover of his brochure is a message that describes exactly what McCuistion's firm does:

Mission

Management

Marketing

Money

McCuistion

The title describes what McCuistion's services can mean to the client as well—money.

Pennington's brochure simply gives the name of the firm ("Pennington Performance Group"), while Tony Alessandra has a photograph with the copy "Dr. Tony Alessandra—Keynote Speaker." (See Exhibit 7.2.) Nido Qubein has his photograph and name.

Although each is different and targeted to a specific audience, they share one thing in common—every cover says "quality." Before anyone reads the contents, its professionally designed appearance

EXHIBIT 7.2

DR. TONY
ALESSANDRA
CPAE
KEYNOTE SPEAKER

says to the prospective client "this is a quality firm . . . they know what they are doing . . . they are worth a significant fee."

CONTEMPORARY BROCHURES

Most contemporary brochures are designed in a press kit fashion. They are $8\frac{1}{2} \times 11$ folded, or 17×11 when opened. They usually have pockets inside to hold additional materials. The advantage of this approach is that the consultant can always add or remove materials. The press kit format can be significantly more economical than a four-color printed brochure that cannot be changed. The press kit holds a variety of materials. If a consultant adds a service, all they have to do is print a sheet and insert it into the package. If the consultant decides to drop a service (perhaps it was not economical) all they have to do is remove the printed sheet. They never have the financial worry of discarding a printed brochure.

Take, for instance, the inserts in Johnson's press kit brochure (Exhibit 7.3). "Reorganizing and Restructuring" is a phase of consulting for CPAs that has only recently come into vogue. With the press kit format that Bill Johnson prepared, he was able to add one $8\frac{1}{2}'' \times 11''$ sheet with minimal cost. If he had a bound brochure that detailed the various phases of his business, he would be faced with discarding all his old brochures and completely rewriting it, instead of just adding a page. Johnson's other inserts have a similar format (Exhibit 7.4).

McCuistion's kit is similar, however, inside he has "stacked" the information on his company (Exhibit 7.5). If one area intrigues a client, all they have to do is pull it out. On the left side are five different categories. On the right side of the kit is information about McCuistion and his television program (Exhibit 7.6).

Pennington has a similar pull-out configuration. (See Exhibit 7.7.) On the right side are several reprints from magazines (Exhibit 7.8). One is from *Executive Excellence* and the other from the *Bottled Water Reporter*. Each enhances his credibility, as does an article McCuistion has included from a local newspaper, *Las Colinas*

EXHIBIT 7.3

Reorganization and Restructuring

FINANCIAL REVERSALS are common in the current business community, and troubled companies typically file for bankruptcy under Chapter 11 of the U.S. Bankruptcy Code. Their petitions are designed to provide the opportunity to reorganize under court protection, and give debtors a respite from their creditors.

Relief from debt is available under the Bankruptcy Reform Act of 1978, and the Bankruptcy Tax Act of 1980, which apply to Chapter 7 (liquidation), Chapter 13 (personal debt) and Chapter 11 (corporate and individual reorganization). All three types of bankruptcy begin with a petition in bankruptcy court.

The need for competent professional counsel in this process is underscored by the fact that only 10% to 12% of Chapter 11 cases emerge in a successful reorganization, according to an estimate by the Administrative Office of the U.S. Courts. The poor success rate lies in part with the overburdened court system, and partly because many companies lack access to timely reliable information.

Johnson & Associates offers its expertise in the highly specialized practice of corporate reorganizations and restructuring. Our staff is familiar with the requirements of a sound reorganization plan and the tax advantages available under the Bankruptcy Code. We are prepared to apply our considerable experience in your behalf.

After a voluntary filing of bankruptcy in the federal district court, the court may appoint a trustee to run the business, or the owner may operate it as a "debtor in possession." At this point, creditors are prevented from collecting debts incurred before the petition filing date. A schedule of assets and debts is filed by the debtor, and claims against the company are filed by each creditor, which may be allowed or disallowed by the court.

Financial reporting for a business in bankruptcy requires knowledgeable personnel. Transactions specifically related to the reorganization must be reported separately from the results of the company's continuing operations. Johnson & Associates complies with the accounting standards and procedures set forth by the Accounting Standards Executive Committee of AICPA in its Statement of Position 90-7, "Financial Reporting by Entities in Reorganization Under the Bankruptcy Code," which applies to any company that files a Chapter 11 petition after December 31, 1990.

Furthermore, we are members of the Association of Insolvency Accountants, a national not-for-profit organization whose membership is actively involved in reorganization practice. The AIA has established a certification program to designate those members such as Johnson & Associates who have attained the highest degree of expertise in the area of business bankruptcy and insolvency. ∎

JOHNSON & Associates
AN ACCOUNTANCY CORPORATION
3878 Carson Street • Suite 101 • P.O. Box 13666 • Torrance, CA 90503 • (310) 540-7477
4200 Rocklin Road • Suite 3 • P.O. Box 300 • Rocklin, CA 95677 • (916) 624-3779

EXHIBIT 7.4

Estate Planning

RE YOU LEAVING your estate to the government or to your family?

Because many of us choose not to consider our own mortality, we put off crucial decisions regarding our estates. Such lack of planning could prove costly to our families and survivors.

Recent studies indicate that many people have not made out a will, the most elemental step in estate planning, nor protected their families from undue taxation. If your estate—including your home, business, real property and other tangible assets—exceeds an individual's $600,000 exemption, your family may be forced to pay estate taxes, as well as probate fees averaging five per cent of the estate, plus court and accounting fees.

At Johnson & Associates our experienced estate planners are prepared to advise you on how to minimize estate taxes, and ensure privacy in the distribution of your wealth to your designated heirs and dependents in the timely manner of your choosing. Many people are surprised to learn that a will does not necessarily protect their estates from government assessments. A will only specifies who receives the property of the decedent. The establishment of one or more trusts may prove to be far more beneficial to you and your family.

The trust is the principal instrument of estate planning. Property administered in a trust and distributed after an individual's death usually is not part of the probate estate, and may not be subject to estate taxes. A living trust is one which is created during a person's lifetime, and may be revocable or irrevocable. A testamentary trust is created upon death through a will or living trust. The specific details and planning will vary from one family to another, but without planning, there is no assurance that the distribution of your estate will be in accordance with your wishes.

Johnson & Associates recognizes that the most important factor in estate planning is the relationship within the family, and we are sensitive to your individual preferences. Our estate planners are also experienced CPAs with tax expertise who can alert you to the tax ramifications of your decisions. We work with your attorneys and advisors to be certain that all tax aspects of your plans are responsibly fulfilled.

The benefits of estate planning must be weighed in each case. But we can help you and your family avoid those unneccessary costs so often incurred in the transfer of property, and assist survivors in the management of your estate in the manner in which you intended. ◼

JOHNSON & Associates
AN ACCOUNTANCY CORPORATION
3878 Carson Street • Suite 101 • P.O. Box 13666 • Torrance, CA 90503 • (310) 540-7477
4200 Rocklin Road • Suite 3 • P.O. Box 300 • Rocklin, CA 95677 • (916) 624-3779

EXHIBIT 7.4 *(continued)*

Operational and Financial Analysis

I T'S SAID, FOR EVERY ILL, there's a remedy. But finding what ails you often requires professional judgment. Just as a physician probes for strengths and weaknesses in his examinations, Johnson & Associates applies the same intense scrutiny to the companies it analyzes. We start with a broad overview, studying the financial and operational systems used by a company. Policies, procedures, and controls are then reviewed in detail.

But that is just the beginning, because our staff knows how to resolve the problems they uncover. While we locate weaknesses and trouble-spots within a company's structure, our objective is to help you improve your company's operation and profitability.

Our business experts are seasoned managers first and foremost, people who have served on the front lines and in the trenches, grappling with the real problems which confront every business. They know where future problems are likely to occur because of their hands-on experience.

As companies grow, they are subject to more regulations at the federal, state, and local levels. A properly conceived control structure eases the stress associated with that growth. We spot the places where companies are hemorrhaging dollars, and highlight those points where stronger checks and balances are needed.

Our analysis includes the study of your insurance coverage, accounting system, and reporting procedures. Due consideration is given to internal controls, and staffing, including hiring practices, compensation and fringe benefits, personnel qualifications, and morale.

In our financial analysis we scrutinize accounts receivable, accounts payable, and credit losses. But our focus is not just the debits and credits, but the management and the controls under which your systems function.

We also search for the undue concentration of resources among customers, vendors, or suppliers, and we study sales trends and patterns to locate vulnerabilities. If there is a computer system in place, we look at its effectivness in producing the information that management needs in a timely manner for budgeting, planning, and tax preparation.

Johnson & Associates believes that "good business is good business"—that the basic rules of organization and control apply to all. Although it's unwise to bury a company in policies and procedures, it's our opinion that when a company "puts it in writing" there's less chance of error, and more chance of success. We can help your company improve its internal operations and become more efficient and profitable in the process. ∎

JOHNSON & Associates
AN ACCOUNTANCY CORPORATION
3878 Carson Street · Suite 101 · P.O. Box 13666 · Torrance, CA 90503 · (310) 540-7477
4200 Rocklin Road · Suite 3 · P.O. Box 300 · Rocklin, CA 95677 · (916) 624-3779

EXHIBIT 7.5

Keynotes and Programs

Articles

Books, Videos, Audios

Quotes from Satisfied Clients

LOOK WHO'S TALKING ABOUT THE BOOK...

SELLING STRATEGIES FOR TODAY'S BANKER: A SURVIVAL GUIDE FOR TOMORROW

"Selling Strategies for Today's Banker is one of the most practical and useful books I have read on the subject of bankers and selling. It is written for bankers by authors who know and understand the dynamics of the banking industry."

Max Cook
Executive Vice President
Missouri Bankers Association

"Dennis and Niki McCuistion have become bank training superstars."

Robert E. Harris
President
Texas Bankers Association

"This may well be the most readable, comprehensive and compelling book yet on the who, what,

EXHIBIT 7.6

McCuistion
& Associates
"Talking about things that matter with people who care."

Dennis McCuistion, CSP

Professional Speaker, Author & TV Celebrity

Specialist: Banking, Leadership, Economics, Strategic Planning and Free Enterprise

- **CONSULTANT**
  Dennis McCuistion, a 35-year veteran of banking and related financial industries, founded **McCuistion & Associates** in Irving, Texas, where he serves as a consultant on financial matters to banks and businesses. During his banking tenure, he was CEO of two banks and served on the board of another.

- **SPEAKER**
  He develops and teaches seminars on banking, economics and free enterprise for financial institutions, corporate clients, conferences, schools and associations across the country. His keynote speeches are filled with humor and inspiration designed to move audiences to action. He has earned the Certified Speaking Professional designation, an award held by fewer than 5% of the National Speakers Association's 3500 members.

- **AUTHOR**
  Dennis is the author of <u>The Prevention and Collection of Problem Loans</u> and co-author of the just released <u>Selling Strategies for Today's Banker: A Survival Guide for Tomorrow</u>. He is a frequent contributor to trade journals and newspaper op-ed pages.

- **TV CELEBRITY**
  He is the host, and executive producer of the **McCUISTION** television program aired weekly throughout Texas, produced by his partner, Niki McCuistion. He is also co-host of the award-winning live T.V. program **Open Line**.

(Topics on reverse side)

601 San Juan Court   Irving, Texas 75062   214/717-0090

EXHIBIT 7.7

What They're Saying About Randy Pennington...

Randy G. Pennington Is Proud
To Have Served The Following Clients:

Randy G. Pennington

Randy G. Pennington is President of Pennington Performance Group, a Dallas-based training and consulting firm. Randy specializes in helping organizations and their people unleash the positive power of integrity, commitment and change. He's worked with many of this country's best managed organizations including Shell, Procter & Gamble, United Telephone of Florida, The Washington Post, Pearle, Inc. Georgia Power Company and Southwestern Bell Telephone to develop practical solutions to complex human resource and business issues. He is co-author of *On My Honor, I Will: Leading With Integrity In Challenging Times,* to be released by Warner Books in the Spring, 1992. Randy can be heard as a syndicated radio commentator on "Ninety Seconds For The '90s" and is an instructor for the Edwin L. Cox Business Leadership Center at Southern Methodist University.

Randy's background is a unique blend of line, staff and consulting experiences ranging from hourly employee to senior management. He holds a Bachelors and Masters Degree in Psychology and has completed Post-graduate work in Organization Administration and Management. Randy is an active member of the National Speakers Association, Secretary of the American Heart Association Texas Affiliate and serves on the board of the Dallas County Salvation Army Adult Rehabilitation Center.

EXHIBIT 7.8

EXECUTIVE Excellence®

THE MAGAZINE OF PERSONAL DEVELOPMENT, MANAGERIAL EFFECTIVENESS, AND ORGANIZATIONAL PRODUCTIVITY

RANDY G. PENNINGTON

Integrity-Driven Organizations

By taking seven steps, you can lead your organization to a new level of integrity in products, services, and relationships.

*H*E'S A REAL BOY SCOUT. Those words were used by a middle manager to describe his boss, and judging from his tone of voice, the comment was not meant as a compliment.

The common belief is that business is war with no rules—no trick is too dirty, no tactic too underhanded, no principle too sacred in this win-at-all-costs world.

In one scene in the movie *Wall Street*, the main character stands before a crowded stock holder meeting and declares, "Greed is good!" The rash of recent business and government scandals support the conclusion that art imitates reality. The desire to succeed has led many to the lure of expediency. The new moral code says, "If others do it, why shouldn't I?"

A Trip Down Memory Lane

Remember when the signature of a craftsman was the quality of his work? Remember when employees automatically used their best judgement to solve a customer's problem? When business deals were consummated with a hand shake? When "The customer is always right" was not a revolutionary concept? Remember when the integrity of an organization's products, services and relationships were the foundation of its success?

Times and values have apparently changed. The book, *The Day America Told The Truth*, reported the following to emphasize just how much: 91 percent of those surveyed admitted to lying about something on a regular basis; 50 percent will procrastinate, in effect doing nothing, one full day out of every five; and 74 percent will steal from those who will not miss it. If these statistics are true, they spell trouble. Deteriorating product quality and customer service are obvious effects. In addition, the trust level among employees may be strained at a time when teamwork is more critical than ever. Most important, customer perception that products and services do not meet stated standards or that the organization does not act in good faith will have an impact on the bottom-line.

Today's consumers are skeptical about the products they buy and the businesses they buy from. The message is clear: *Organizations must maintain the trust of their customers, employees, suppliers, and communities if they hope to succeed. And to do that, they must ensure the integrity of their products, services, and relationships.*

Integrity In Action

Integrity is more than ethics. It is the strict adherence to a set of principles that insures success. Integrity goes beyond a belief in moral principles to guide all aspects of personal and organizational performance. Integrity-driven organizations provide quality products and services out of duty; act ethically because it is consistent with their beliefs; and cultivate trust, commitment, and loyalty among customers, employees, and suppliers because it builds strong partnerships.

As a result, they experience fewer conflicts over the implementation of strategic decisions; more effective response when crisis situations arise; and increased trust, loyalty, and support from customers, employees, suppliers, and the community.

Johnson & Johnson, Lennox Heating & Air Conditioning, Mary Kay Cosmetics, JC Penney and Ben & Jerry's Ice Cream are a few of the many examples of integrity in business today. To identify other examples, ask:

• *Which organizations and leaders come to mind when you think of ones you can trust?*

• *Which organizations overdeliver on their promises of quality products and services?*

• *Which organizations and leaders can you count on to do what is right even when they are negatively affected?*

• *Which organizations hold their employees accountable for acting with integrity?*

• *Which organizations and leaders can be counted on to act consistently with stated beliefs and values?*

EXHIBIT 7.8 *(continued)*

MANAGEMENT

▼

Being A Good Scout Is In
In The '90s

by Randy Pennington
Pennington Performance Group

The words "He's a real Boy Scout" were used by a middle manager to describe his boss. Judging by his tone of voice, the comment was not meant as a compliment. That statement, or some variation thereof, has become synonymous with the belief that business is a war with no rules. Danny DeVito's character in the recent movie, "Other People's Money," sums up the goal of a win at all costs approach to business—"He who dies with the most toys wins."

Does that view hold true in real life? Apparently so. "The Day America Told The Truth" (Prentice Hall, 1991) reported the following:
• 91 percent of those surveyed admitted to lying about something on a regular basis.
• 74 percent will steal from those who will not miss it.
• 62 percent of the high school seniors surveyed believe that bankrupt businesses are under no moral obligation to repay their debt.

Inc. Magazine (February 1992) reported that 61 percent of respondents to its "Scout's Honor" Honesty Poll believed it is OK to "get around the law if you don't actually break it." One reader described the activity as "aggressive tax avoidance."

Unfortunately, businesses and business leaders who operate in this manner are guilty of another error that could affect their survival . . . not listening to their customers and communities.

The January 16, 1990 edition of *Parents* Magazine reported that 78 percent of respondents in a poll expressed a desire to return to "traditional values and old-fashioned morality." That desire is reflected in the actions of consumers. People have grown tired of products and services which do not live up to the promises advertised. They are demanding honesty,

integrity and fair dealing from the companies with which they do business. Those perceived as even remotely negligent will continue to draw the wrath of the public, media and regulatory groups. In other words, being a "good scout" is in in the '90s.

Eighty-Three Million People Can't All Be Wrong

Mention being a "good scout" and many will conjure up a picture of a young boy or girl dressed in uniform and doing a good deed. Others will remember summer camp, merit badges and knot tying. Hardly the stuff that prepares you for business survival in these turbulent times. But, look again. Scouting also teaches survival skills, self-discipline and core principles that insure long-term success. For instance:
• The Scout motto is "Be Prepared." That is good advice in a world where markets, technology, financial resources and regulatory requirements are changing faster than ever.
• The Scout oath talks of principles such as doing your best, doing your duty, helping other people and keeping yourself strong and awake. Anyone surviving in today's economy will tell you that it is almost impossible unless you do your best. Customer service is just another way of describing the need to help others. The same applies to involvement in community activities. The water companies which donated products to the Desert Storm Operation this time last year were following the oath. And, every operation must maintain their strength and stay awake for new opportunities if they hope to survive.
• The Scout law encourages us to be trustworthy, loyal, helpful, friendly, courteous, kind, obedient,

People (Exhibit 7.9). Even though the publication may not be the *New York* or *Los Angeles Times,* it still packs credibility because it is "media."

McCuistion also includes speech/seminar typics that he and his wife (Nikki) can present (Exhibit 7.10). Both are in the consulting field.

These press kit formats allow the client to browse quickly through the consultant's qualifications and read whatever they want. There is no need to go from front to back with a long, cumbersome brochure.

Qubein's brochure is packed with credibility. He has an extensive client list (Exhibit 7.11) and another insert that shows prospects the wide variety (and sizes) of audiences he has addressed (Exhibit 7.12)

Qubein also has two pages of endorsements from clients and he has a reprint of an article (credibility) that explains his philosophy and techniques (Exhibit 7.13).

Pennington includes a tri-fold, 8½ × 11 brochure in one of the press kit pockets. It is inexpensive and has two prime messages. On one side it gives a rundown of the programs Pennington presents (Exhibit 7.14). The other side is filled with quotes from pleased clients (Exhibit 7.15).

Alessandra's kit contains articles he has penned for various industry trade papers, and feature stories that have been written on him—both build credibility. (See Exhibit 7.16.)

This press-kit approach is being utilized frequently because it saves time for the busy executive, who has less time to spend than ever before. With a long brochure, the executive has to spend an inordinate amount of time reading before he finds out who he is dealing with and what qualifications they have.

Content for Brochures

A brochure or kit will not close a sale, but it does leave an important impression—positive or negative. The way the brochure looks is as important as what it says.

EXHIBIT 7.9

The McCuistion challenge: Get serious Dallas!

Gambling on their belief that people want to be informed about issues that affect them, business consultants and Las Colinas residents Dennis and Niki McCuistion plunged into the world of television talk shows three years ago.

Not the glitzy, screaming, sensational type; but discussions about serious issues with informed people. "Talking about things that matter with people who care" remains the theme of the program which debuted when Channel 27 agreed to offer the midnight hour Saturday nights.

With Dennis hosting and Niki as producer, eight shows emerged. One featured assistant Dallas County District Attorney Norman Kinne discussing the controversy which arose after the wife of Methodist minister Walker Railey was attacked in their home. Another featured Ravi Batra, author of *The Great Depression Of The 1990's.*

Response to the pilots prompted KDTN-Channel 2 PBS affiliate to offer an hour on Sunday mornings. Now winding up its second season, the McCuistion program can be seen Sundays at 1 p.m. and again at 11 p.m.

"We are building a following and our ratings are very good," said Niki. "We believe that the power of television, when combined with the understanding of important issues, can make significant, positive differences in the lives of people who watch."

Dennis and Niki also speak professionally and conduct training seminars around the country. Financial backing thus far has come from the McCuistions themselves and from several of their clients. While they benefit from use of Channel 2's studio and technical expertise, the show foots its own production costs. The McCuistions hope opportunities for underwriting will grow along with the program's audience.

Two shows taped this season were: "The Politics of Breast Cancer," featuring Nancy Brinker of the Komen Foundation; and "Rape: Is It Ever Over?" These programs marked executive producer Niki's fourth and fifth appearance as co-host.

"Warning: Is Breathing Hazardous To Your Health?" aired June 9; and "The Politics of Breast Cancer" aired June 16. Reruns will carry the McCuistions to season three in October, when they'll be back with new hard-hitting programs.

What lies ahead? The McCuistion Program is beginning to appear in markets outside of Dallas/Fort Worth. Already airing in Waco, Killeen and College Station, the show will soon be seen in El Paso, too.

"We've always thought of McCuistion as a Texas program which looks at both state and national issues," says Nikki.

"We're solutions-oriented to the extent of addressing issues and making viewers aware of ways to get involved," she adds. "Tune in and discover how the many issues of the 90's affect you personally and how you can change your world."

EXHIBIT 7.10

KEYNOTES AND MOTIVATIONAL PRESENTATIONS

Niki Nicastro McCuistion, CSP

- **EITHER LEAD, FOLLOW OR GET OUT OF THE WAY!**
  A challenging audience participation presentation on building leadership based on the foundation of integrity, mutual trust, respect and the shared vision and cooperation that empowers followers to commit to the organization's mission and achieve results.

- **INTEGRITY DRIVEN SELLING STRATEGIES**
  Selling in a competitive and challenging economy demands salespeople be more knowledgeable of their customers' business and its competitors, more in tune to their customers' needs and more willing than ever before to develop win-win, long-term customer - salesperson relationships. This participatory presentation outlines what it takes to succeed in sales today by meeting and exceeding your customers' expectations.

- **TOTAL QUALITY SERVICE: YOUR BEST SALES STRATEGY**
  How do some companies avoid time consuming and expensive mistakes, profit while others go out of business, gain strong market share while their competition suffers, and report gains, not losses? This practical, idea-packed presentation gives you how-to strategies and techniques to build a quality service program, empower staff and management to give superior customer service and develop teams that really listen to customers in a total quality service culture of participation, trust and integrity.

- **DEVELOPING THE HIGH PERFORMANCE TEAM: CREATING AND INSPIRING CHANGE, QUALITY AND PRODUCTIVITY**
  Creating an empowered organization with each member commited to continuous improvement and change may well be the success challenge of the '90s. This highly interactive presentation gives both management and staff specific tools to increase productivity, enhance performance and build self-confidence, and a road map for developing and working in teams that embrace change.

- **LEADERSHIP AND PEAK PERFORMANCE: A PLAN FOR ACTION**
  This keynote covers the ten characteristics of peak performers and how to attain them. It encourages the participants to commit to specific plans which meet their own personal or business goals.

- **FINANCIAL INSTITUTIONS: SIX GREATEST CHALLENGES OF THE '90s AND HOW TO MEET THEM**
  Our research has identified the six most important challenges that financial institutions will face in the '90s. More importantly, this program recommends six specific solutions which will allow financial institutions not only to survive, but to thrive.

© **McCuistion**   214/717-0090

EXHIBIT 7.11

A Message That's Right For America's Business Community.

As one of America's leading professional speakers, Nido Qubein has shared his wisdom, wit and insight with millions of people. He has spoken at more than 4,000 engagements in the past dozen years, in over 400 cities across the country and around the world. And year after year, corporate and association clients of all sizes invite him back. Because they know they can depend on Nido for excellence, on every occasion.

A Sampling Of Clients:

Corporations*

A. O. Smith Harvestore
Achievers Canada
Allied Safety Supply Company
Aluminum Distributors Company
American Can Company
AT&T
Amoco Fabric Company
Analytics Corporation
Ancilla Systems
Archway Cookies
Arvin Industries
Associates Corp. of North America
Associated Inns of America
B. B. Walker Shoe Company
Bama Pie Corporation
Bank of America
Barnhill Construction Co.
Bassett Furniture Company
Bedding Plants, Inc.
Best Western Hotels
Blacksmith Furniture Shop
Blount International, Ltd.
Blue Bird Wanderlodge, Inc.
Blue Cross and Blue Shield
Boling Chair Company
Borden Dairy, Inc.
Brayton International, Ltd.
Broyhill Furniture Industries
Builder Marts of America
Burris Furniture Company
Cambridge Savings & Loan Assn.
Capp Homes Corporation
Carlton Furniture Companies
Carlyle & Company Jewelers
Carolina Beauty Systems
Carolina Telephone Company
Carté Cosmetics

Castle & Cooke, Inc.
Chatham County Corporation
Chicago Pneumatic Tool Corp.
Chilton Corporation
Clarke Printing Company
Coachmen Industries
Command Performance
Cotton States Insurance
Coulter Electronics
Cox Broadcasting Company
Craddock-Terry Shoe Corp.
Craven Construction Company
Culp, Inc.
Curtis-Matheson Corp.
CUNA Mutual Insurance Group
Data General Corporation
Diamond Shamrock Corporation
Dible Management Institute
Dollar Rent A Car
Domino's Pizza Corporation
Durkee Foods
Dresher, Inc.
Edward Weck & Company
Erwin-Lambeth Furniture, Inc.
Evans Products
FTD, Inc.
Farm Bureau Insurance Company
Federal Land Bank of Louisville
Federal Land Bank of St. Paul
Federated Investors
Feld Truck Leasing Company
General Business Services
General Cassette Corp.
General Electric
Georgia Pacific
Glemby International
General Electric Info. Services

EXHIBIT 7.11 *(continued)*

Gold Medal Products Company
Greyhound Food Management, Inc.
Great American Seminars Corp.
Heublein, Inc.
Holiday Hair Fashions
Horizons Cable TV
Hubbard Farms
INA Bearing Company
INA Bearing Company of Canada
Image Improvement Corporation
Image Products Company
Industrial Housekeeping Systems
Integon Insurance Corporation
J.C. Penney's
John Harland Company
Kable News Company
Lacks' Stores, Inc.
L. G. Balfour, Inc.
Lampart Table Company
Land O'Lakes, Inc.
La-Z-Boy Chair Company
Life Insurance Co. of Georgia
Lyles Chevrolet Company
M & R Seal Corporation
M & T Bank
Maxon Industries, Inc.
Malden Mills
McKee Baking Company
McDonnell Douglass
Michigan Bakery Supply Co.
Mid-Atlantic Stihl, Inc.
Mid-State Tile Company
Miller Brewing Company
Milliken & Company
Minnesota Stihl, Inc.
Mobile Chemical Company
Mobile Home Industries
Moog Hydra-Point Corporation
Mooney Industrial, Inc.
Moore Business Forms
Mountain Bell Telephone Co.
Mr. Transmissions, Inc.
Nabisco
National Electronic Card Co.
National Electronic Distributors Assoc.
Norman Perry Lamp Company
North American Watch Company
North State Telephone Company
Northrop Corporation
Olympic Stain Corporation
Orkin Exterminating Company
Parkdale Mills
Porter Paint Company
Princeton Industries
Profit Freight Systems

Preferred Savings & Loan
Prudential Insurance Company
Pulsar Time
R. W. Moore Equipment Company
Rock-Tenn Company
Rockwell International
Rollins Protective Services
Romac & Associates
Royal Mark, Inc.
Scandinavian Design Stores
Schewell Furniture Company
School Pictures, Inc.
Schwaab, Inc.
Service Merchandise Company
Sherwood Medical Industries
Snyder Paper Company
Southern Trust Corporation
Southland Corporation
Spartan Stores
Star Manufacturing
State Farm Insurance Companies
Steelcraft Corporation
Stihl, Inc.
Superior Value Company
Swiss Colony Stores
Tennessee Valley Authority
Texas Corporate Supplies, Inc.
The Cooper Group
The Dana Corporation
The Falk Corporation
The Waymakers Group
Thermo King Corporation
Thomasville Furniture Company
Tidy Car, Inc.
Time Management Center
Tri-D Corporation
Tyson Foods
United Commercial Travelers of America
United States Furniture Industries
United States Leasing Corporation
ValCom Computer Company
Vallen Corporation
Vision Dynamics, Inc.
Walsworth Publishing Company
Watson-Bowman & Acme Corp.
Western Electric
Westwood Furniture Company

*This list of corporations includes only those that invited Nido to do one or more meetings for their employees and/or customers. It does not include the hundreds of corporations which sent representatives to hear Nido at public seminars and association conventions.

EXHIBIT 7.11 *(continued)*

National Associations
Adhesives Manufacturing Assn.
American Camping Association
American Feed Mfgrs. Assn.
American Furniture Mfgrs. Assn.
American Metal Stamping Assn.
American Pharmaceutical Assn.
American Society of Assn. Executives
American Society of Safety Engineers
American Trucking Association
Assoc. General Contractors of America
Credit Union National Assn.
Edison Electric Institute
Electronic Industries Assn.
Farm & Industrial Equipment Inst.
Farm & Power Dealers Assn.
Fibre Box Association
Food Marketing Institute
Grocery Mfgrs. National Assn.
Health Industries Distributors
Independent Buyers Association
Institute of Internal Auditors
Life Insurance Underwriters
Marking Device Association
National Apartment Assn.
National Assoc. of Furniture Mfgrs.
National Auctioneers Association
National Beauty Salon Assn.
National Home Furnishings
National Machine Tool Builders
National Paper Converters
National Spa & Pool Institute
National Speakers Association
National Tool Association
National Turkey Federation
Potato Chip Snack Food Assn.
Printing Ind. of America
Real Estate Leaders of America
Retail Bakers of America
Safety Equipment Distributors
September Days Club Assn.
Sheet Metal & Air Conditioning
Society of Mfgr. Engineers
Specialty Tools and Fasteners
Student American Pharmaceutical

State Associations
Assoc. Pennsylvania Constructors
California Beer Wholesalers
California Rental Association
Carolinas Travel Council
Connecticut Savings Banks Assn.
Credit Management Assn. of Greater
   Washington
Dairy Products Institute of Texas
Georgia Association of Educators

Georgia Data Processing Assn.
Georgia Farm & Power Equipment Dealers
Georgia Wholesale Grocers
Illinois Credit Union League
Indiana Auctioneers Assn.
Iowa Credit Union League
Kentucky Credit Union League
Michigan Assn. of Nurserymen
Minnesota Health Care Facilities
Missouri Credit Union League
New Hampshire Bankers Assn.
New Jersey Automobile Dealers
North Carolina Assn. of Ins. Agents
North Carolina Dairy Products
North Carolina Hotel Managers
North Carolina Motor Carriers
North Carolina Savings & Loan League
Oil Dealers of Washington
Pennsylvania Auctioneers Assn.
Saving League of Wisconsin
Tennessee Credit Union League
Tennessee Oil Jobbers Assn.
Texas Dairy Association
Texas Recreational Vehicles
Wisconsin Credit Union League
Wisconsin State Telephone Assn.
Virginia Bankers Association
Virginia Credit Union League
Virginia Farm & Industrial Dealers

International Associations
Int'l Data Processing Management
Int'l Foodservice Manufacturers
International Management Council
International Order of The Golden Rule
Meeting Planners International
Optimist International
Sales & Marketing Executives Int'l

Regional Associations
American Federation of Advertising Clubs
Carolinas Farm Power Equipment
DPMA Regional Association
Eastern Data Processing Management
Intermountain Assn. of Hardware Dealers
Southern Dairy Food Manufacturers
Southern Decorators Products
Southern Furniture Mfgrs.
Southern Textile Assn.
Southeastern John Deere Dealers
Southeastern Poultry and Egg

The above list of Association clients does not include scores of Chambers of Commerce, educational institutions, service and professional societies, and a host of other organizations.

EXHIBIT 7.12

GROUP	GROUP SIZE	LOCATION	ASSIGNMENT
Prudential Insurance Company	1200	Orlando, FL	Making four keynote addresses to Prudential's star salespeople plus four sales seminars is not an easy task. Creative Services and Nido Qubein were entrusted with the assignment, which resulted with Vice President Pat Buckley calling the meeting their "best ever."
General Electric Information Services	600	Honolulu, HI	Only General Electric's top producers attended. Nido gave a short, entertaining keynote on the first day . . . and an intensive personal profile lab session on the second day analyzing individual strengths and weaknesses.
Mobile Chemical Corporation	25	Key Biscayne, FL	The Design Products Division of Mobile assembled its zone sales group for an intensive workshop. Nido developed a tailored presentation showing how industrial salespeople can penetrate the market profitably.
Wrangler	95	Miami, FL	The merchandising and sales departments of Wrangler Boyswear engaged Nido Qubein for help in organizing and producing their last two national meetings . . . as well as training presenters in advance and speaking himself during the sessions in Miami.
Diamond Shamrock Corporation	40	Naples, FL	This was a challenging assignment. The salespeople came from all over the world. And Nido's task was to communicate effectively, using methods that can apply internationally, the key steps to profitable selling strategies.
North American Watch Company	38	New York, NY	How does one train and inspire a group of top-notch salespeople who market some of the world's finest time pieces? It's a challenging assignment. Nido carefully prepared a full-day workshop, designed to introduce a system for persuasive selling, and to familiarize the sales team with customer behavioral tendencies.

Company	Number	Location	Description
Integon Insurance Corporation	75	Various locations nationally	Integon's management charged Nido to design, create, and administer a sales/management training program aimed at elevating skills for better performance in an increasingly competitive market. The project included the development of cassettes and written handouts.
Nabisco	60	Dorado Beach, Puerto Rico	The group consisted of bakery managers from across the United States along with top management. Nido concluded the conference with an address defining the profile of a results-oriented manager in today's economy.
Thermo King Corporation	180	Various locations nationally	Thermo King hosted three regional management meetings for all of its distributors in the United States and Canada. As part of a highly sophisticated multi-media production, Nido's role included the presentation of a message that closed the meeting on a high note.
U. S. Furniture Industries	1,000	Various locations nationally	U. S. Furniture Industries owns and operates eight different companies with plants from coast to coast. Since 1976, the company has had Nido on a retainer to develop and present quarterly sessions to front-line supervisors, middle to top management, and sales group.
Wisconsin Savings League	200	Stevens Point, WI	Never before had the day-long program highlighted a single trainer, but this time, the Wisconsin Savings League brought their statewide branch managers to learn from Nido Qubein. The day, with input from the League, provided a total system for effective interpersonal relations.
ValCom Computer Stores	100	Various locations nationally	A division of Valmont Industries, ValCom wanted to bring together its franchisees to four regional locations nationally. Nido was highlighted at each meeting as a management consultant who brought forth a wealth of practical information.

221

EXHIBIT 7.12 (continued)

GROUP	GROUP SIZE	LOCATION	ASSIGNMENT
State Farm Insurance Companies	350	**Asheville, NC**	Here Nido addressed State Farm's Millionaires Club — their most outstanding sales representatives. In an after-dinner speech he inspired the group to continue seeking its standard of excellence, and provided a four-point system for personal growth.
Moore Business Forms	700	**Cerromar Beach, Puerto Rico**	On two different occasions, Moore entrusted to Nido the opportunity to address its Top Achievers Club. As the largest company in its field, Moore wanted more than a simple motivational speech.
Stihl, Inc.	260	**Virginia Beach, VA**	Stihl is the world's largest manufacturer of chain saws. At its United States headquarters, Nido provided a retail sales training program for all of the Stihl distributors and their salespeople. His delivery was so well received that numerous repeat engagements were scheduled.
INA Bearing Company	35	**Various locations internationally**	Nido developed a total sales training program, including audio visual materials, and personally held sessions with INA's industrial salesmen. He has an on-going agreement now to counsel with management and to train the salesforce.
Borden Dairy	400	**Houston, TX**	Academic lectures were out of the question. This was the annual strategic planning conference and Borden needed a powerful message emphasizing corporate growth and individual development. Nido Qubein was their choice.
Heublein's	120	**Hartford, CT**	The Spirits Group decision-makers were assembled at Heublein's headquarters for a demanding five-day seminar. Nido's responsibility was to close the last morning of the meeting with a tailored presentation on effective communication skills.

Princeton Industries Corporation	250	Various locations nationally	This highly successful manufacturer of fund-raising products employed Nido over a three-year period to guide its top management in developing total organizational and training systems. Services included seminars, workbooks, cassettes, and a host of other personalized tools.
Cox Broadcasting Company	32	Atlanta, GA	Cox Broadcasting is one of this nation's largest independent radio and television networks. They asked Nido to address their top management convention with a carefully tailored presentation aimed at introducing the group to sophisticated leadership skills.
Carté Cosmetics	150	High Point, NC	For this direct sales company, Nido created and presented the programs for two Management Institutes. In addition, he counsels regularly with top management on various topics including recruiting, marketing, advertising, training, and personal development.
AT&T	120	New York and San Francisco	On three occasions when AT&T assembled groups of their sales management teams, their choice for a trainer was Nido Qubein. His challenge was to develop special sessions to aid AT&T personnel in marketing their services effectively.
Marking Device Association	630	Various locations nationally	This national association engaged Nido to speak at its annual convention and its three regional meetings. The main focus was on training its small-business members to use direct mail effectively.
Milliken & Company	250	Spartanburg, SC	When Milliken's Interior Furnishings Division developed a promotional program with Eastern Airlines, they invited some of America's largest manufacturers and retailers to national orientation conferences. The professional speaker that Milliken assigned to keynote and conclude these sessions was Nido Qubein....a speaker they have utilized many times since.

EXHIBIT 7.13

PROFILE

Speeches, writings combine to give clients the big picture

Educating business

by Joann Cassell

Circus animals are trained. People are educated.

Management consultant Nido Qubein illustrated the difference with a story about a trip to a fast food restaurant. "I was waited on by an obviously bright, well-trained young woman, and I ordered a milk shake and an apple pie. 'Sir,' she asked me, 'would you like a dessert to go with that?,'"

Qubein, 40, chairman of Creative Services Inc. of High Point, an international consulting firm specializing in employee development, said the exchange told him that some employer's training program was paying off. "She was obviously told to try to sell a dessert with every order, and she was operating exactly as trained. American corporations are spending millions to train, not educate, their employees. You have to teach [employees] how to learn, how to proact and react — training only shows them how to handle a specific situation."

Creative Services has five full-time writers who help Qubein develop proprietary employee development programs. For a major bank with 4,000 employees, his company might create a complete system of learning from tellers to top management. For a machine manufacturer, he might devise an educational program for the sales force, including written materials and audiovisual aids.

'**W**e can create a learning system for any industry that has people, whether they sell bearings or financial systems. We don't sell off-the-shelf programs; we talk to top management about their objectives, then we create fully integrated, customized programs for each client. That's the difference between us and many other employee development consultants," said Qubein, who calls himself a "change agent."

Despite his emphasis on designing comprehensive learning systems, Qubein's fame began — and continues to grow — as a motivational speaker. He speaks about 100 times a year for undisclosed fees. He is one of nine recipients of "The Cavett," considered the Oscar of the speaking profession. In 1986, he was inducted into the International Speakers Hall of Fame. A past president of the National Speakers Association, he continues to be active as chairman of the National Speakers Association Foundation.

From his plush office and private recording studio, Qubein turns out a steady stream of motivational tapes and inspirational books distributed worldwide by Prentice Hall and Nightingale-Conant. But he emphasizes that those tapes and books cannot take the place of an ongoing educational program. "We sell expertise. We don't sell books and tapes. To me, you

"**We don't sell** off-the-shelf programs; we talk to top management about their objectives, then we create fully integrated, customized programs for each client," said management consultant and motivational speaker Nido Qubein, chairman of Creative Services Inc. in High Point.

Photo by Julie Knight

don't read a book and develop yourself to your fullest potential," said the author of more than 30 books, including *Get the Best from Yourself: The Complete System of Personal and Professional Development.*

Polishing his English speaking and writing skills required years of practice for Qubein, who came to the United States from his native Lebanon in 1966 to attend Mount Olive College. Friendships made as a counselor at Camp Cheerio, High Point's YMCA camp in Roaring Gap, brought Qubein to High Point College. He received a bachelor's degree in human relations there in 1970 and a master's degree in business from the University of North Carolina at Greensboro in 1973.

In 1971, Qubein started a small publishing company with $500 in savings. He wrote, edited and collated leadership materials, which he then sold by direct mail. "People began to buy, and then they began to say 'Hey, would you come speak to my group,'" he said. "I started speaking in 1973, and I was soon giving more than 300 presentations a year."

EXHIBIT 7.13 *(continued)*

By 1978, Qubein said, the business had reached a plateau. "I was giving 300 talks a year to companies like AT&T and Nabisco. But I realized I wasn't doing anything important. The value of inspirational talks is limited — they work for a while, but pretty soon, you go back to doing things the way you did before. In fact, motivation can actually cause frustration because people are really looking for education. Education must be repetitive to work, and it must allow for practical application of what you're learning. Companies will send employees to seminars, but they don't allow their people to use what they've learned."

He expanded into management consulting, using his speaking engagements as a way to get people interested in learning more. "As I began to expand, I found an incredible hunger for education. Once upon a time, you just had to make the best tables to make a good living. Now you have do more — you have to know how to keep employees and how to work with them to be successful," Qubein said. "Imagine what happens if we could change the behavior of just 2 percent of your employees with this program, perhaps another 2 percent next time. Unless you have a short view, the question is not whether a company ought to develop an employee education program but whether you can afford not to."

But in too many businesses, Qubein said, "The dailiness of life takes over and [executives] find themselves dealing with issues as they arise, rather than planning a management strategy and employee development programs. People tend to come to us when they have a pain — their people aren't selling, their turnover is bad. Often it's a positive pain: They've reached a plateau in growth, and they don't know where to go next."

Most executives don't know how to create their own employee education programs or how to find someone to do it for them. More than $6 billion is spent on consultants each year, said Qubein, who estimates his multimillion dollar business has only scratched 1 percent of the potential corporate market.

"I go to a dentist to get my teeth cleaned and to a mechanic to get my car fixed," he said. "Companies who aren't large enough to have their own employee development programs can still work with a specialist."

Although he consults for multibillion dollar corporations like AT&T and General Electric, most of his clients are small- to medium-sized companies with five to 100 salespeople. All his business comes by word of mouth, Qubein said, and about three-quarters of his clients are repeat customers. A fee is negotiated by the project, and Qubein remains involved to some degree in each project Creative Services handles.

"You can look at the cost of an employee education program as a percentage of sales or by how much it costs per person. But you have to know [the client] how that investment relates to other investments — the speaker at your seminar may be expensive, but he probably costs less than the open bar before dinner," he said.

"The client wants to know 'What's in it for me?' I believe you can measure the performance [of an employee education program]. It won't be as statistical as production figures on a factory line, but you can see the results in sales and customer satisfaction. The byproduct ought to be a happier employee who is less likely to leave."

In most cases, Creative Services creates the program, then turns its implementation over to the client. "The ideal is for us to go in and do a needs analysis and find out where the company wants to go. Then in a year or two or three, we leave and they take over," he said.

For Bama Foods, a Tulsa, Okla., manufacturer of apple and cherry pies for the snack food industry, Qubein developed a sales and marketing program, did strategic planning and created the Bama Institute for employee development. As part of the project, he wrote scripts for Bama's chief executive officer so she could record her own motivational tapes for employees. "You can't have any ego in this business," said Qubein, who also turns executives into "instant experts" by ghostwriting their books.

For First Citizens Bank of Raleigh, he is developing complete educational materials for sales and customer service. "They had a training program, but it was mostly in technical areas. We talk to the employees about attitude and communication. You don't teach, you educate people to learn. You can't drill a hole in someone's head and pour the knowledge in. But through continuous repetition — with in-person seminars, audio cassettes, written insider reports — it will stick."

With two or three exceptions, Qubein deliberately has avoided the furniture industry. "First of all, I want to be able to enjoy living in High Point. I didn't want to see a client every time I went out anywhere," he said. "Second, for the most part, the furniture industry has not made a complete commitment to its people yet. That's changing, though, I think."

If Qubein enjoys living in High Point, it is clear the feeling is mutual. He recently was awarded the 1988 Triad Rotary Citizenship Award and the 1988 High Point College Alumnus of Year Award. He is past president of the Furnitureland Rotary Club, chairman of the 1988-89 American Cancer Crusade, trustee of Westchester Academy and serves on the board of visitors for High Point College.

As important as his business and community activities are, Qubein said his family is top priority. He and his wife are expecting their fourth child. He leaves work shortly after 5 p.m. for a jog and dinner at home. He doesn't work nights or weekends unless he is speaking out of town, and he takes two months off every summer. "Clients say, 'What an easy job, Nido. I can't take all that vacation.' But I tell them, one, I have good people working for me, and, two, that what I do is so intense, I would burn out if I didn't take a break."

Another priority is the Nido Qubein Associates Scholarship Fund, started in 1971, when Qubein was fresh out of school. It has provided scholarships to 175 students at North Carolina private colleges, including High Point College. About 100 area businesses also contribute to the fund.

"That gives me great joy. I really have a passion for these scholarships. I need to help other people because so many people have helped me," Qubein said. "God has given me a gift for living, and I believe it requires me to spend one-third of my life learning, one-third serving and one-third earning. As long as your goals are consistent with values, I think this is a good business in which to serve, yet learn and earn." □

EXHIBIT 7.14

Keynotes:

On My Honor, I Will: Leading With Integrity. Integrity is the foundation on which long-term success is built. Learn practical steps for developing integrity-driven leaders and organizations. Discover why integrity is the single most important factor in mobilizing your organization for commitment and change.

Toto, I Don't Think We're In Kansas Anymore. The world has never changed faster than it's changing today. Learn two truths, three "P's" and six lessons for effectively managing change and insuring success.

The Five Most Important Words For Success In The Nineties. Successful organizations and individuals actively manage their future. Learn five words to help you direct your energy, why they are important and how to make them work for you.

WORKPLACE 2000.™ Preparing For Tomorrow's Challenges Today. How will the successful organization of the future look? Discover the answer to this question and more. Learn the issues that will affect your organization and strategies to insure your success in the future.

Consulting Services

Let Randy work with you to design and implement a systematic approach for managing change, building commitment and becoming integrity-driven.

Seminars and Workshops:

INTEGRITY DRIVEN™ Leadership. Integrity is the foundation for successful leadership. Learn specific skills to build employee trust, empower action, and help the organization maintain integrity in its products, services and relationships.

The COMMITTED PERFORMER.™ Discover why commitment is the key to long-term success and learn three habits that help you succeed. This workshop promotes individual commitment, develops skills that enhance effectiveness and recognizes that organizational success depends on individual success.

Building Committed Organizations. Discover the characteristics of committed organizations and the five groups to whom commitments must be made and honored to insure success. Learn how to accomplish the five critical tasks for building a committed organization.

WORKPLACE 2000.™ An in-depth opportunity to determine how your organization should look in the future and learn a five-step model to get you there.

Find out how Randy can work his magic for you.

PENNINGTON PERFORMANCE GROUP
4000 WINTER PARK LANE DALLAS, TEXAS 75244
TELEPHONE 800 779 5295 IN DALLAS (214) 980 9857

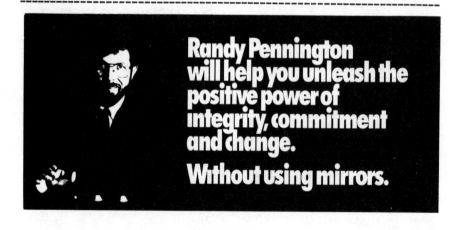

Randy Pennington will help you unleash the positive power of integrity, commitment and change. Without using mirrors.

EXHIBIT 7.15

Its not magic. Just unbelievable results, right before your eyes.

Randy is a high-content speaker, workshop leader, author and consultant with a "human" style.

He provides practical solutions to the challenges of:

— Building and maintaining *integrity* in your products, services and relationships

— Building individual and organizational *committment*

— *Managing change* and positioning your organization for success in the future

No illusions here. He knows what really works.

Over the past fourteen years, Randy's worked with industry leaders such as GE, Georgia Power, Procter & Gamble, Shell, Hitachi, Pearle and Southwestern Bell to help solve their most complicated and sensitive business and human resource issues.

His background is a unique blend of line, staff and consulting experiences that enable him to focus on what really works.

Randy's first book, On My Honor, I Will: Leading With Integrity In Challenging Times, has been described by Former US President Gerald Ford as "A blueprint on how leaders became successful by following the path of honor and integrity. A challenge to the next generation to reach the top by embracing the same high principles."

His commentaries on important issues facing American business are heard on "90 Seconds For The '90s."

He makes an amazing difference.

"We asked Randy to speak to 650 of our people and the results were amazing. His presentations were of consistently high quality. The content was directly on target... In short, he was a hit."

James C. "Bing" Brown
Manager, Information Department
Salt River Project

"Randy is excellent as both a presenter and facilitator. He is humorous and knowledgeable. He is energetic, and he instills in members of the audience the same enthusiasm for a subject, as he has."

Kay L. Wolf
Assistant Vice President, Law
United Telephone System

"Randy Pennington is a dynamic and exciting presenter. Our members are experts on professional speakers and Randy received "excellent" ratings across the board. He delivers what he promises and more!"

Marilyn Monroe, CAE
President
Texas Society of Association Executives

"Randy took the time to learn our issues and focus on specific "how to's." He produces high quality materials to go along with his quality presentations. Our members think he's great and the staff finds working with him a pleasure."

William F. Deal, CAE
Executive Vice President
International Bottled Water Association

"Working with Randy is a special experience. You get more than you bargained for. He believes in giving something more—100% is not quite enough."

Jane Beauchamp
Director, Human Resources
Charter Hospital of Savannah

EXHIBIT 7.16

Selling Strategies

By Dr. Anthony J. Alessandra
Alessandra & Associates, Inc.
La Jolla, CA

Fact-finding:
How to ask the right questions

Are you envious of a fellow salesperson who picks the right questions to ask in a fact-finding situation? Probing—asking the right questions at the right time—is essential to success in sales. Probes help prospects "open up." When prospects feel free to reveal feelings, current situations, finances, needs, and desires, the salesperson knows how to help them, service the business, write additional business, and obtain referrals.

Amazingly, the fine art of asking questions is seldom taught. Law schools typically instruct students on productive ways to use questions within the courtroom where a witness has sworn to tell the truth, but these cases have little bearing on the world outside the courtroom where people are not obliged to answer.

In the sales world, finely honed skills must be applied in order to obtain meaningful and truthful information.

Through skillful questioning, you initiate and maintain conversation that leads to sales and builds your image as a professional. No matter whether your prospects are reticent or talkative, your probing skills help you to uncover and identify their needs.

Keep in mind the following general strategies as you select the questions to ask your present and potential prospects.

Questions must be properly timed. If your prospects are not in the proper frame of mind to receive questions, you will not get accurate or complete answers.

Questions should not be asked too quickly or too slowly; timing is important in getting answers. After asking a question, allow enough time for your client to think and come up with an answer. Asking questions too quickly gives the impression of impatience and comes across more as an interrogation than a sales interview. On the other hand, asking questions too slowly can lead to a quick case of boredom.

Have a questioning plan. Although it is not generally advisable to memorize specifically worded questions that you will ask in a particular sequence to every client, it is productive to have a questioning strategy—particularly in a client service interview. You should have a clear idea of what you want to ask in order to get the information required to do a good job.

A list of the points you want to cover, a "survey sheet," allows you to explore fruitful areas as they arise in the conversation. When you leave your planned questions to explore other areas, you can use your list to bring you back on track. Remember that you only need a reminder of the information you desire. You do not need specifically worded questions.

Ask permission to ask questions. This is a good rule of thumb: Even though you feel that you have the right to ask prospects questions in your role as their advisor, you will find that the simple courtesy of asking permission will put them at ease. This show of respect sets a positive tone for a sales presentation. It is a first step toward building trust, and will allow an honest, straightforward exchange of information.

Move from broad to narrow questions. "Can you tell me a little about your financial plans for retire-

ment?" is an excellent example. This broad, open-ended question allows your client total freedom to answer whichever way he or she wishes.

Clients may not answer with sharply defined plans of action, but they will indicate areas of concern and interest to the salesperson who listens. From the answers, specific needs become obvious, and you will know how to follow-up with specific questions.

Your ability to listen carefully to the response will guide your choice of the next question. You will know how to narrow your inquiry based on the previous response. For instance, your second question might be, "You mentioned that you would like to invest your pension funds in a small business when you retire. Would you mind elaborating on the kind of business you have in mind?" Subsequent questions may narrow even further to explore in more detail the needs and concerns of your client.

Build on previous responses. Simply stated, listen carefully before questioning. Rather than becoming preoccupied with what you want to ask next, and missing most— if not all—of what your prospects are communicating to you, concentrate on what they say. This information can be used to frame subsequent questions, based on your client's responses.

By building on previous responses, you show that you are, in fact, listening to what they are telling you. Also, you get the opportunity to explore areas of interest to your prospects that you, on your own, might not have chosen to explore had you not truly listened.

EXHIBIT 7.16 *(continued)*

Selling Strategies

By effectively mastering the fine art of questioning, a professional salesperson fills the role of problem solver, counselor and consultant.

Use common language. Keep your questions free of slang and technical jargon that may or may not be understood by your prospects. In addition, avoid flowery, formal or legal language. In phrasing your questions, keep in mind the famous K.I.S.S. formula — Keep it Short and Simple. Also avoid "hundred dollar" words that you believe might impress your prospects.

By using simple language, devoid of superfluous terminology, your questions will be easy to understand, and more likely to result in accurate and straightforward information.

Balance the number of questions that you ask. Asking too few questions can be seen as shallow. For instance, you might ask, "How are you?" Or "How's your job treating you?" And after receiving answers to these questions, move right into discussing your own interests. It doesn't take long for prospects to see you for what you really are — a shallow, ritualistic questioner only utilizing questions as springboards for your sales presentation.

On the other hand, asking too many questions without sharing some of yourself can be seen as an interrogation. It creates an information imbalance in which your prospects provide you with too much information — and you do not give enough. This increases interpersonal tension and decreases trust. Always try to balance the number of questions you ask with the information that both you and your prospects need.

Questions should not be manipulative. They should not limit your client's personal autonomy, force them into an answer, or put them on the spot. "How does your morning look for a meeting this week?" is better than asking, "Would you prefer to see me at 10:00 a.m. on Tuesday, or at 3:00 p.m. on Wednesday?"

Effective, non-manipulative salespeople realize the importance of protecting the dignity of their prospects. They know that if they insult peoples' intelligence with blatant manipulation, they will be poorly received and less likely to close sales.

Keep your questions non-threatening. Threatening questions such as, "How much money do you want to spend on...?" (when asked at the start of a sales interview) usually will raise tension and decrease trust. Other sensitive areas involve annual income, investments, marital status, health, religion, etc. Questions which embarrass (if answered truthfully) encourage avoidance of the truth. Beware of answers when probes touch sensitive areas; if your prospects seem uncomfortable with the question, and you don't really need the answer, move on to a different subject.

Provide a rationale for sensitive questions. When you must touch on sensitive areas, be sure to explain why you are asking the question. Phrase the question in as non-threatening a manner as possible. With proper preparation, prospects can anticipate the question and be ready to answer. Suspicions vanish and anxieties subside. If a client remains anxious, back off a bit, explain your purpose, and ask a second time. Just be sure that you need the information causing your client's uneasiness.

Ask "benefit" questions. If you want your initial questions to produce the most useful and complete information, structure them to ask about the benefits or end results the prospects want to achieve, rather than the specific policies or amounts of coverage.

Focusing your discussion around benefits allows prospects to speak freely, and at the same time, provides you with more latitude in designing meaningful solutions to satisfy their needs. Structure your questions around the bottom-line benefit that your client is trying to achieve.

Maintain a consultative atmosphere. Remember that your ultimate role in the sale process is that of an advisor. Do not ask questions in an interrogative, rapid-fire manner; you are not a prosecutor with your prospects on the witness stand. High pressure usually is counterproductive.

Use a relaxed and quiet tone of voice, giving prospects time to contemplate your questions -even if it means a period of silence. By pausing and allowing them time to think, you will get more accurate and complete replies.

Allow your prospects to completely answer each of your questions without interrupting. Above all, show empathy and understanding during the entire sales process. This applies not only to the words you use, but in the way you say them and the non-verbal signals you project.

The non-manipulative approach to selling relies on skillful questioning by the salesperson. In order to help prospects solve their problems, you have to uncover what those problems are. By effectively mastering the fine art of questioning, a professional salesperson fills the role of problem solver, counselor and consultant.

The final result is more sales, more satisfied prospects, and more public respect for your profession.▲

EXHIBIT 7.16 *(continued)*

master salesmanship®

The newsletter for professional salespeople

**VOL. 10 ISSUE 4
FEBRUARY 15, 1988**

Conversational Selling: The Non-Manipulative Approach to Sales

by Dr. Tony Alessandra
President, Alessandra & Associates

S ALESPEOPLE are among the highest paid professionals in our society. Why, then, do so few people respect sales as a career? The answer, in a word, is *pressure!*

Tension-producing pressure causes traditional salespeople and their clients to feel uneasy, displeased and distrustful of their sales interaction. But such pressure is NOT an integral part of selling. It does not have to go along with the job. This is what conversational selling is all about.

Both the old high-pressure and the new conversational philosophies recognize four basic stages in the sales process: Information-gathering, Proposal, Confirmation and Follow-through. But the relative amount of time spent in each stage of the process is significantly different.

Stage 1. Information-gathering. In the information-gathering stage, the salesperson and client find out if there is something the client wants or needs that the salesperson can provide. The high-pressure (traditional) salesperson spends more time in small talk and then, acting on the assumption that the client wants/needs the product or service, launches into the presentation (pitch).

The conversational (progressive) salesperson, in order to build a solid, accurate informational base, spends more time on defining client needs than on any other part of the sales process. This phase is divided into three parts:

1. Planning. Maximizes the efficient use of your time by making sure you're pursuing the right prospects (markets). Involves territory, time and account management; market planning and analysis; prospect planning and call preparation.

2. Meeting. Develops person-to-person rapport and begins a "business friendship."

3. Studying. Encourages the client to provide pertinent information such as business needs and objectives, financial status, personal "behavioral" style and so on.

Stage 2. Proposal. Both traditional and conversational (progressive) selling methods allocate about equal amounts of time to the proposal or presentation, but that's where the similarity ends.

The traditional salesperson gives a standard presentation to all clients, regardless of their individual needs. In the progressive approach, the proposal is custom-tailored to the client's specific business situation and personal style.

Stage 3. Confirming the sale. In this stage, the buyer makes a commitment to implement the agreed-upon solution.

In high-pressure sales transactions, the majority of time is spent overcoming buyer objections and trying to

---

What to do when a customer says, "NO"

When a customer says he or she doesn't want to buy, professional salespeople don't take this refusal personally. Instead, they look for ways to turn the "no" into a "yes."

Experience has taught these salespeople that a simple question such as, "Why not?" can often uncover a prospect's reason for not buying. A customer may have misunderstood the terms of the sale or have a problem that can be easily resolved.

Other valuable questions you may want to ask are, "What can I do to change your mind?" or, "Are you satisfied with the price I've quoted?"

If the customer still says, "No," ask permission to call on him or her again in the future. You have nothing to lose and everything to gain.

---

close the sale despite the resistance of the "stubborn" customer. The tension level soars. Problems arise because the salesperson has inadvertently pressured the buyer into revealing his or her hidden objections at this late stage of the sale. (The best time to deal with customer objections is early-on in the information-gathering stage, because objections are an important source of information.)

The conversational salesperson doesn't need to hustle for the close or push for a commitment, because the solution has already been agreed upon, and confirming the sale becomes a question of "when and how," not "if."

Stage 4. Assuring customer satisfaction. At this point, the salesperson makes a commitment to the buyer to provide the promised product or service, and to keep in touch with him or her throughout their business relationship. Traditional salespeople tend to minimize the concept of continual service. Their casual acquaintance with the client fades, so that the seller has to reestablish rapport the next time a sales call is made.

The conversational salesperson never lets the relationship fade in the first place. He or she makes a commitment to the buyer to provide service and assistance in the spirit of customer satisfaction.

Tony Alessandra is one of America's premier sales and communications speakers. He has written many articles and several books, including the popular Non-Manipulative Selling published by Prentice-Hall. He has been featured in films produced by Walt Disney and McGraw Hill, including the award-winning Power of Listening film, and in many audio and video cassette programs. For a listing, contact: Alessandra & Associates, Inc., PO Box 2767, La Jolla, CA 92038. (800) 222-4383.

EXHIBIT 7.16 *(continued)*

THE·SQUARE·YARD

The professional journal of the American Floorcovering Association

| October 1990 | Volume 14, Number10 , $3.00 |

PROJECTING A PROFESSIONAL SALES IMAGE

by Dr. Anthony Alessandra

Have you ever seen yourself on TV or video tape? Have you heard your voice on a tape recorder? Have you examined photographs of yourself? How did you look and sound - to yourself? Were you projecting the type of image you would like others to see? These self-images are very important because they give you an idea of how you may be coming across to other people, either positively or negatively.

Projecting an appropriate image to other people significantly hastens the development of trust and rapport, with people.

With an appropriate image, other people will feel much more comfortable and much more at ease around you, thus making it easier for you to communicate with them. On the other hand, if your image is inappropriate, it will create a roadblock that will severely hamper effective communication.

Salespeople who attend to the guidelines of image tend to be more successful than those who do not. Those salespeople who look and act like professionals have a decided edge over those who do not convey a professional image.

The critical importance of the image you project to others is underscored by the well-accepted fact that the famous debate between John F. Kennedy and Richard M. Nixon was won by Kennedy primarily because of his physical image, not by the verbal content of his speech. That turned out to be a major turning point in that presidential elec-

tion. With that in mind, let's take a closer look at the six critical components of your professional image.

Dr. Anthony Alessandra

FIRST IMPRESSIONS

"First impressions are lasting impressions." We have all heard that saying before, but have you ever given it serious thought? Have you ever contemplated the ramifications of your first impressions on other people - the way you dress, your voice, grooming, handshake, eye contact, and body posture? The way you choose to manipulate each of these various factors greatly affects how other people will initially perceive you.

It is an unusual individual who does not make particular value judgments about a person with a heavy Brooklyn accent, a weak handshake, sloppy grooming, poor hygiene, bad vocabulary, poor posture, or ill-fitting clothing. Take the risk of asking one or more of your close friends if you are guilty of any of these peccadillos. If so, first thank your friends for their honesty, and then immediately do something

to correct any of your image deficiencies.

DEPTH OF KNOWLEDGE

This area refers to how well you know your subject - your particular area of expertise. How well do you know your company, your industry, your competition, and your customers? You should make every effort to learn as much as possible about your particular area of expertise. Take advantage of any training programs that your company or industry may offer as well as doing your own independent study. By increasing your depth of knowledge, you will command respect from your customers, co-workers, and competition by projecting an image of intelligence and credibility.

BREADTH OF KNOWLEDGE

This area deals with your ability to converse with others in fields outside *(continued on page two)*

American Floorcovering Association
13-154 Merchandise Mart, Chicago, IL 60654
(800) 776-3566/FAX: 312-644-2787
Edward Korczak-Publisher
Janet L. Milakis-Editor/Writer
Susan Ing-Assistant Editor

EXHIBIT 7.16 *(continued)*

T H E · S Q U A R E · Y A R D

Professional Sales Image

(continued from page one)
of your own particular area of expertise. When you are willing and able to talk with people about topics that are of interest and importance to them, those people will feel much more comfortable being in your presence. In fact, people will go out of their way to talk with you. By increasing your breadth of knowledge, you will increase your circle of influence with various types of people.

FLEXIBILITY
Flexibility is your willingness and ability to interact effectively with other people on their level. You practice flexibility every time you slow down with another person who does not feel as comfortable moving as fast as you do. You also practice flexibility when you take time to listen to a personal story from another person, rather than getting right down to the task at hand.
Flexibility is required because of the fact that people are different and need to be treated differently. You develop open and honest relationships with others by being tactful, reasonable, and understanding.

ENTHUSIASM
If you want others to show enthusiasm, you must project that quality yourself. It doesn't just happen. Enthusiasm is like a disease; it's catching - positive or negative. When you outwardly show enthusiasm yourself, the same attitude will rub off on others - and vice versa. The choice is yours. Which will you choose?

SINCERITY
This is the final aspect of a professional image. This simply means that you cannot and should not, fake it.

Above all else, be sincere in your interactions with other people and project that sincerity to them.

If you come across as insincere to others, it will have a more damaging effect on your relationship with them than

if you violated all the above components of image in the first place.
From the beginning to the end of every transaction with another person, you are on stage. Every word, gesture, expression, and impression that you project will be seen and evaluated, consciously or subconsciously, by others. That image you project will facilitate or impede your success with others.
Therefore, go through great pains to make sure that the image you project in each and every transaction is an image that helps facilitate and foster open, honest and trusting communications. Project a professional sales image.

Dr. Anthony Alessandra is one of America's premier sales and communications keynote speakers. Since becoming a full-time speaker in 1979, he has delivered more than 700 professional speeches and has authored five books. For a free catalog please call or write to: Alessandra & Associates, PO Box 2767, La Jolla, CA 92038., or call 800/222-4383; in California 619/459-4525.

SUBTLE SELLING
by Dr. Anita Jacobs

As we try to persuade others to see things our way, we're "selling" our point of view about a product or service or an idea. Sales and marketing professionals recognize that they often utilize a wide array of communication styles in their persuasion efforts.
Sometimes we speak with carefully chosen words and with the sound of our voice. As individuals, we can be significantly more effective if we increase our understanding of the subtle nuances of the very significant image we project - our spoken image, the "Speaking Salesman."

A good Speaking Salesman voice pace is a moderate tempo (not too fast or slow) with a varied rhythm utilizing a mixture of short, succinct sentences and longer, explanatory statements.

Our voice is a unique gift. It reflects our personality and it is said to be the "melody" of our soul.

A subtle way to gain your listener's respect and an advantage for you is to

match your client's speech without obviously imitating him. This creates the impression that you are like him which helps put him at ease and be possibly more receptive. To be efficiently heard, use a moderate volume level and try to match the clients voice level, except if his volume softens due to uncertainty or increases due to anger.
You sincerely want your clients to understand that you value what they say and care enough to really understand their point of view. Your voice should have a good low comfortable (continued on page six)

EXHIBIT 7.16 *(continued)*

Conversational Selling:

The Non-manipulative Approach to Sales

Salespeople are among the highest paid professionals in our society. Why then, do so few people respect sales as a career? The answer, in a word, is pressure.

by Tony Alessandra

Tension-producing pressure causes traditional salespeople and their clients to feel uneasy, displeased and distrustful of their sales interaction. But such pressure is *not* an integral part of selling — it does not have to go along with the job. This is what conversational selling is all about.

Both the old high-pressure and the new conversational philosophies recognize four basic steps in the sales process: information-gathering, proposal, confirmation and follow-through.

But, as you can see in the diagram that follows, the relative amount of time spent in each stage of the process is significantly different.

Information-gathering

In the information-gathering stage, the salesperson and client find out if there is something the client wants or needs that the salesperson can provide. The high-pressure (traditional) salesperson spends some time in small talk and then, acting on the assumption that the client wants/needs the product or service, launches into the presentation (pitch).

The conversational (professional) salesperson, in order to build a solid, accurate informational base, spends more time on defining client needs than on any other part of the sales process. This phase is divided into

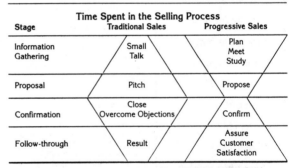

Traditional and Progressive, or relationship selling approaches both require the same amount of time and effort. The difference lies in what activities you emphasize.

three parts:

1) **Planning.** Maximizes the efficient use of your time by making sure you're pursuing the right prospects (markets). Involves territory, time and account management; market planning and analysis; prospect planning and call preparation.

2) **Meeting.** Develops person-to-person rapport and begins a "business friendship," based on flexibility, cooperation and trust.

3) **Studying.** Encourages the client to provide pertinent information such as business needs and objectives, financial status, personal "behavioral" style and so on. This allows the salesperson to thoroughly understand, and respond to, the specific client situation.

Proposal

Both traditional and professional selling methods allocate about equal amounts of time to the presentation, but that's where the similarity ends.

The traditional salesperson gives a standard presentation to all clients, regardless of their individual needs. In the professional approach, the proposal is custom tailored to the client's specific business situation and personal style. Each presentation is different because each reflects the buyer's unique combi-

continued on page 8

2

EXHIBIT 7.16 *(continued)*

Food For Thought:

"A lot of practices have evolved because they're easy to manipulate — require no brains, no theory. But, the biggest losses and biggest gains cannot be measured. The cost of an unhappy customer can't be measured. Yet these unknowable costs are precisely the activities that must be managed."

— W. Edwards Deming, management consultant, and quality guru, his quality management theories led to the rebuilding of Japanese industry in the 1950s and '60s.

Non-manipulative Selling

continued from page 2

nation of circumstances.

Confirming the Sale.

In this stage, the buyer makes a commitment to implement the agreed-upon solution.

In high-pressure sales transactions, the majority of time is spent overcoming buyer objections and trying to close a "stubborn" customer.

The tension level soars. Problems arise because the salesperson has inadvertently pressured the buyer into revealing his or her hidden objectives at this late stage of the sale. (The best time to deal with customer objections is early on, in the information-gathering stage, because objections are an important source of information.)

The conversational salesperson doesn't need to hustle for the close or push for a commitment, because the solution already has been agreed on, and confirming the sale becomes a question of "when" and "how," not "if."

Assuring Customer Satisfaction

At this point, the salesperson makes a commitment to the buyer to provide the promised product or service, and keep in touch with him or her throughout their business relationship.

Traditional salespeople tend to minimize the concept of continual service. Their casual acquaintance with the client fades, so that the seller has to reestablish rapport the next time a sales call is made.

The professional salesperson never lets the relationship fade in the first place. He or she makes a commitment to the buyer to provide service and assistance in the spirit, as well as the the letter, of customer satisfaction.

Dr. Tony Alessandra is an internationally renowned speaker, author and consultant on professional sales and sales management. He is based in La Jolla, California.

By assuring the satisfaction of each customer, the progressive salesperson builds a clientele that magnifies strength and sphere of influence. Nurturing professional relationships gives back what the seller puts out in terms of time, effort and concern. Not only does it lead to more sales, it allows you feel good about your occupation and helps reestablish the image of selling as an honorable and respectable profession.

Traditional vs. Progressive Sales Relationships

Traditional Selling	Relationship Selling
• Casual Acquaintance	• Business Friendship.
• Topics are social or general.	• Business topics are appropriate.
• Dialogue is limited.	• Dialog is open.
• Little is known about each other.	• Mutual professional respect is shown.
	• Attitude is I win/you win.
• Attitude is often I win/you lose.	• Professional courtesy is shown.
• Personal courtesies are shown.	• Interest is shown in needs and goals.
• Interest is sporadic and spontaneous.	• Follow-through is expected.
• Additional meetings are not expected.	• Meetings are usually brief and businesslike.
• Meetings happen at any time.	• Appointments are made.
• Disagreements are a threat.	• Disagreements are opportunities for mutual problem-solving.

8

Content should be centered around:

1. An idea as to how your company operates
2. The problems, situations, etc. you are prepared to handle
3. Any specialties
4. Background/qualifications.

Consultants should avoid stating fees in the brochure. Aside from becoming outdated, it allows prospects to prejudge services and make a decision before the consultant is ever met.

If a consultant is putting one together, the following questions should be asked before anything is written:

1. What audience are you trying to reach? Who are the present and potential customers? What are their needs? What will they buy? Why? The brochure's thrust should be towards them.
2. Who is going to design it? How many colors? What's the budget?
3. Who is going to print it? What's the quality of the printer like? How many are going to be printed? Over what time period are they expected to be used?

The first step is writing. The most important facet of the brochure is that it should address the potential client's needs. Clients are going to be interested in only those things that relate to them. How can you solve their problem? For example, suppose a consultant is in the money management field—the client's needs are seeing their portfolios grow in value with relative safety. Does the content of the money manager's brochure address those two prime needs? If it does not, it may fall short as a sales tool.

Once again, freelance writers can be found through ad agencies, journalism schools, newspapers, or the chamber of commerce. Designers can be found through references (if you see a brochure you admire, ask the company that produced it about the designer), yellow pages or even through printers. Match the designer to your brochure. In other words, if a designer specializes in putting together inexpensive, two color productions and you are looking at a four-color piece, think twice before you hire them. Ask for samples of previous work and for names of previous clients. Design is critical. It can ruin a quality piece or make it.

If the brochure requires photography, the designer can usually assist in finding one. Printers are another source. Remember, not all photographers are good at shooting people, and not all "people" photographers are good at taking shots of objects.

When the brochure is printed, retain possession of the original art (called mechanical boards). When someone else has them in their possession they can be lost. If the designer retains it, you are almost forced to utilize the same person again. If you were unhappy with the cost, timetable, and so on, you may want to change. If the printer retains it, you may find yourself in an awkward position as well. Insist on having the boards (and negatives) returned to you before paying the invoices.

The following checklist will help in planning and printing a brochure and/or kit:

18-Step Brochure Kit Checklist

1. Determine need—do you need one?
2. Determine budget.
3. Will it be a press kit version or a fold?
4. Find writer, examine past work, negotiate fee.
5. Supervise writing of copy, including cover copy.
6. Begin designer selection.
   a. Ask writer for suggestions.
   b. Ask printer for assistance.
   c. Check other companies with quality work for ideas as to who might do work.
   d. Call local ad agencies for freelancers.

7. Interview designers.

   a. Examine previous work.

   b. Get input from designers on brochure approach.

   c. Is the designer flexible? Will they listen to you?

   d. Determine and negotiate fees.

8. Hire designer.

   a. Send groundrules, your involvement, deadline.

   b. Sign letter of agreement detailing due dates and deadlines.

9. Design stage.

   a. Decide on stock, layout.

   b. Agree on printer and why this particular one selected.

   c. See rough layout.

10. Hire photographer, if needed.

    a. Consult printer, designer, ad agency, public relations agency, other businesses that have put together brochures with good photography.

    b. Make sure photographer can shoot what is required; that is, people, objects, or whatever is required.

11. Finalize brochure layout.

    a. See and approve comprehensive brochure layout.

    b. Have mechanicals or boards produced.

12. Find printer.

    a. Consult designer.

    b. Consult photographer.

    c. Talk to other businesses.

13. Select printer.

    a. Decide on printed quantities.

    b. Get three written, competitive bids.

    c. Negotiate cost.

    d. Put in writing that boards must be returned to consultant's firm.

14. Approve boards and send to printer.

15. See blueline/brownline for approval.

16. See color key and approve (if brochure in color).

17. Have designer supervise printing.
18. Brochures and boards delivered.

In designing the cover of the brochure, remember it is like an advertisement. What it says may get a prospect to open it—or put it in the trashcan. Brochure cover guidelines:

1. Think about the audience. Who will read it?
2. What needs does the audience have?
3. How do the needs tie into the consultant's services?
4. Can those needs be answered and translated into benefits?
5. Can the consultant offer any of those benefits?
6. Can any of the benefits be offered on the cover?
7. Can the cover benefit be fit into five-to-seven words?
8. Will the prospect understand the benefit on the cover?
9. Is it misleading?
10. Can the consultant follow up the cover line inside and live up to it?

To answer 10 and determine what should go inside the brochure, ask the following questions:

1. Does the body copy go along with the cover copy?
2. Is it easy to understand?
3. Is it easy to follow?
4. Is it written on a one-to-one basis. That is, does it sound like one person talking to one person, and not one consultant talking to a company or room full of executives?
5. Is it factual?
6. Will it interest the prospect?
7. Does it have a unique selling proposition (USP)? A USP is present in every product and/or service. It is the one thing

that sets a consultant's practice apart from his competition, such as fast service, a money-back guarantee, expertise in a specific area that no one else has, or some other aspect.

8. Does it explain the consultant's service?
9. Does it address the client's needs?
10. Does it contain background information on the consultant's firm?
11. Does it promise enough to pique curiosity?
12. Can those promises be delivered?
13. Would the consultant choose this company and consultant if he or she were the client?

Brochure Cover Letters

A cover letter or note from the consultant should always accompany the brochure and/or kit. The letter conveys an image of the consultant to the prospect. If, for instance, the consultant and client have just had an amiable chat on the telephone and the brochure follows, the note that introduces the brochure should be amiable, too. A letter with a touch of humor can frequently win over a client and show them a side of the consultant they did not know existed.

Whether the letter is humorous or not, there is a format to letters that can easily be mastered by consultants. Each can be put together via a four-step process. In reality, every letter is a sales letter. Each is selling something. It may be a product or service—or it may be a consultant's company and its service. An effective sales letter is no different from a good advertisement. Traditionally, in an ad there are four words that comprise a winning structure:

1. Attention
2. Interest
3. Desire
4. Action

This is called the AIDA formula. To begin, the letter writer has to grab the reader's attention, just as an advertisement does. It may be through a provocative or humorous statement, or possibly via some mutual association they share.

The Key. That opening statement (*attention*) should address or hit upon the prospect's needs. For instance, "how would you like to boost productivity without incurring additional cost?" Or, "is your company's market share what you want it to be? If not, perhaps you're missing one key ingredient . . ."

Be Provocative. Use statements that pique curiosity. That's how attention is generated. The interest statement usually adds to the opening. It goes into something that the writer can offer to the recipient. For instance, "maybe that one ingredient you are missing is a potent advertising message to your customers. I'll create a powerful space ad and/or sales letter offering for you as I have done for some of the top company's in the country . . ."

The attention-getter may only be a sentence or two, the interest can go on for a paragraph or more. It's laying out, in generalities, the services that the letter writer can offer. The benefits follow in the "desire" section: "With this new service your company will reach a customer base it has never before tapped . . . your company will generate 50 percent more business from your existing clientele . . ."

The Close. The close is merely a statement that causes action on the part of the recipient. For instance, "we have the top data processing specialists in our company on hand for the next two weeks. I would like to bring them in and have them spend a short time with you and your DP department so they can provide you with some insight into how productivity can be improved."

Notice, the last step requires action. It sets a time limit and forces the recipient to act. The action may not come specifically from the prospect. The action may be caused by the consultant calling, reiterating the action step that was spelled out in the letter, and asking the prospect what day may be most convenient for the meeting.

Every effective letter has these four ingredients. Whether they are short notes or two-page "pitches," those that work can be divided into the four areas.

Take a simple thank you note:

Dear _____:

I enjoyed the conversation and the lunch—great restaurant and a fascinating discussion about an extremely promising company.

John and I discussed the project and we came up with a number of preliminary ideas that I think you'll find quite interesting.

Each has tremendous potential and will make a significant impact on your profits in the next 12 months.

Both of us will be free towards the end of next week, and we'd like to come by with our productivity analyst to give you a better idea of the approach we have formulated. I think you'll find it exciting—and an excellent tool.

I'll give you a call to see if we can set a mutually convenient time.

Once again, thanks for an entertaining and productive lunch.

Best

Notice how AIDA format is developed in the letter. The same approach is used in the following letter:

Dear _____:

What single investment appreciated approximately 80% greater than bonds, 66% higher than stocks, and 74% more than real estate?

The answer—the investment that the John L. Sloan company made in our consulting services last year.

To be precise, we were brought into the Sloan firm to solve some specific problems in the productivity area. Like many companies, Sloan had watched its sales increase but its profits diminish.

What was wrong? Could it be fixed? And, more importantly, how does it relate to your company? After all, you are in a different industry.

What we found at Sloan was a problem that many firms in every industry share . . . a common problem that many companies share . . . a problem that is growing daily and eating into production and profitability. But, it is a problem that can be remedied—if companies know what it is and how it is hindering performance.

I'd like to tell you more about it, how it may be impacting your company and the possible solutions. I think it could make a significant impact on your profitability in the coming year.

I'll call to see if we might get together for a few moments to discuss our findings. Incidentally, I've included a brochure that will give you some insight into our firm and the type of work we do.

Sincerely yours,

Provocative? Of course, and it is typical of what every letter should be like. Whether it is a cold call piece of correspondence or a thank you note for lunch, they all share one common characteristic—they paint an image of the writer and their company.

That image translates into how the client perceives the consulting firm and the value they bring to the table. Correspondence, newsletters, brochures, speeches, media attention. They are all key elements in reaching and selling clients. And, most important, they are critical influencers when it comes to clients deciding exactly how much your services are worth.

Index